Eighth Army Versus Rommel

Tactics, Training and Operations in North Africa 1940-42

James Colvin

Helion & Company Limited

Helion & Company Limited
Unit 8 Amherst Business Centre
Budbrooke Road
Warwick
CV34 5WE
England
Tel. 01926 499 619
Email: info@helion.co.uk
Website: www.helion.co.uk
Twitter: @helionbooks
Visit our blog at blog.helion.co.uk

Published by Helion & Company 2020
Designed and typeset by Mary Woolley (www.battlefield-design.co.uk)
Cover designed by Paul Hewitt, Battlefield Design (www.battlefield-design.co.uk)

Text © James Colvin 2020
Images © as individually credited
Maps drawn by George Anderson © Helion & Company 2020

ISBN 978-1-913336-64-6

British Library Cataloguing-in-Publication Data.
A catalogue record for this book is available from the British Library.

For details of other military history titles published by Helion & Company Limited contact the above address, or visit our website: http://www.helion.co.uk.

We always welcome receiving book proposals from prospective authors.

Contents

List of Illustrations

List of Maps

Acknowledgements

The drawing (Image 1) of Captain Basil Liddell Hart originates from his memoirs published by Cassell; the photograph (Image 2) of Colonel Fuller is from *Boney Fuller: The Intellectual General* by Anthony Trythall, also originally published by Cassell; the photograph of John Harding (Image 3) comes from *Harding of Petherton* by Michael Carver, originally published by Weidenfeld and Nicholson, as does the photograph (Image 5) of Lieutenant General O'Connor, Major General Creagh and Brigadier Harding. I am indebted to the current copyright holder of all these works, the Orion Publishing Group, for their co-operation, all attempts at tracing copyright holders having failed. My thanks are also due to Amberley Publishing for permission to reproduce photographs of Lieutenant General Auchinleck, Major General Campbell and Brigadier Gatehouse.

Preface

This book has its origins in the University of Buckingham's external MA degree course in Military History, and my thanks are due to Professor Saul David who led the course and to Dr Matthias Strohn, the tutor assigned to me. The latter's interest in the questions raised encouraged me to continue the research, and Professor David has been most generous and helpful in his comments. Contacts made on the course led me to Christopher Dorman-O'Gowan, son of the late Major General Dorman-Smith, who was kind enough to go through the narrative to correct some errors of fact and reassure me that from his perspective my efforts were, in many respects, not too far off the mark.

After meeting Chris Camfield of Toronto in the Royal Armoured Corps archives at Bovington while we were researching our separate subjects, he very kindly read through and edited each chapter as I produced them. His interest and enthusiasm did much to sustain me through the considerable challenge of making sense of conflicting accounts of events, and if the result is at all readable, the credit is his.

A number of friends were especially helpful, in particular Simon and Angus Tweedie, who encouraged me to continue at a point when time and enthusiasm were in short supply. Mike Geerts, Richard Moon and Ben Sharp also all assured me that the project was worth pursuing. My wife Caroline was busy with her own creative work during the later stages — Julia is at time of publication twelve months old — and they will both no doubt let me have their critique quite soon. It goes without saying that the project would seem pointless without them or my elder daughters, Clare and Susannah.

The days spent in The National Archives, the Imperial War Museum, the John Rylands Library, the Churchill Archive Centre, the Liddell Hart Centre for Military Archives and Bovington Tank Museum would have been an ordeal without the assistance and efficiency of the staff. They were without exception helpful and co-operative and made the prospect of another session with boxes of documents something to look forward to. Special thanks to Andrew Webb at the IWM and Katie Thompson at the Bovington photographic archives for their help in dealing with my technical illiteracy.

James Colvin
15 August 2020

Introduction

On 21 June 1942 Churchill was in conference with Roosevelt at the White House when General George Marshall, Franklin Roosevelt's Chief of Staff, entered the Oval Office and handed the president a pink slip. Roosevelt read it and passed it to Churchill without comment. It informed the latter that the Afrika Korps had captured Tobruk and taken 30,000 prisoners. It was the most bitter blow Churchill was to suffer during 1939-45. As he wrote later, 'Defeat is one thing, disgrace is another.' After the fall of Singapore earlier that year, it was the greatest British military disaster of the Second World War.

It was also the culmination of a series of military setbacks in North Africa. It had been a puzzle since the beginning of the year why, despite reinforcements and changes of command, the Eighth Army was unable to compete with the Afrika Korps. Neither the Chief of the Imperial General Staff in London, Sir Alan Brooke, nor the Commander in Chief in the Middle East, Lieutenant General Claude Auchinleck, could understand why the Eighth Army and the commanders of its armoured units consistently failed in action. The commanders on the ground were themselves quick to criticise each other and their immediate superiors, and when neither they nor training manuals could provide solutions, individual regiments were obliged to improvise their own, introducing a variety of tactics that often served only to make cooperation between units more difficult. Blame for their misfortunes was put on inadequate equipment and on Rommel's unnerving talent for warfare. All found themselves in a demoralising series of setbacks and retreats, even when their own unit appeared to have fought successfully.

The performance of the army as a whole and the question of why the Afrika Korps appeared to regularly outperform British troops at brigade and divisional level has attracted less attention than the argument over whether Claude Auchinleck, Commander in Chief Middle East from July 1941, or Bernard Montgomery, succeeding him in command of the Eighth Army in August 1942, deserved the greater credit for the eventual defeat of Rommel at Alamein that November. At the time British failures were blamed on inferior equipment and generalship, and, later, on a poor grasp of mechanised warfare, in particular an inability to concentrate armour or to combine tanks with artillery and infantry. But even in June 1942, when British equipment had improved and British commanders were fully aware of the need to combine all arms, the Eighth Army still suffered its catastrophic defeat at Tobruk, a rout to Alamein and a desperate struggle to halt the German threat to the Middle East, where failure could have changed the course of the war. Responsibility for the loss of Tobruk was heaped on the shoulders of Auchinleck's field commander, Lieutenant General Ritchie. Not even he claimed he was blameless, but it is clear that fault lines ran wider than through one individual. The failure of senior British officers to learn appropriate lessons from experience is a puzzle, and the thinking behind the organisational and tactical choices that were made is something of a mystery. Holding individuals to account is easy enough, but it should be recognised that the commanders involved were committed men, less ambitious for themselves than for the cause in which they fought, and the ability of many showed later in the war or in post-war careers. The perspective of the future Field Marshal Michael Carver, who as a young staff officer knew and worked with most of them, was that though they 'were not supermen, they were neither better nor worse than those who succeeded them. They were faced with a form of warfare that was completely novel to all, for which their training and experience was of little value'.[1] But the fact remains that the conditions of North Africa were novel to both sides and while the Germans successfully met the challenge, constantly refining their practices through experience, the British were in 1942 still fumbling towards solutions. On examination it is clear that inherent deficiencies in organisation, training and command derived less from individuals than from the army and the culture in which the leaders worked. In particular the evidence seems to show that it was the army's institutions and its culture that made it extraordinarily difficult to establish a commonly understood doctrine of mechanised warfare. The reasons behind this deficiency, and how the army fared against professional opposition that had come to radically different tactical concepts, are what this book hopes to make clear.

At the outbreak of war in 1939 the British army in North Africa was composed entirely of regular troops whose men had volunteered for up to twelve years' service under officers largely of upper middle class backgrounds. The replacements that appeared from February 1941 were composed of those who had volunteered in the months immediately before or after the outbreak of war plus a proportion drawn from the first batch of conscripts, but these new units had been formed on cadres drawn from the pre-war regular and Territorial army and their ethos was very much of that style. National characteristics are often reflected in armed forces: in pre-war British middle class society and its army the characteristics included a deeply rooted patriotism and an unbounded confidence in Britain and its Empire, a class divide ameliorated by paternalism, a belief in the virtues of the amateur, and a penchant for clubbability.

---

1   FM Lord Michael Carver, *Dilemmas of the Desert War*, (London: Batsford, 1986), p. 143.

These features of the pre-war British officer corps, their common education and background, produced a culture and mindset in the regular army that was to influence the relationships between the senior commanders, and even the tactics they employed and the decisions they made. The British army shifted in character through the war, inevitably so, as it changed from a long service regular force to a mass citizen army drawn from a much wider base, but for the three years to mid-1942 its pre-war spirit dominated, and since the character of its early leadership was to prove both a strength and a weakness it repays examination, from the education of its young officers to the training and relationships of its senior commanders.

Throughout the 1930s the British army lacked both prestige among the public and resources from the state. It was a poor third behind the RAF and the Royal Navy in the queue for modernisation: the annual budget in the mid-thirties for armoured vehicle development covered the cost of no more than three tanks. Mechanisation and the introduction of armoured fighting vehicles had forced all major armies of the period to reconsider tactics and doctrine, and Germany and Russia, defeated in the

1. Captain Basil Liddell Hart, 'the best known military writer in the world', in 1938. (Orion Publishing Group)

First World War, approached the issues with minds more receptive to new ideas than the victors. In Germany, the Versailles restrictions on equipment forced the military to look more creatively at maximising their effectiveness despite limited resources. In Britain lack of equipment tended to stultify thought and restricted activity to the traditional role of defending the empire. Creative thinking amongst British junior and middle ranking officers was not improved by the attitude of the two most vociferous military theorists, Basil Liddell Hart and J.F.C. Fuller.

These two saw themselves as revolutionaries rather than reformers, antagonistic to the military establishment and ultimately preferring to work with the press and politicians rather than the recognised military order. They became contentious figures in military circles and while their influence on British military practice was profound, it was not always beneficial, for some who appreciated the need for progressive thinking took their cue from Liddell Hart's and Fuller's radicalism and adopted their remedies uncritically. There have been many analyses of their thinking: the intention here is to trace their impact on doctrine and tactics as evidenced by contemporary reports and war diaries.

After the defeats of 1940 in Norway and France, success against Italian forces in North Africa encouraged British commanders to believe that by and large their management of armoured forces was going along the right lines, though it was acknowledged that German troops would prove a greater challenge than the Italians. When Rommel attacked in April 1941 the gulf in ability between the two armies was evident but could be explained by his superiority in numbers of tanks, and by the withdrawal of experienced British troops to other fronts. Further reverses were ascribed to weaknesses in equipment and leadership. But by the end of the winter battles of 1941-42 it was clear that a change in practice was essential if the Eighth Army was to compete with the Afrika Korps. The object of this narrative is to discover why this conclusion was so delayed and why the remedies were so poorly chosen. Original letters, reports and war diaries demonstrate how and why change came so late, and the sources have been as far as possible quoted rather than paraphrased, to give the flavour and attitudes of the time. They also illustrate the determination with which the men of the British Army fought. Inevitably, most written sources come from officers rather than the men, and if it appears to a reader that the narrative is overly 'officer-centric', the close relationship between officers, NCOs and men in the British army of the time should not be forgotten.

1

Culture and Institutions

The British army and its officer class received a hostile press in the years running up to the Second World War. For much of the interwar period, civilian grief for the tragedy of the casualties of trench war, contempt for the perceived idiocy of the war's management, and horror at the waste, combined to reduce the status of the army in the eyes of the working man to a level as low as in the Victorian age. Retrenchment reduced the army of 1918 to a fraction of its Great War establishment and the 'Ten Year Rule' of 1920 (renewed to 1932) assumed no major war for the next decade, thereby negating planning and funding for anything other than defence of empire and confining the army's role to that of an imperial gendarmerie. When in the 1930s political instability and military threats developed on the continent, the army still came no higher than third in priority for defence expenditure, behind Britain's traditional safeguard, the Royal Navy, and the new dimension of aerial warfare. Throughout the thirties, the failure to provide funds to bring the army up to date or up to strength gave ever more credence to the cartoon character of Colonel Blimp, the personification of a defective military culture and of an institution said to be class ridden, tradition bound, inefficient and unwilling to innovate. As a career for most officers, the army offered little benefit beyond 20 years employment and a modest pension.

Background and Officer Education

The British divisional and corps commanders of Eighth Army prior to Montgomery's arrival in August 1942, the leaders faced with the challenge of desert warfare and therefore the critical group of the period under discussion, came from a very narrow demographic and range of experience. They were born (with only one exception) between 1891 and 1895, were almost all public school educated, introduced as eighteen year olds to their profession at the Royal Military College at Sandhurst, or at Woolwich if they aimed for the artillery or engineers, and thrust into the First World

War soon after the age of twenty.[1] Their first years in the army were not the anticipated colonial policing with the regiment of their choice but the maelstrom of the Western Front, and it was not until the war was over that their formal military education began. Their experience until then had been of the primacy of the regimental system, the value of artillery in supporting infantry attacks, and a glimpse of the future as the tank and aircraft made their first appearances. Their reasons for choosing a military profession no doubt were varied, though few are recorded as showing early military ambition. An upper middle class young man who could expect a moderate family inheritance in due course would find the army or navy an acceptable way to pass the intervening years in a profession that, importantly, fulfilled the obligations of service, duty and patriotism instilled by family, school and society. A good proportion of them were looking for a reasonably relaxed way of life in a world where trade was considered vulgar unless it was the family brewery or firm of stockbrokers, and where respectable professions were limited to the law, civil service, academia, politics or the church. Certainly a private income was necessary to supplement army pay and to give a reasonable standard of living but provided one's funds matched the lifestyle of one's chosen regiment adequate comfort would not be too difficult to achieve. The men who were to command in North Africa and who joined the army before 1914 would have needed a private income of £1000 a year if they chose and were accepted by the Guards, £750 if the cavalry, and £200 or more as an infantry officer, though there were significant variations between regiments in each category.[2] After 1918 private incomes were often hit by rises in taxation or reduced revenue from landed estates, and many regiments curtailed their social and recreational activities to accommodate officers in reduced circumstances. Among the Guards, Rifle Brigade and cavalry, regiments did not necessarily relax their requirements.

As late as 1939, 85 percent of Sandhurst and 91 percent of Woolwich entrants came from the public schools,[3] where reverence for tradition, hierarchy of rank and privilege, Spartan communal living, and early experience of command through the prefect system chimed well with military ethos.[4] Sport, in public schools centred

---

1   The exception, Major General William Ramsden (b. 1888), was GOC 50th Division in 1942.
2   Anthony Clayton, *The British Officer* (London: Routledge, 2007), p. 135. The pound in 1914 was worth more than one hundred times its 2020 value according to the Bank of England inflation calculator.
3   Jeremy Strang, *The British Army and the People's War* (Manchester: Manchester University Press, 2000), p.22
4   David Turner, *The Old Boys*,(New Haven & London: Yale University Press, 2015), Chapter Five, ebook loc 2962. The schools were public in the sense that they were open to the paying public rather than financed by and catering exclusively for the sons of the wealthy. Their establishment followed the Clarendon Commission's Report of 1861 and the Public Schools Act of 1865, when the structure of seven leading charity schools was reformed so that they became independent under boards of governors free of influence of the Crown, government or church. These were joined within a few years by another dozen

around the team games of rugby and cricket, had its character building value affirmed by authorities from Plato onwards. The cult of sporting activity and the precedence that character and physique thereby took over intellect and knowledge had its pitfalls: 'playing the game' is all very well, but as one observer has said, 'In politics, business and war, the rules invariably change with each generation and those playing the old game lose.'[5]

The public schools' prefect system inculcated a powerful sense of responsibility, duty and service.[6] It was in the 1920s considered self-evident that a public school background prepared a young man for command,[7] and not merely because gentility and a military career were associated from the time that the landed and professional class produced most of the officers for fighting services.[8] The schools tended to be authoritarian, dominated by team games and physically tough. One former subaltern from a soccer playing public school told the writer that the physicality learned on his school playing field was considered excessive in the army, and he found himself sent off for foul play in his first match for his regiment in 1930. Bernard Montgomery left St Paul's in 1906 having learnt that 'life is a stern struggle, and a boy has to be able to stand up to the buffeting and setbacks.' Another future field marshal and Chief of the Imperial General Staff, Gerald Templer, 'loathed and detested' his four years at Wellington, where he was badly bullied,[9] and after which Sandhurst was a delight. It was a common joke among the more cynical that public school boys coped remarkably well in jail. But with a romantic concept of service, and encouragement for the gifted amateur personality rather than the technical specialist, the public schools cast their leavers in a mould that seemed well suited to a soldier's career.[10] Churchill's first appointee to Chief of the Imperial General Staff, John Dill, noted that 'men will follow and work better for some lad who is a gentleman, it has always been so'.[11] One

independent schools under the auspices of a 'Headmasters' Conference'. By the end of the century over sixty schools were members of the Headmasters Conference, educating 20,000 pupils, approximately one percent of the age group at the time. Although the public schools tended to share a common Christian ethos and Victorian notion of public service and duty, as individual selective establishments they also acquired differing social status depending on fashion, location and fee structure.

5   Turner, *The Old Boys*, Chapter 4, E-book loc. 1990
6   A public school of 500 boarding pupils would likely be organised on a 'house' system, each house perhaps of 80 pupils, its non-academic activities and discipline largely run by prefects selected by the house master. This typically resulted in pupils learning both deference to authority and responsibility for subordinates.
7   Allport, *Browned off and Bloody Minded* (New Haven & London: Yale University Press, 2014), p. 84.
8   David Boyd, *Elites and their Education* (Windsor: NFER Publishing Co., 1973) p. 123.
9   John Cloake, *Templer. Tiger of Malaya: The Life of Field Marshal Sir Gerald Templer* (London: Harrap, 1985), pp. 12-13.
10   Gordon Ross, *'Breathless Hush in the Close', The World of the Public School* (London: Weidenfeld & Nicholson,1977), p. 61.
11   Allport, p. 97.

of the most progressive soldiers of the interwar years and the first Commandant of the Royal Armoured Corps, Lieutenant General le Quesne Martel, thought that 'of course the good type of public school boy made by far the best officer'. He believed that 'The main requisite of an officer is that the men shall be proud to serve him',[12] and that 'It is quite true that the secondary [i.e. non-public school] schoolboy is handicapped. He has led a sheltered life. He usually lives at home and runs home to his mother if he is in difficulty. The stern test of fending for himself which the public schoolboy has had to face is denied him.'[13] At most public schools, the 'stern test' included cold baths, corporal punishment, a degree of bullying and what Victorian writers delicately called 'beastliness'.[14] Martel did however concede that the best secondary schoolboys overcame the handicap of their education and were better than public schoolboys of below average capability. Promoting from the ranks did not appeal to him: 'The older and more senior NCOs [in the Royal Tank Corps] were not given commissions. They have their own line of promotion, which is far better than making them junior officers except in very special cases.' Martel expressed his views robustly, as one might expect from the rugby playing army champion boxer that he was, but they were not exceptional at the time, and antediluvian though these attitudes may appear now, they were widely held and accepted without resentment by the majority, then and later.

Academic achievement at public schools was centred on the Classics. However beneficial this might be to intellectual development – one Classics scholar who later achieved high military rank wrote that 'Its emphasis on the Socratic method, combined with a naturally argumentative character, had always led me to question the accepted, established answer, method or regime'[15]– it was not directly relevant to the army's requirement of mathematics, science and language for entry to the military colleges at Sandhurst or Woolwich. Most public schools therefore held 'army classes' which though considered intellectually inferior by classics scholars answered the need for a broader education. If a candidate failed to make the grade in the army class, he still had the traditional option of a 'crammer' which would coach him for the Sandhurst entry exam. By the end of the nineteenth century, public school army classes had improved to the extent that the proportion of entry to Sandhurst directly from crammers had fallen from 68 percent in 1895 to 52 percent five years later.

12   Lieutenant-General le Quesne Martel, *An Outspoken Soldier* (London: Sifton Praed, 1949), p.173.
13   Lieutenant General le Quesne Martel, *Our Armoured Forces*, (London: Faber & Faber, 1945) p.104.
14   Bernard Montgomery's grandfather, Frederick Farrar, a master at Harrow, later headmaster of Marlborough and Dean of Canterbury Cathedral, wrote a famous account of schooldays in late Victorian England, *'Eric, or Little by Little'*, chronicling the pitfalls of public school life.
15   Field Marshal Lord Carver, *The Apostles of Mobility: The Lees-Knowles Lectures of 1979* (London: Weidenfeld and Nicholson, 1979), p. 11.

The relative status of the public schools was fairly subjective. Three of the most prestigious, Eton, Westminster and Winchester, were also the oldest, derived from medieval foundations. The others, with a social status reflecting that of their localities and their age, were divided between those derived from schools founded in the 16th century, mostly by Edward VI, the foundations of the 17th and 18th centuries, and the bulk established in the 19th century. Among this last group were such as Uppingham, the innovator of the 'house' system and a founder member of the Headmasters Conference that supervised the public schools, Radley, unkindly described as 'a school for the sons of Oxford grocers', and Lancing, established principally for the offspring of High Church Anglican clergymen. Eton and Harrow ranked at the top level socially, Eton, Winchester, Westminster and St Paul's were among the most academic, Wellington and Cheltenham were the most oriented to producing army officers. Although those from a less prestigious establishment might feel reasonably comfortable with most other ex-public schoolboys, it did not follow that they were regarded as on the same level by Etonians or Harrovians, who if they entered the army tended to maintain their social distinction after Sandhurst through their choice of regiment. Documented examples of any resulting social discord are rare, mentioned generally as an aside, but a vivid instance early in the Second World War is the behaviour in the Sherwood Rangers, a socially elite Yeomanry (i.e. Territorial Army cavalry) regiment towards some new colleagues: they 'hadn't been to Eton or Harrow, worked for a living and didn't keep horses or hunt twice a week so they had nothing to talk about and were pretty roughly treated'.[16] The poet Keith Douglas is now perhaps the best remembered individual from this regiment. Diaries and reminiscences from other members of this exceptionally well documented unit contain numerous references in the early years of the war to both deliberate and unconscious social discrimination, on occasion via 'unintentional condescension through exaggerated politeness', as one post war commentator has described it.[17] Ironically enough, one of those harassed early in the war for not being quite the right sort, Stanley Christopherson, ended the war as commanding officer of the Sherwood Rangers, leading them in Normandy and later.

Of the twenty British educated men of major general rank or higher who served as British formation commanders in the Middle East prior to Montgomery's arrival

---

16 James Holland (ed.), *An Englishman at War, .The Diaries of Stanley Christopherson* (London: Bantam Press, 2014). Other published accounts of life in this regiment include *Alamein to Zem Zem* by Keith Douglas and *Tank Action* by David Render. The Afrika Korps' Friedrich von Mellenthin was disappointed to find that a prisoner he captured in 1943 was not David Stirling of the SAS but the CO of the Sherwood Rangers, who he described as a 'typically arrogant' British officer.

17 Sir Antony Beevor, *Inside the British Army* (London: Corgi Books, 1994), p. 71.

in August 1942, five were educated at Eton or Harrow,[18] five at Wellington.[19] No other school provided more than two.[20] Two were educated outside the public school system.[21] It is worth noting at this stage that the close association of Old Harrovians and Old Etonians may account in part for the relationship in the Eighth Army between Lieutenant Generals Norrie (Eton) and Gott (Harrow), each regularly consulting the other before accepting the instructions of the army commander, Ritchie (Lancing). It would have been surprising if the intimacy of the school tribe, with its concomitant barrier to outsiders, were not continued in the army, tribal group solidarity being transferred to the regiment, and other regiments often regarded as either in or out of an extended tribe.

The Military Colleges – Sandhurst and Woolwich

Other than Royal Engineer officer cadets sponsored by the War Office for the second and third years of an engineering course at Cambridge, and Royal Artillery cadets who had a similar privilege, few pre-1939 officers attended university, or even countenanced it. The leaders of 1939-42 would have been of undergraduate age in 1914 but beyond it by 1918. Many of their subordinates who were part of the post Great War officer entry found the cost of further education beyond their means, and with uncertain prospects in civilian life settled for a military career instead. This is not to say that they were intellectually mediocre. 'Shan' Hackett, for example, had entertained notions of becoming a don and later in life became Principal of King's College in London but, perceiving in the early '30s the likelihood of war, settled for a military career. Michael Carver's father's faltering business put university out of reach and left him, as he saw it, with a choice of the church or the army. Harold Pyman was one of the very few to choose both university and a military career. All three were brigadiers by 1945 and achieved high rank later.

18 Wilson, Gott, Gambier-Parry, Messervy and Norrie. Norrie, when ordered to dismiss his subordinate and fellow ex-Etonian, Messervy in June 1942, refused to do so and passed the responsibility back to Ritchie.
19 Auchinleck, Freyberg, O'Connor, Beresford-Peirse, Creagh. The last three worked together as the Corps and Divisional commanders of 'Operation Compass', the sole success of the pre-Montgomery period. Of the other pivotal figures in 'Compass', Caunter and Dorman-Smith had gone to Uppingham while Harding had escaped public school altogether.
20 These others were Wavell (Winchester), Neame and Cunningham (Cheltenham), Godwin-Austen (St. Lawrence's), Lumsden (The Leys), Campbell (Sedbergh), Renton (unidentified), Gatehouse (Bedford), Pope & Ritchie (Lancing).
21 H.R. Briggs (educates in the USA), Ramsden (Bath College).

After 1918 Sandhurst did provide something between 'high grade secondary education' [22] and university[23] while Woolwich, the college for prospective engineer and artillery officers, was noted for its demands for mental capacity and hard work. Robin Dunn passed top of his course at Woolwich in 1939 and ascribed his later success in civil life to the education and work habits he learned there rather than at his school, Wellington.[24] Entry to both Sandhurst and Woolwich was by competitive examination for which the candidate needed a pass in the School Certificate to be eligible, and 'without a good pass, there was not much hope of achieving high enough marks in the exam to qualify for a place.'[25] Sandhurst's substantial fees of £200 a year (in 1921, equivalent to £10,000 a year today) could be reduced to £20 by winning one of twelve annual prize cadetships. These were competitive and demanding: Horatius Murray, a grammar school scholarship boy, found the work needed to win his award 'dwarfed all other considerations for that year.'[26] Candidates could also apply for a reduction in fees to as little as £15 a year. All candidates went before an Interview Board which would determine whether a candidate was acceptable and which could override success in the examination if not satisfied or, conversely, recommend waiving of fees to encourage an application. Intelligence was certainly valued, but 'Character', presumably believed to be available in greater quantity than brains and a reasonable substitute, was highly rated: Dunn was told by the Commandant of Woolwich, General Jumbo Goschen,'Three qualities are required of an officer; courage, physical fitness and brains – in that order.' Dunn recalled that he 'often thought of that remark during the war years.'[27] One candidate for Sandhurst, asked why he did not wish to follow his father's distinguished career in the Royal Engineers, was congratulated on his reply, 'Because I don't have the brains', which was taken as demonstrating he was just the right sort of chap for the infantry regiment for which he was aiming.[28]

The mix of social class among officer cadets at Sandhurst after 1918 was wider than is often assumed. At Sandhurst in 1932 John Hislop, the son of an NCO, discovered:

22 Boyd, *Elites,* p. 125.
23 Col. Roderick Macleod & Denis Kelly (ed.), *The Ironside Diaries, 1937-40* (London: Constable, 1962) p .46.
24 Sir Robin Dunn, QC, MC. Winner of the Sword of Honour in the last term of Woolwich's existence 1939, and Lord Justice at the Court of Appeal 1980-84.
25 John Archibald Hislop, *A Soldier's Story, Memoir of a British Officer in the Indian Army, 1935-1947* (Newhaven: Newhaven Publishing, 2007), p. 19.
26 John Donovan (ed), *A Very Fine Commander: The Memoirs of General Horatius Murray* (Barnsley: Pen and Sword, 2010) p.10
27 Sir Robin Dunn, *Sword & Wig* (London: Quiller Press, 1993) p.10. In case Goschen sounds like a buffoon, it should be noted that he was a good friend of the future CIGS, Alan Brooke, who was extremely discriminating in the company he kept. Remarks of this nature were often intended to be humorously self-deprecating.
28 Personal account.

[T]he Gentlemen Cadets were a complete cross-section of British society from the top aristocracy to the working or lower classes... In my term we had a marquess, one or two 'honourables' and then members of the upper, middle and lower middle classes plus the Army cadets; the latter include some middle-class men, as the Gentleman ranker still exists, but they were, in the main, intelligent working class men, some of whom on arrival at Sandhurst had difficulties with their aitches and with their knives and forks. However there was no snobbishness at Sandhurst; that was just not allowed.

It would of course have been poor form for socially assured cadets to display any hint of disdain for their fellows but that did not mean they were entirely comfortable in the company of men of equal military but inferior social rank: Peter Carrington, at Sandhurst in 1937, fresh from Eton and destined for the Grenadier Guards, wrote to his father that

Most of the junior [cadets] seem to be most 'what the dame would call not top drawer'. About 50% [of fellow cadets] are quite shattering but probably quite nice. There is one piece of work unfortunately called Brown and whenever he opens his mouth [he] puts his foot in it in broad cockney. The 50% would probably if they met you in the holidays call you sir...they talk about serviettes and sauce instead of gravy and are always saying "pardon".[29]

Snobbery comes in many forms, and after his first month at Sandhurst Michael Carver described his fellow cadets to his housemaster at Winchester:

They are a mixed lot, not all as stupid as one is led to suppose, quite a number of good men, plenty of medium and one or two pretty nasty, For the first time really I can begin to observe in detail the difference between the outlook of Win. Coll. and Portsmouth Grammar. The place overflows with chaps from Wellington, and their outlook does not really correspond with the Wykehamist; quite what the radical difference is I don't quite know, but I hope to find out.[30]

Carver's housemaster kept the letter and returned it to Carver 41 years later when he was a Field Marshall and Chief of the Defence Staff.

Eric Dorman-Smith graduated from Sandhurst in 1914 and perhaps speaking of his own rather than the post-1918 generation, thought British officers were reasonably representative of national life, 'most from the wealthier middle class, not the insular

29   Christopher Lee, *Carrington: An Honourable Man* (London: Penguin-Viking Books 2018), p. 67.
30   Field Marshall Lord Carver, *Out of Step* (London: Hutchinson, 1989), p. 21.

aristocracy, which doesn't really exist in Britain'.[31] Sandhurst was egalitarian in that, once admitted, all members were firmly reduced to the same plane, and once admitted, students belonged. Distinctly meritocratic by entry, ability and work at Sandhurst were rewarded by improving the cadet's chances of getting his choice of regiment. A modest background was no handicap, and though individuals' social distinction might be evident, it would be reflected in the selection of regiment on leaving Sandhurst rather than being significant during the two-year course. And the public school atmosphere of Sandhurst allowed those who had been otherwise educated to acquire the social skills that fitted them into the culture of an officers' mess. In an army where the bulk of a career would be spent with a single regiment, it was clearly preferable that a common set of social habits was maintained. English restraint, good manners and the public school spirit prevailed, rather than codified regulations. Though not perceived at the time, the most serious failing was that military training was very basic, and in effect taught cadets how to be first class private soldiers, omitting formal leadership or much tactical training – cadets being gentlemen no formal leadership training was thought necessary, and training for living in the field or field exercises was left to the regiments.[32]

In comparison, the background of German officers up to 1933 was more socially exclusive and had been for generations. Despite efforts as early as 1808 to throw open the officer corps to talent irrespective of origin, by 1865 two thirds of the Prussian officer corps was still of 'noble' blood.[33] The later nineteenth century expansion of the army to cope with a likely war on two fronts obliged recruitment of officers from broader occupational circles and by 1914 reduced the proportion of nobility to 30 percent, but since educational and other requirements[34] remained in force, this did not greatly narrow the social gap between the officer corps and the rest of the army. The distinction was severe and pains were taken to maintain it – during the Great War only about 300 combat proven sergeants rose to regular officer rank, and to prevent others crossing the line, two further ranks intermediate between officer and NCO

31 Churchill Archive Centre, Barnett Papers, BRNT1, Dorman-Smith to Barnett, p. 72.
32 Clayton, *The British Officer*, p. 197.
33 Whilst the British aristocracy could be defined as the approximately 500 families with a seat in the House of Lords, German nobility was much more numerous, and perhaps corresponds to the 'insular aristocracy' referred to by Dorman-Smith. Until 1919 German nobility conferred upon the holder legal rights and privileges varying according to the state of which the holder was a citizen. There were grades of nobility but essentially the individual was identified as noble by the 'von' or 'von und zu' before their family name. Nobility could be withdrawn from an individual for certain offences – murder, and marrying outside one's social rank, among them.
34 Officer candidates were required to hold the educational *Abitur*, thus excluding the vast majority of the population, and the Prussian officer corps had the right to elect candidates for officer entry to the army. Regiments ruled on the appropriate private income for officers, and the commanding officer and the Kaiser had the right to adjudicate on the suitability of officers' brides.

were introduced. Unsurprisingly, this innovation was considered something of an insult by the men in the ranks and has been described as 'a powerful corrosive of unit morale and a major factor in final collapse.'[35]

The 100,000 man Reichswehr of 1920 had places for only 4,000 of the 34,000 regular officers of 1918. Pre-induction testing and unit service in the ranks now became a requisite for new officers (annual intake was about 200). The necessary educational qualification of the *Abitur* still restricted the vast majority of the population from entry. The Reichswehr retained the old army's regimental election procedure for entry of new officers, maintaining the requirement for social graces and vetting of their prospective brides as before. The social exclusivity of the German officer corps therefore continued: in 1932 almost 24 percent of the officer corps was still of 'noble' origin. Their introduction into army life was not gentle. Friedrich von Mellenthin could trace his pedigree back to 1225 and to a nephew of Frederick the Great as well, but he still had to spend four years 'under hard conditions'[36] in the ranks and with others take tests for officer cadet potential before he was promoted to corporal, let alone commissioned.[37]

The Regiment

The tribalism that began at school and continued after Sandhurst through choice of regiment was a dominating characteristic of the British army. Men of similar private means and social standing tended to congregate in regiments where they would find likeminded souls, continuing the pattern of schooldays. Family traditions reinforced the tendency and it was a cliché that there was no such thing as a British Army, just a collection of regiments. From the time of Marlborough 'the regiment as an entity, in spite of obvious disadvantages, had endured as the basic organisation of the British army.'[38] The Napoleonic Wars barely refined this system and the essential structure of individual regiments, minimal supporting troops and a virtually non-existent staff lasted unchallenged until the end of the nineteenth century. Structural inefficiencies exposed by the Crimean war were remedied only slowly. The Cardwell reforms of the 1870s did abolish the purchase of commissions but disregarded lessons that might be drawn from the American Civil War or Prussia's victories in Europe in favour of reorganising battalion sized units for the role of winning and policing the

---

35   Macgregor Knox, *Common Destiny* (Cambridge: Cambridge University Press, 2000) p. 205.
36   Major General F.W. Von Mellenthin, *Panzer Battles* (London: Futura Publications, 1979) p. xii.
37   Dr. Matthias Strohn, *The German Army and the Defence of the Reich* (Cambridge: Cambridge University Press, 2011) p. 116.
38   Field Marshal Lord Carver, *The Seven Ages of the British Army* (London: Weidenfeld and Nicholson, 1984), p. 60. Carver adds, 'Its psychological advantages have to be weighed against its administrative cost and inflexibility.'

Empire. Until the Boer War of 1899-1902, infantry equipped with modern firearms were usually adequate to deal with opposition met in colonial fields, rarely had much need for support from artillery and could often use locally raised rather than British cavalry. There was little need for all arms co-ordination, and minimal practice of it. A mix of sound discipline, cohesive regimental spirit and not infrequently inspired leadership led to a tradition and expectation of success that fed upon itself to overcome the occasional difficulty. Every regiment could identify a moment in its history where it had performed a notable feat, every officer regarded it as his duty to instil regimental pride in his men and most hoped for the opportunity to add to the story. It was what Major General Dorman-Smith described with approval as 'the idealistic and romantic world of regimental life, where unselfish duty to a limited cadre was the rule and competition was impossible and unproductive in any case',[39] a concept that survived the Great War intact. Nonetheless, loyalty to the regiment or arm could have its disadvantages: 'cap badge competition', as one commentator has termed it, was 'often the crippling bugbear of the British army of the time and long after.'[40]

After 1918, the possibility of another European war was discounted and the army reverted to policing the Empire. Officers on regimental service abroad for years at a time did risk becoming parochial in outlook. Determinedly patriotic, they concentrated, in a paternal and squirearchical fashion, on management of their men, with emphasis on duty, professional competence, teamwork, loyalty and competitiveness through sport. Experience of, but lack of engagement with, the different cultures of the Empire developed a tolerant chauvinism and a somewhat stereotyped view of foreigners. Deployed in small units and equipped mainly for internal security, practice of new military technique was impossible, and except through courses at Staff College or independent reading there was little opportunity to keep up with technological and tactical changes. The prime function of battalions left in Britain was to provide personnel for the overseas sister battalion of the regiment so British based units were poorly manned and concerned with basic training only,[41] and often not much of that. The Director of Military Training complained at the CIGS' Staff Conference of 1927 that 'some young officers have to go for private tuition at military crammers because their COs don't train them. In one division, only two days of tactical training were carried out in a year, at a time when half the officers would be absent anyway.'[42]

Few exercises of brigade or divisional strength were held in the 1930s. Lieutenant General 'Tiny' Ironside, CIGS in the first months of the Second World War, records ruefully that 'There was no doctrine for the training for 20 years and practically no

39 John Rylands Library, Dorman-O'Gowan Papers, GB133GOW/2/3/1, letter to 'Larry', 3 April 1958.
40 Major General Mungo Melvin, *Manstein*, E-book, Chapter 3, loc1770.
41 Macleod & Kelly, *Ironside Diaries*, p. 288.
42 The National Archives (TNA) WO 279/57: Staff Conference at Camberley, 17-20 Jan 1927, p. 52.

manoeuvres.'[43] Without modern equipment or the prospect of it, or any planning for a European conflict, only sporadic thought was given to how a mechanised force might be handled, and, outside the Royal Tank Corps, the issue was ignored at regimental level. Those serious about their work followed the writings of J.F.C. Fuller and Basil Liddell Hart, but theories, however well argued, bore little relation to the realities of military life. Most younger officers accepted poor pay and slow promotion as drawbacks in an otherwise respectable profession which did at least include travel, reasonable company and considerable free time among its benefits. Lieutenant General Sir Francis Tuker later observed that regular officers of the period were 'to a great extent, only part time soldiers ... the twenty years between 1919 and 1939 may aptly be termed the Ice Age of military thought. There was virtually no study of war whatsoever.'[44] And by 1939 Ironside lamented the 'absence of a tactical doctrine, lack of uniformity of training, and uncertainty as to organisation.'[45]

2. Colonel J.F.C. Fuller, 'a totally unconventional soldier, prolific in ideas, fluent in expression, at daggers drawn with received opinion, authority and tradition', c. 1919. (Orion Publishing Group)

43   Macleod & Kelly, *Ironside Diaries*, p. 242.
44   Lieutenant General Sir Francis Tuker, *The Pattern of War* (London: Cassell, 1948), p. 11.
45   Macleod & Kelly, *Ironside Diaries*, p. 391.

Infantry regiments could be divided into several strata, being classed, informally, as 'good' or 'not very good', or 'smart' or otherwise.[46] Social divisions within the army affected deployment. Notably, it was axiomatic that the battalions of foot guards, famed for their discipline and reliability, in war served with other Guards battalions, under a brigadier from a Guards regiment. A division including two or more Guards brigades would be under a major general of foot guards' background. The Household Division (comprising the Guards regiments and the Household Cavalry) held a monopoly on certain appointments, such as command of the London District and of regimental districts. These carried automatic command of Territorial brigades and thus an additional opportunity for promotion. When in 1943 it was clear that armoured warfare would dominate, a number of foot guards regiments were converted to tanks and formed into a Guards Armoured Division that excluded cavalry or RTR regiments. An infantry trained Guards officer was appointed to command the division, and not even Montgomery was able to move him.

The battalions of the Rifle Brigade, the Kings Royal Rifle Corps and some of the light infantry regiments, collectively known as The Greenjackets, with a tradition of elitism derived from their specialist role a hundred years or more previously, were considered socially on a par with the Foot Guards if not necessarily so well-funded. They had a reputation for professionalism and were also reputed to be quick to look after the career prospects of their members: 'where two or three are gathered together wearing black buttons, there shall they form a clique', claimed Lieutenant Howard of the Ox and Bucks Light Infantry.[47] A useful idiosyncrasy of rifle regiments was that their own version of army drill made it difficult to transfer officers from other regiments, ignorant of the practice, to them. 'Pip' Roberts, from the most classless of front line units, the Royal Tank Regiment, in August 1942 commanded a brigade in 7th Armoured Division and was later to become probably the outstanding British divisional commander of the war, but in 1942 he found his new divisional commander, a Greenjacket,

> Not an easy person to get to know, and I had certainly established no rapport with him when we had last met. I always got the impression that everyone and

46   Capt. J.R. Kennedy, *This Our Army* (London: Hutchinson, 1935), p. 117.
47   Even at a junior level, Lieutenant Michael Howard of the Ox and Bucks, in 1946 was dismissive of his line infantry colleagues ('the officers seem a moderate crew') and felt he would have much more in common with Rifle Brigade officers than with any of the others there, since he would 'speak more of the same language on all subjects.' A number of them duly arrived including to his pleasure three Old Etonians. He was later distressed when 'John Bayley, a delightful Guardsman, was demobbed three weeks ago – that only leaves Robin in the mess to attempt to make intelligent conversation with.' Michael Howard, *Otherwise Ocuppied* (London: Old Street Publishing, 2010), pp. 24, 69, 162, 286.

everything with 'black button' connections was certainly all right. Anything or anyone else was doubtful.[48]

Raleigh Trevelyan joined the Rifle Brigade during the war and 'straight from school and therefore impressionable, I had it dinned into me day and night that I belonged to a crack regiment; only Guards and one or two others in the cavalry could be tolerated.'[49]

Even at the very highest level Rifle Brigade sentiment influenced opinion and appointments. In August 1942 Churchill's reluctance to see Montgomery appointed to command Eighth Army was based on the opinion of the Foreign Secretary Anthony Eden, late Rifle Brigade. Eden preferred Lieutenant General Gott and then, after Gott's death, Lieutenant General 'Jumbo' Wilson, both also Rifle Brigade soldiers. It was only when the CIGS Sir Alan Brooke pointed out 'that it was not astonishing that Eden should select old Green Jacket officers' that Churchill accepted Brooke's view that Montgomery might be an acceptable choice.[50]

In the line infantry, regional distinctions did of course add to the cohesive, family, tribal culture, and nowhere more than in the Scottish regiments. Liddell Hart recorded a conversation with a senior British officer in June 1942:

> He spoke of the extraordinary degree to which "feudalism" still prevailed in Scotland. In these scattered districts it was only the "Laird" who could lead them – they were unwilling to accept the leadership of anyone who had made money and come into the district. They made exceptions for ministers and schoolmasters, for 'although these were not on the same level, they had been accustomed for generations to regard them as "teachers" and were therefore ready to accept them as officers.[51]

And Lieutenant Val McCallum, ordered up to a Highland regiment to replace a casualty at the height of the battle of Alamein, was sent back by the colonel because he was a Lowland officer.[52] Scottish regiments, especially Highland regiments, were more prestigious than English, to judge by the numbers of titled officers and royal patrons they attracted, and on that basis regiments recruited in the North West and

48   Major General G.B.P. Roberts, *From the Desert to the Baltic* (London: Kimber & Co., 1987), pp. 91-92. The reference is to the black buttons on the dark green dress uniforms of rifle regiments, including some Light Infantry regiments. Post 1939-45, the term is 'black mafia'.

49   R. Trevelyan, *The Fortress: Anzio 1944* (London: Leo Cooper, 1956), p. 48.

50   Alex Danchev & Daniel Todman (eds.), *War Diaries 1939-1945 Field Marshal Lord Alanbrooke* (London: Weidenfeld & Nicholson, 2001), p.291

51   Liddell Hart Centre of Military Archives, Liddell Hart Papers, LH11/1942/41 Talk with Thorne, 3/6/42, Mil. Attaché in Berlin 1932-35.

52   Jon Latimer, *Alamein* (London: John Murray, 2002), p. 235.

the Midlands were the least socially elevated.[53] One might observe that the two outstanding leaders of 1939-45, Montgomery and Slim, both began their careers in the distinctly unfashionable Warwickshire Regiment. Location was not the only dividing line: in England, long established English infantry regiments, identifiable by their lower numbers, tended to reflect more prestige, at least in their own eyes, than the more recently raised. Much of the English line infantry was known by their smarter colleagues as 'points of the compass' regiments, a reference to the prevalence of North, South, East or West in their titles. Regiments reflected the quality of their commanding officers – few were inadequate – and had their own characteristics as well, to the extent that when Montgomery was commanding a brigade of an English, a Scottish and an Ulster battalion, he did not lay down detailed instructions as to how his colonels should train their battalions since 'The needs of battalions vary and what suits one battalion does not always suit another.'[54]

Within each of these levels there was healthy competition, jovial leg-pulling and a common argot, but between them, differences in manners and attitudes could, occasionally, disrupt relationships and the few instances documented may reflect a larger number of unrecorded incidents.

Cavalry regiments, like the Guards, would only accept young officers with private means, as pay was poor and the cavalry lifestyle in England expensive. They too were less likely to be posted abroad in peacetime. A proportion of those drawn to the cavalry unquestionably found the culture of equestrian pursuits the principal attraction of army life. The cavalry had a reputation for a relaxed view of the military profession – Field Marshal Archibald Wavell is said have claimed 'I was once attached to a cavalry regiment. I only heard one order given at any time. It was, "Trot on, Algy".'[55] A carefully cultivated nonchalance was certainly to be outwardly their rule in the desert war, expressed in an informality in dress,[56] and to quote one who did achieve high rank, writing in 1973, 'To be thought of as an 'ambitious' soldier was, in the eyes of most cavalrymen before and even after the last war, to be condemned.'[57] As with the infantry, there could be significant differences between outwardly similar units: Major General 'Pip' Roberts noted of the 7th and 8th Hussars in North Africa that the Seventh performed their duties excellently but the Eighth 'while very charming

53   David French, *Military Identities. The Regimental System: The British Army & the British People, c. 1870-2000* (Oxford: Oxford University Press, 2005), pp. 165-167.
54   Imperial War Museum (IWM), Montgomery Papers BLM11 & 13, 11/1.
55   John Rylands Library, Manchester. Dorman-O'Gowan Papers, GB133GOW1/2/6, Letter to 'Larry', 3/4/58.
56   A colleague of Robin Dunn in North Africa was quite typical in wearing 'suede desert boots, corduroy trousers, a knee length tweed covert coat and an Old Etonian silk scarf round his neck to prevent desert sores from the sweat.' A very battered service cap was the only piece of official uniform. See Dunn, *Sword & Wig*, p. 32.
57   IWM, London, 7533 General Strawson, *General Sir Richard McCreery*, privately published, p. 28.

and trying their best with great courage always seemed to get into a mess, sustained very heavy casualties, and were continuously being "withdrawn to refit".[58] The cavalry's resistance to giving up their regimental horses has been overstated. It was the lack of armoured vehicles that prevented mechanisation rather than sentimentality for the military use of the horse, and since they could afford their own horses, their recreational equestrian activities were unaffected by conversion to armour. They were concerned, however, over the threat to their role. In the absence of any official doctrine on mechanisation, the writings of military theorists in the 1930s carried enough weight to arouse suspicion that cavalry regiments might be abolished, their cherished traditions abandoned, and their role changed to supporting infantry or even converting to infantry as 'tank marines' instead of inheriting the freely manoeuvring and decisively charging role of the *arme blanche*. This fear was to have an unfortunate effect on their equipment and deployment.

The Royal Tank Corps was a victim of retrenchment after 1918, being reduced from twenty battalions to four. Given the mechanical deficiencies of early tanks there was no immediate role for tracked vehicles in policing the empire, and they lost some of their armoured cars either to the RAF, to co-ordinate with aerial policing work in Britain's newly acquired responsibilities in Iraq, or to the cavalry, as a token of mechanisation in England and Egypt. It has been claimed that in the wave of cuts after 1918 a number of substandard infantry and other wartime officers had been detached from their regiments for their regiments' good and transferred to the Tank Corps. True or not, this would have had only a short term effect and certainly Vyvyan Pope who transferred in 1920 from the North Staffordshire Regiment was delighted with the change: 'I had fled from dull, gentlemanly and inefficient stagnation; here I found a confused and riotous vortex out of which might emerge anything.'[59] At Staff College in 1922 Frederick Pile was approached by 'the great armoured expert, Colonel "Boney" Fuller', who, when he learnt that Pile was finding that the more imagination or original research he put into his papers, the lower his marks, said, "why don't you join the Tank Corps? They like bright ideas there." Though the lists were closing in less than a week, Fuller assured Pile he could get him in and duly did so.[60]

Of the transferring regular officers who were to become prominent in the early Tank Corps only Charles Lindsay had begun his career in a 'smart' regiment, following his father into the Rifle Brigade. He had appreciated early on the importance of the machine gun's firepower and had been midwife at the birth of the Machine Gun Corps in 1915, then made a natural progression to the Tank Corps, which clearly was all about adding mobility to firepower. Other early recruits to the tanks who later reached very senior positions were Charles Broad and Frederick Pile, both gunners,

58   Roberts, *Desert to Baltic*, p. 27.
59   Ronald Lewin, *Man of Armour: A Study of Lt. General Vyvyan Pope* (London: Leo Cooper, 1976), p. 43.
60   General Sir Frederick Pile, *Ack Ack* (London: Harrap, 1949) p. 25.

Vyvyan Pope from the North Staffordshires, and John Crocker from the Middlesex Regiment, while Percy Hobart and le Quesne Martel were both Royal Engineers, and Ray Briggs came from the Machine Gun Corps. Cavalry and Guards officers did not feature at all in the new entry. As a recent creation, the Tank Corps lacked (or was free from) history and traditions and its undefined role but potential for mobility developed into a rivalry with the cavalry: the threat from the cavalry's point of view was that the Tank Corps might become not just another arm like the artillery, but another service like the RAF, and one that would absorb them and discard their cherished traditions. Antagonism was mutual and continuing: in Egypt 'in 1938 & 9 the R[oyal] T[ank] R[egiment] were accusing the cavalry of only being able to use polo ponies and sticks. The Cavalry referred to the RTR as garage mechanics,'[61] and Michael Carver, a Tank Regiment officer, describes the formation of the Royal Armoured Corps in April 1939, intended to bring the two together, as resulting at best 'in an uneasy alliance.'[62] The object had been to share management of basic training and recruiting, and establish one voice in the War Office. However the cavalry retained control of their officer selection – not for any valid military reason but to ensure continuity of their individual regimental style and regimental family atmosphere, one result being that there was no exchange of officers between cavalry and tank regiments to share experience. Royal Tank Regiment officers came from a much more varied background than their cavalry equivalent: Martel, the first Commandant of the RAC, recorded that

> about one third were public school boys, one third were carefully picked secondary school boys and we obtained the remaining third from older men who had already launched out into the world before the war.[63]

Regimental training continued independently, there was in North Africa no cross-fertilisation of ideas between cavalry and RTR before Montgomery's arrival, no attempt by the cavalry in the same period to examine the RTR's infantry support role and no instance through the war of a Royal Tank Regiment officer being appointed to command a cavalry regiment. Only one instance before 1944 of a cavalry officer commanding a Royal Tank Regiment has come to light. But the separatism of the cavalry came under pressure to adapt. A letter written in North Africa in April 1942,[64] from the commanding officer of the 9th Lancers, reveals the intensity of regimental jealousies and identity: Lieutenant Colonel Burne could not help:

---

61   Churchill Archive Centre, Cambridge, Lt. Gen Galloway Papers, GLWY 1/6, letter to Eric Sixsmith.
62   Field Marshal Lord Carver, *Out of Step* (London: Hutchinson, 1989) p. 49.
63   Martel, *An Outspoken Soldier,* p. 173.
64   TNA WO 169/481 9 Lancers War Diary, draft letter 22 April 1942 from Lt-Col E..O.|Burne.

[F]eeling increasing alarm at each new A.C.I. [Army Council Instruction] that comes out, adding, each one, another nail to the coffin of the individual cavalry Regiment. The compulsory black beret (hallowed by no good British Tradition),[65] the posting of officers to the R.A.C and not to a regiment, the forbidding of canvassing for the officer young entry, these are but a few examples. The argument that the popular regiments get a monopoly of the best class of officer is but a point in favour of the old system. Under the new system the R.A.C. will not get good officers at all. The powerful Trades Unions of the Guards Brigades [sic], and the Rifle Regiments will see to that. This stamping out of individual regimental existence is admittedly in conformity with practice in continental armies but is contrary to all British ideas. The Englishman is the inventor of the club, the club system is inherent in his blood, and not unnaturally he likes to belong to the best club. A good regiment is regarded as a good club by both officers and men, and round it are built up innumerable welfare associations, and social service societies. Is it imagined that Regimental private funds, News Letters, Regimental and Wives Associations, Old Comrade Associations and the rest, will operate in favour of the R.A.C?'

There is no indication as to whom or even whether the letter was sent, but at that time Lieutenant General Norrie commanding XXX Corps, Major General McCreery, Commandant of the RAC in Egypt, Major General Lumsden, GOC of 1st Armoured Division, and Brigadiers Carr, commanding 22nd Armoured Brigade, and Fisher, commander of 4th Armoured Brigade from mid-June, were all present in North Africa and were all former COs of a Lancer regiment. One might reasonably guess that these sentiments and the letter were directed to those quarters. Montgomery a few months later was also to use the term 'trades union' pejoratively to describe elite regiments, informing a staff officer that he was downgrading a certain formation (the 1st Armoured Brigade) as part of the process of 'destroying the desert trades union ... a very tight trades union operation which was governed by the 'cavalry', the Guards and the Greenjackets, and all the old sweats who thought they were very superior people.'[66]

The Royal Artillery's reputation had been enhanced by the Great War and many very senior positions between the wars were filled by its officers. Milne, Montgomery-Massingberd, Ironside and Brooke were all gunners and all Chiefs of the Imperial General Staff within a dozen years, while Pile, a contender for CIGS and originally a gunner, was appointed to the key pre-war post of GOC Anti-Aircraft Command.

---

65 The black beret was the RTR's distinctive uniform and was to become Montgomery's favoured headgear.
66 Nigel Hamilton, *Monty: The Making of a General, 1887-1942* (London: Hamlyn Paperbacks, 1992), p. 729.

Ironside was an unhappy choice for CIGS,[67] being more of a front line soldier than a staff officer, but he and his fellow gunners all, except perhaps Montgomery-Massingberd, showed an open mind to military developments, though frustrated by lack of funds and regimental vested interests and suffering criticism from politicians and journalists. In 1923 the Royal Horse Artillery, the Field Artillery and the Garrison Artillery had been merged into the Royal Regiment of Artillery but the Royal Horse Artillery which like the Rifle Brigade had a historically elite, specialist, role and tradition with lighter, more mobile guns and an association with the cavalry, managed to retain its identity. It continued to attract the more lively and generally more socially elevated type of officer, some of whom, in the less prosperous world after 1918, wished to avoid the expense of a cavalry regiment – it was occasionally said of them that they were 'poor, proud and prejudiced'.[68] To be selected to join a RHA regiment was something of an honour and was known as being 'awarded one's jacket', a reference to the ornately decorated dress uniform of the RHA. The field artillery regiments, their role to support the infantry, were less glamorous, and the anti-aircraft, coastal and garrison artillery even less so. Of all the regiments and Corps, the Royal Artillery supplied by far the greatest number of British 1939-45 generals (38), followed by the Royal Engineers (23), reflecting not only the pre-eminence of these arms during 1914-18 and the large number of battalion equivalent units in these two corps from whom senior officers would eventually be selected, but also perhaps their greater seriousness and professionalism, the number of university graduates among them and their suitability for the vast number of senior administrative and planning roles during 1939-45.[69] But to some in the army artillery officers in general were not always distinguished by their personalities: even after 1945, they were in some eyes characterised by 'a certain ordinariness'.[70]

Amongst infantry, cavalry and armoured units, the striking variations in the numbers of senior officers produced by different regiments must indicate differences in regimental culture and attitude to the profession. The Grenadier Guards produced eight generals between 1939-45, as many as the Coldstream, Scots, Welsh and Irish Guards combined. The Rifle Brigade produced seven, while Scottish infantry regiments outperformed English: the Cameron Highlanders produced eight, the Cameronians six and the Highland Light Infantry five. Most other infantry regiments produced between two and four. The eighteen pre-war cavalry regiments produced only four generals between them in contrast to the Royal Tank Regiment which, with four pre-war battalions from which to draw candidates, produced nine, of whom seven commanded divisions or corps in action, much the highest proportion of any regiment.

---

67   He had long been promised command of the BEF, for which he was well suited, but
      for personal and political reasons this went to the then CIGS Viscount Gort, whom he
      replaced. He was not successful at working in Whitehall with Churchill.
68   Dunn, *Sword and Wig*, p. 11.
69   Richard Mead, *Churchill's Lions* (Stroud: Spellmont 2007), pp. 526-7.
70   Beevor, *Inside the British Army*, p. 375.

Pay for regimental officers was barely subsistence level. A lieutenant in the 1930s was paid ten shillings (50p) a day, which when stationed in England would cover not more than his mess bills, and he could expect to spend at least ten years at this rank.[71] His rate was only a shilling (5p) a day more than in 1670, though admittedly then it also had to cover the cost of a horse.[72] Private means were necessary to make life tolerable in Britain, but in India or the Middle East, the two major foreign postings, living was very much cheaper and a reasonable lifestyle could be achieved. In the Indian Army and East African regiments or in attachments to units such as the Sudan Defence Force, pay was more generous as well. If in need of funds, it was often possible to find a position in a regiment posted abroad to replace an officer who preferred to stay in England[73]. As a captain in India in the 1920s with only his Great War gratuity to supplement his pay, John Harding could live comfortably and finance two polo ponies but a decade later found himself struggling to make ends meet as a married major dependent on his pay in England.[74] In England in 1939, 2nd Lieutenant Dunn's allowance of £150 a year from his father meant he could keep two hunters but only if he was extremely careful with his mess bills, largely giving up drink.[75]

Promotion in the army up to lieutenant colonel was dependent on vacancies within the regiment that the young officer had joined. Immediately after the Great War, the numbers wishing to continue an army career created a logjam: George Davy, a twenty year old gunner lieutenant, was told in 1919 he was welcome to remain in the army but since promotion within the Royal Artillery was by seniority he would not move beyond captain before he was 45.[76] He eventually succeeded in transferring to a cavalry regiment where advancement came sooner. Until the mid-1920s promotion as far as lieutenant-colonel remained a matter of seniority within one's regiment rather than ability, and changing the system roused controversy, for many felt that competition for a post between fellow officers would damage regimental cohesion. Discontent at the change showed at the CIGS's Staff Conference at Camberley in 1927, to judge by the CIGS's defence of it: 'I want to speak about the fact that promotion to command a battalion is now by merit. There was a great howl about promotion by merit some time ago. Now, we hear nothing of the praise side of it; we only hear the complaint side of it.'[77] Below lieutenant colonel, the ambitious and able could evade the process of seniority by accepting a higher rank in another regiment if a vacancy appeared earlier than in one's own, a system known as 'accelerated'

71   £1 in 1930 equates to £64 in 2019, according to the Bank of England inflation calculator, making a 1930 subaltern's salary the equivalent of £10,000 p.a. today.
72   Carver, *Seven Ages*, p. 29.
73   Carver, *Out of Step*, p. 34.
74   Field Marshal Lord Michael Carver, *Harding of Petherton* (London: Weidenfeld & Nicholson, 1978), p. 39.
75   Dunn, *Sword and Wig*, p. 16.
76   Liddell Hart Centre for Military Archives, GB0099 Davy Manuscript memoirs & notes
77   TNA WO 279/57: Staff Conference at Camberley 17-20 Jan 1927, p.53.

promotion. Montgomery for one took advantage of this, though it was regarded as slightly 'pushy', or 'careerist', the respectable ambition of most being to command their own regiment – the future Lieutenant General O'Connor twice refused accelerated promotion into other regiments in order to have a chance of commanding a battalion of his own, the Cameronians.[78] Some officers, from the Rifle Brigade in particular, were reluctant for social reasons to move even temporarily to what they considered an inferior regiment,[79] and no example of a Guards officer serving in another regiment outside another Guards battalion has come to light: their attitude to line infantry was summed up not long ago in a reference, by a (post-war) Coldstreamer in conversation with the writer, to 'fish and chip' regiments.

The promotion rate was a real grievance for many regimental officers. A lieutenant could expect to spend 10 or 12 years at that rank and salary. As one commentator wrote, 'To keep an officer at the restricted, repetitive work of a subaltern during all these years is to risk destroying him body and soul.'[80] Generous leave and a light workload were only a partial recompense. For the ambitious, promotion to general was at least partly dependent on which regiment the officer belonged since the first hurdle, promotion to colonel within the regiment, was more easily crossed in those regiments where a higher proportion of officers left the army early. In practice this meant the regiments whose officers could afford to leave on inheriting the family estate. In 1933-4 the average age of Guards officers on promotion to lieutenant colonel was 40, in the cavalry 44, infantry 46 and artillery 48.[81] Given the four year posting as a commanding officer and the retirement age of 55 for those who had not reached general rank, the window of opportunity for promotion to major-general therefore varied from eleven years for a Guards officer (55-(40+4)) to three for a gunner (55-(48+4)), and therefore the senior ranks of the army were likely to be disproportionately dominated by the Guards and cavalry and under-represented by line infantry and artillery. War Office attempts to remedy matters by moving officers from one regiment to another through accelerated promotion were 'almost wholly unsatisfactory'[82] according to one critic and could cause bad feeling because it deprived an opportunity for those already in the regiment that the transferee joined. Regimental idiosyncrasies and traditions could make transfers difficult: rifle regiments' drill was only one of the distinctions in uniforms and practices that made interchange between

---

78 John Baynes, *The Forgotten Victor: General Sir Richard O'Connor* (London: Brasseys UK, 1989) p. 270.
79 Their most distinguished leader of the period, Lieutenant General 'Strafer' Gott', criticised this attitude, on the grounds that it was 'one's duty to accept and do all one could to raise the standard of some other regiment, however poor one privately thought it, and never to patronise it'. R. Vernon, ed., *'Strafer' Gott, A Tribute* (Winchester: Culverlands Press, n.d.), p. 23.
80 Kennedy, *This Our Army*, p. 82.
81 Kennedy, *This Our Army*, p. 85.
82 Kennedy, *This Our Army*, p. 90.

regiments and arms complicated and expensive, the difference in the cost of living of different regiments being also significant.

As a career, the army was not attractive to those ambitious for wealth or, given the uncertainty of promotion, position. Equally, it was not the last resort of the underachieving or the unemployable. It did offer social status, with a choice of levels from the Foot Guards to the Pioneer Corps, congenial company, responsibility, work that could be challenging and was of import if often routine, and very reasonable opportunity for leisure. This could take almost any shape. After the Great War, Eric Dorman-Smith spent his leaves on the Continent where he became a close friend of Hemingway and his set. Indeed, thanks to his war record he became something of an icon to them, featuring in Hemingway's early writings. George Davy, somewhat younger, was shy about revealing his talent as an artist, 'because one might be thought peculiar'. If he had known the future Field Marshal Brooke's passion in life was bird watching, he might have been less self-conscious, as it was, only after retirement as a senior officer did he find real fulfilment, as a painter and sculptor.[83] Michael Carver, in the thirties, and no great lover of regimental life but a classical scholar, took the opportunity of his posting in Egypt to visit the sites of the ancient Greek world. On the whole the army respected intelligence and ability and was tolerant of idiosyncrasies, provided the individual was not 'unsound', 'a troublemaker', 'too clever by half', or 'a wrong 'un '. Sir Michael Howard, explaining in later years that he had been too shy to admit at his interview with the Coldstream in 1941 that his reason for applying to join was that he liked their regimental march, was told by his former interviewer, 'My dear boy, why didn't you tell me? We would have been *delighted*!'[84] Most appreciated the availability of horses, one of the major perks of the army,[85] riding being an expensive pastime in civilian life where grooms as well as animals had to be paid for. Carver and Dorman-Smith, neither at all in the conventional mould, were as enthusiastic as their contemporaries about hunting while at Sandhurst – a full blooded, life endangering and reputation enhancing activity in the days before hard hats, body protectors or air ambulances, corresponding to amateur club rugby today in terms of physical demands, nerve and commitment.[86] Abroad, polo substituted for hunting, though there was a pack of hounds at the Staff College in Quetta in India, in

83   Liddell Hart Centre for Military Archives, Davy Papers.
84   Sir Michael Howard, *Captain Professor* (London: Continuum, 2006), p. 53.
85   Ability to ride was essential for all officers before mechanisation – Major General Anthony Deane Drummond, DSO, MC & Bar, joined the Royal Signals from Woolwich in 1937 because it was an inexpensive corps and 'because two horses, or "chargers" were the automatic right of every officer in the unit.' *Obituary, Daily Telegraph*, 5 Dec 2012. Riding lessons remained compulsory at least for Royal Marine and Foot Guard officers into the 1950s.
86   e.g. Lt. Gen Norrie's tribute to 'Jock' Campbell recalling the fight at Sidi Rezegh for which Campbell was awarded his VC: 'A fine horseman and a great man across country... I can remember him so well reveling at the smell of gun powder and saying to me with a glint in his eye "this is really better than fox hunting."' See IWM, Campbell Papers, n.d.

emulation of the Drag Hunt at Camberley, and in England different forms of racing supplemented it: Herbert Lumsden, later to command X Armoured Corps under Montgomery, won the Grand National, and the future Field Marshal John Harding had never ridden before enlisting but learned to compete enthusiastically in amateur races. Infantry, cavalry and gunner teams competed on the polo field, to the fury of the cavalry when another arm won.

3. The future Field Marshal Harding demonstrating army equestrianism, 'full blooded, life endangering and reputation enhancing', in 1929. (Orion Publishing Group)

One might argue whether it was altogether desirable to have, as a significant proportion of officers, individuals whose view of soldiering was as an agreeable and honourable occupation with excellent recreational facilities rather than as a serious profession demanding as much intellectual dedication as that of the doctor, the lawyer or the engineer. But one should recognise the virtues of the British officers who emerged from this culture and these institutions. They were competent, honest, patriotic, immune to political extremes, self-sacrificing and careful of the lives of their men. Their country did little to prepare their army for the Second World

War, and they were forced into a scramble to catch up. Whatever criticisms can be made of them, they could not be accused of then lacking commitment. Loyalty to their regiment meant they would persevere in an army which paid them poorly, was inadequately equipped and which many of them regarded at times with a degree of cynicism.

Staff College

In the nineteenth century, focus on the regiment as central to army life, and as the limit of promotion for most, led many officers to disparage those who took a broader view of military affairs and whose ambition went further, and thus created a division between 'staff' officers and 'fighting' soldiers. The divide was exemplified by the followers of Garnet Wolseley, the scientific soldier of the late Victorian period, and those of the Duke of Cambridge, Commander in Chief from 1866 to 1893. The ability of staff officers was sometimes questioned, and their personalities also: 'The College has been called hard names – a Forcing House for Unpleasant People', wrote Major Godwin-Austen in 1928.[87] But twenty five years earlier the consequences of raising an army of 250,000 for the Boer War, with staff officers sufficient for only 90,000, had finally confirmed the need for a General Staff with clear definitions of roles and qualifications, amid a growing awareness that 'soldiering was something more than filling in the time between breakfast and lunch'.[88] From 1906, appointments to the new General Staff were reserved for those who had passed Staff College, and successful service on the Staff was to be rewarded by accelerated promotion. Immediately, the number of applications to Staff College rose – in 1908 141 candidates applied for 36 places whereas in the late nineteenth century there had sometimes been not even two for each vacancy. The Great War aroused criticism of the Staff – the journalist Sir Philip Gibbs complained of 'the high stupidities, the narrow imagination, the deep, impregnable, intolerant ignorance of the Staff College men' – though in fact the Staff had coped fairly well with the problems of expanding the army by several million. After being closed for the duration of the war, the College reopened in 1921 with much fiercer competition for entry and by 1926 there were 440 applicants for 22 places. Nonetheless, a solid body of opinion still held that 'real' soldiering began and finished with the regiment. Senior elements of the army tried to ensure that talented young officers were not deterred from applying, and also to ensure that less academic soldiers were not excluded.

Major Godwin-Austen's 1927 history of the Staff College was clearly intended to encourage prospective applicants. Its viewpoint was endorsed in a foreword by the CIGS, Field Marshal Milne. It listed successful graduates from the past, emphasized

---

87   Major A.R. Godwin-Austen, *The Staff and the Staff College* (London: Constable, 1927) p. xi.
88   Godwin-Austen, *The Staff*, p. xi.

good fellowship, excellent sport, and stimulating work in an institution that was progressing confidently into the twentieth century. It reads rather like the prospectus for a fairly new university keen to attract bright but not radical students and included hints on preparation for the entrance examination. It says much about attitudes of the time. An emphasis on sport, in particular on the Drag Hunt, 'the mainstay of the life of the Staff College',[89] represents the relaxed, uncompetitive, collegiate, atmosphere. Care is taken not to put off 'the ordinary "mutton-fisted" regimental officer' by appearing 'highbrow'[90] – which Godwin-Austen feared an official description of the College as 'a school of progressive military thought' was likely to do. He hoped that this 'flowery description' would not encourage young Staff Officers 'thereby to take themselves too seriously but carry on the good work naturally and unaffectedly.' He reassures them that 'The Public School spirit, in fact, is apparent', especially in deflating those with 'a mistaken notion of intellectual superiority.'[91] In his final paragraph he rather piously hopes resentment against the Staff is disappearing but expects leg-pulling from regimental officers to continue – 'may the Staff see to it that no justification arises for any jest with a sting.'[92]

The records of the Staff Conference at Camberley that year, chaired by the CIGS Field Marshal Milne, echo this perspective and shed light on the army as well.[93] On the attitude of regimental officers to the College, a Colonel Thorpe observed:

> The Staff College exists for the higher training of officers, whether as staff officers or as commanders … There are lots of officers I know who do not wish to go on the staff but would rather command their battalion or regiment. Therefore they stay in the regiment.[94]

Colonel Karslake on the other hand thought 'that the majority of officers are now really ambitious and feel that, unless they can get a p.s.c., their chances are nil.'[95] Colonel Finlayson pointed out that 'there are always certain fellows who cannot do examinations – first class fellows in the field, first class leaders and thoroughly knowledgeable, who just fail in the examination.' As matters stood, these could bypass the entrance exam through a nomination from their CO but should 'possess a good personality, and must be above the average in tact, ability, character and power of command.'[96] To avoid suspicions of string-pulling at the final selection, their details

89   Godwin-Austen, *The Staff,* p. 292.
90   Godwin-Austen, *The Staff,* p. 245.
91   Godwin-Austen, *The Staff,* p. 287.
92   Godwin-Austen, *The Staff,* p. 300.
93   TNA WO 279/57 Staff Conference at Camberley, 17-20 Jan 1927.
94   TNA WO 279/57: Staff Conference at Camberley, 17-20 Jan 1927, p. 43.
95   TNA WO 279/57: Staff Conference at Camberley, 17-20 Jan 1927, p. 49.
96   TNA WO279/57: Staff Conference at Camberley, 17-20 Jan 1927, p. 45 (p.s.c. – passed staff college).

would be anonymised before being considered by the Army Council. But Lieutenant General Gillman thought nominations through an officer's CO had the disadvantage that 'many commanding officers have themselves failed to get into Staff College or have a distinct aversion to what they dub a "brass hat"',[97] and could be unresponsive to a request for a nomination.

Faced with this diversity of views, Milne was at pains to confirm that there was no intention of following the admission procedure practised in France (the only comparable foreign Staff College) which involved a demanding series of written exams and interviews, and he emphasised that the current system would continue, subject to fine tuning. It is clear that the matter exercised the minds of regimental officers, and that there was at least a healthy freedom to express opinions.

In the 1920s and 30s the Staff College was not a think tank for tactics, nor was it designed to produce a reserve of brainpower to be deployed as needed, nor was it an arena where careerists could make their mark. It did not teach a doctrine and had no guiding philosophy. It was not technically or politically educated enough to see beyond the remit provided by the government of the day and was therefore unable provide answers to problems that would be posed in the near future. It did not tackle questions to which freelance military theorists were ready to provide answers. Tactics were taught on paper or through 'TEWTS', Tactical Exercises Without Troops, rather than on exercise with full sized units and formations. The standard method was through 'syndicates', when candidates were divided into groups to work out among themselves the solution to a problem, after which the 'staff college solution' would be announced. It was an approach that would be likely to encourage a consultative style of leadership, and Brigadier Eric Dorman-Smith, sent by Lieutenant General Auchinleck, C-in-C Middle East, to check on Eighth Army's leadership in February 1942, did indeed report on a 'syndicate' method of command that was currently in practice, and which he identified as one of the 'slovenly' practices that were then contributing to the army's difficulties.[98]

In the field, at brigade level the role of principal staff officer was filled by the brigade major, a highly responsible post that marked out the officeholder as a competent figure. At divisional and higher levels, the custom was to have one principal staff officer for general staff ('G') duties of planning and issuing orders, and another for administration ('A' and 'Q'). At divisional HQ, this post was titled GSO1 and was held by a colonel, at Corps level it was titled Brigadier General Staff and held by a brigadier. These posts rarely had the power of command in the absence of the formation commander. In contrast, the German army had a tradition of formation commanders empowering their chiefs of staff to plan and give orders to subordinate formations even when they were commanded by men of superior rank. The senior commander could therefore absent himself from headquarters to observe conditions at

97   TNA WO279/57: Staff Conference at Camberley, 17-20 Jan 1927, p. 50.
98   GB133GOW1/3/1, letter 1/6/64 to de Guinguand.

the front, greatly assisting speed of decision making. Some British commanders were beginning to appreciate these advantages during this period, and some staff officers were unofficially beginning to take these responsibilities upon themselves.

Overall, between the wars the Staff College's outlook was constricted by the army's primary role of policing the empire, and its tolerance, good humour and fellowship reinforced the common culture of the men who would be leading it for the next twenty years. It did teach them 'best practice' in administration and organisation – staff work throughout the Second World War was of high standard. It winnowed out those who lacked the intellectual capacity for high command. Its graduates were blessed with a confidence in their country that allowed them to wait upon events and to be prepared to respond when required. There was enough irreverence to encourage independent thought. With an upper age limit for entry of 33, and a directing staff only ten years older, the atmosphere was intended to be collegiate and cooperative among both students and directing staff.[99] This easy, relaxed manner of command permeated the army – what Godwin-Austen described as 'the peculiarly British spirit of humour bubbling through it. Everyone is expected to do a job of work without making heavy weather, or taking it, or himself, too seriously.'[100] But it could be argued, and was later said by some, that Staff College was an inadequate preparation for the challenges of the Second World War:

> The extraordinary ambivalence of our commanders and their inability to seize upon the occasion can only be due to the training they had been given and especially to that given at our Staff College in England... Excellent staff officers emerged, men capable of the highest efficiency, [but] astonishingly few capable fighting commanders for a war of manoeuvre ... the diagrammatic rigidity of 1918 artillery governed battle and minds became conditioned by it.[101]

This was perhaps a dig at Montgomery as much as a criticism of Staff College, for as will be seen there was no shortage of British commanders wedded to the idea of manoeuvre warfare. But they lacked a unifying doctrine, and though they prided themselves on their flexibility and capacity to improvise, their differing policies never produced the coherent pattern of tactics that was required.

One might reasonably say that up to 1933 the army was less class ridden and no more tradition bound than its future opponent, efficient in its primary role of safeguarding the Empire, aware of its shortcomings and lacking only resources to innovate. Although an unsatisfactory home for those individuals who saw themselves

99 Though three decades later Dorman Smith recalled drive and ambition as the rule at Staff College, 'where anything went, influence, social position and downright climbing on one's neighbour's back by hook or by crook.' Here he is perhaps, as elsewhere, himself the exception that proves the rule. John Rylands Library, GB133GOW2/3/1.

100 Godwin-Austen, *The Staff*, p. 296.

101 Lieutenant General Sir Francis Tuker, *Approach to Battle* (London: Cassell, 1963), p. 144.

as freethinking radicals and were frustrated by resistance to change, it went to some lengths to accommodate their idiosyncrasies and respected their talents even if it was unable to make full use of them. But one cannot ignore the repeated complaints of senior officers in the war years – Montgomery and Brooke in particular – bemoaning the shortage of able men who could be promoted to divisional or corps command. However agreeable its institutions and ambience, and no matter how dedicated its officer corps when put to the test, the British army of the 1930s lacked the professional edge of its chief opponent.

Commonwealth Forces

A significant proportion of British troops in North Africa came from the Empire, supplying most of the infantry divisions as well as supporting troops. The alacrity with which the self governing Dominion countries within the Commonwealth had joined in the declaration of war against Germany had been heartening for many Britons. But along with the Dominions' right to choose to participate came the right of their senior commanders to appeal to their own Government if they thought a proposed operation was unsound and put their troops unduly at risk. That said, there was never a task accepted by the New Zealand and Australian divisions that was not undertaken wholeheartedly. Cultural and social differences had some effect on relationships but were quickly overcome and mutual respect established. One Australian wrote after attending an Officer Cadet Training Unit in Cairo:

> When I came to the OCTU I thought, like most Australians, that an Englishman could be only one of two things – a tailor's dummy or a man on the dole. I now know he is a quiet, likeable fellow who just doesn't think it necessary to act tough.[102]

The informality of Australian discipline bemused many British officers. Major General Douglas Wimberley of the 51st Highland Division rotated his battalions through the 9th Australian Division in September 1942 for experience in the front line and found when he visited that the Australians were 'all half naked and burnt brown as berries. They took a bit of getting used to. I was dressed as a General and they treated me in the most "matey" way.'[103] Australian soldiers, on first name terms with their own officers, were astonished to find that Scottish soldiers had to salute theirs even in action, but differences did not prevent a strong mutual respect. The Sherwood Rangers, an exceedingly 'smart' Yeomanry regiment, took especial care prior to action to polish their brasses in sight of Australian troops, purely to provoke

---

102 Christopher Seton-Watson, *Dunkirk – Alamein – Bologna: Diaries and Letters of an Artilleryman 1939-1945* (London: Buckland Publications Ltd, 1993), p. 109.
103 Quoted in Barr, *Pendulum of War*, p. 262.

a response.[104] Sergeant Wardrop of 5RTR, who fought in the front line from 1940 to 1945 and whose principal recreational activities were amateur boxing and bar room brawls, came across Australians in the closing stages of El Alamein:

> I watched the Australians as we drove through and didn't they look tough, most of them had on only boots and shorts, a rifle and bayonet and a tin hat. They were dirty and unshaven, but at that moment I wouldn't have said 'boo' to the smallest one I could see.[105]

New Zealand troops in contrast combined good turnout and smart behaviour with battlefield competence well up to Australian standards. Both contingents were proud of the reputation of their ANZAC forbears in the previous war and aimed to live up to them. Their commanders were careful to keep their formations intact, refusing to allow British commanders to detach their brigades and employ them independently in the name of flexibility. In the end, flexibility went in the other direction and British brigades were assigned to the New Zealand and Australian divisions when operations made it necessary, and from Alamein onwards the New Zealand infantry division was, uniquely, given its own (British) armoured brigade. The New Zealand performance is epitomised by the two Victoria Crosses awarded to Captain Charles Upham. But like the South Africans their leadership was hampered by being recruited from a small base, and when they were without their Major General Freyberg, their organisation could miss a beat.

Neither Morshead of 9th Australian Division, nor Freyberg of 2nd New Zealand Division, ever commanded a corps and at times were discontented serving under British corps commanders less experienced than themselves. Morshead and his division returned to the Pacific after Alamein but the New Zealanders stayed on in Eighth Army, highly esteemed by Montgomery. They continued to be led, wounds permitting, by the legendary Freyberg, his formation swelling almost to Corps dimensions but still nominally a division.

South African soldiers impressed British commanders, being fit, enthusiastic, and 'full of guts' in Auchinleck's words.[106] But South Africa was a divided nation with (in 1941-42) a single figure majority in Parliament for keeping the country in the war. Their military leaders became notorious for minimising the risk to their troops of any operation, in part from the fear that casualties could mean votes lost and political problems at home.[107] Their formations had been raised from a very small base and their units at battalion level sometimes lacked training and skills.[108] Their

104 Keith Douglas, *From Alamein to Zem Zem* (London: Faber & Faber, 2009), p. 137.
105 George Forty (ed.), *Jake Wardrop's Diary* (Stroud: Amberley Publishing, 2009), p. 71.
106 JLR AUC133/516, Letter from Auchinleck to Arthur Smith 4/12/41.
107 JLR AUC133/581, Letter from Auchinleck to Brooke 25/12/41.
108 JLR AUC133/509, Letter from Auchinleck to Arthur Smith 3/12/41 'The South Africans are **not** trained and are much too unwieldy ... they don't **know** yet.' See also Dunn, *Sword*

divisional commanders and staffs proved either inexperienced or uncooperative, and they were widely if unjustly blamed for the sudden collapse at Tobruk in 1942.[109] Auchinleck described the two South African divisional commanders as 'not very easy to convince of realities.'[110] From the South African point of view, British commanders were unconvincing both militarily and as individuals: Brigadier Hartshorn found Auchinleck rude, humourless and arrogant and was told by his divisional commander Dan Pienaar at a time when he was supposed to be co-operating closely with 201st Guards Brigade, "You know the three things I hate in this world—British lords, British generals and these bloody Guards!"[111]. Both Pienaar and his fellow divisional commander Brink were Afrikaners who with their families had suffered a spell in concentration camps during the Boer War, though according to a recent historian they had emerged from the experience with 'relatively little' dislike for the British.[112] It was not until Montgomery arrived that Pienaar admitted to respect for a British superior.[113] All British commanders, both in North Africa and in the earlier campaign against Italian forces in East Africa, had great difficulty in persuading their South African colleagues to conform to plans. Lieutenant General Norrie's verdict in July 1942 was that neither 1st nor 2nd South African divisions had been properly trained or fitted for mobile operations, and that 'over half their Commanders need replacing by really young men.'[114]

All three of these Commonwealth contingents lacked confidence in British command during the setbacks of the summer of 1942. Lieutenant General 'Strafer' Gott as XIII Corps Commander was universally admired by his British subordinates but held in no particular respect by his New Zealand juniors, and Dan Pienaar of 1st South African Division was positively hostile to him, though Gott seems to have thought his charm had won him over. Freyberg flatly refused to install his division as the garrison of Mersa Matruh or to reorganise it into battlegroups as Auchinleck wished in June 1942. Willoughby Norrie, commanding XXX Corps, had difficulties persuading both Brink of 1st South African Division in November 1941 and Pienaar in July 1942 to follow instructions. Norrie's replacement, Ramsden, had similar problems with Pienaar and also with Morshead of 9th Australian Division. Ritchie reported in the crisis of June 1942 that Pienaar's division was 'not at the moment

and Wig, p. 38.
109 Brawls in Cairo bars were not far short of a recognised form of recreation for troops on leave, and one of the most legendary is said to have been sparked in July 1942 when an Australian met a South African, and offered him a chair with the words, " 'Ere, 'ave a seat mate, you must be knackered after running all the way from Tobruk."
110 JLR AUC133/696, Letter to Ritchie 10/2/42.
111 E.P. Hartshorn, *Avenge Tobruk*. (Cape Town: Purnell & Sons, 1960), p. 171.
112 David Brock Katz, *South Africans versus Rommel* (Guilford, Conn.: Stackpole Books, 2018), p. 232.
113 Katz, *South Africans Versus Rommel*, p. 248.
114 TNA WO 216/85: Norrie's Report, 12 July 1942.

in fine fighting trim'.[115] That such serious rifts should occur so frequently suggests that they were more than clashes of personality or legitimate military differences of opinion, something more like an antipathy on the part of the Commonwealth troops to certain aspects of the British Army. It is an unremarked facet of Montgomery's leadership that these problems disappeared when he took command.

India produced the largest Imperial contingent in North Africa, its 4th, 5th and 10th Indian Infantry divisions, and 3rd Indian Motor Brigade amounting in numbers to almost as many as the rest of the Commonwealth combined. The Indian Army was on a different footing to the Dominion forces, run by British officers, mostly paid for by the British-run Government of India and subject to the same conditions of use as British troops. In 1940 their battalions were largely led by British officers with a number of Indian officers in junior regimental positions. The best Indian Army regiments were famously good, the Ghurkhas (who though ethnically not Indian came under Indian army organisation) being of course the exemplar, but years of garrison duty in an extreme climate, in the days before air conditioning or refrigeration, took its toll on the health and energy of some of their English officers. Central India in particular became known as 'the Sloth Belt', reflecting the prejudice or scepticism in the minds of some of the British Army about their peers from some Indian units. At the most senior level, there was a view that dated back to Kitchener's alleged comment of 1898 that the Indian army existed as a means of outdoor relief for the British middle classes. After two spells in India Montgomery was unimpressed by the Indian Army and ignored 4th Indian Division's desert experience and high morale to give them only a secondary role at Alamein. He later vetoed their commander's promotion to lieutenant general despite Francis Tuker's excellent performance, though Tuker's forthright expressions of opinion could verge on truculence and may have been a factor in the decision. Montgomery was not alone in his prejudice against Indian Army officers. 'Strafer' Gott reportedly described Corbett, Auchinleck's Chief of Staff, as 'the stupidest man in the Indian Army, and that's saying something'. Auchinleck, an Indian Army officer himself, was something of a lonely figure in North Africa since he lacked the extensive network of contacts normal among British officers and relied too much on the few with whom he was comfortable.

Indian Army officers and men both came from highly stratified, class conscious societies where in a military context relationships could be based on mutual respect and trust even if there was no social contact: 'It was the cardinal belief of British officers that their Indian troops would go "through thick and thin for an officer they had decided was the right kind"'.[116] Other British officers were generally impressed

115 I.S.O. Playfair, *The History of the Second World War: The Mediterranean and the Middle East*, vol. iii (London: HSMO, 1966), p. 281.
116 Philip Mason, *A Matter of Honour: An Account of the Indian Army, its Officers and Men* (London: Jonathan Cape, 1974), p. 391.

by Indian troops. J.W. Ramster, not a professional soldier, met Indian soldiers in Egypt in 1942 and 'found them to be the best coloureds [sic], very well educated and never push themselves. Have earned a grand name for themselves in the desert.'[117] His troopship had called in at Capetown where he was disconcerted by the treatment of the black population in South Africa by whites, who, outnumbered ten to one, he thought were frightened of them. In Egypt he noted South African troops' refusal to talk to the Indians. Coming after the fall of Tobruk, this did not impress Ramster.

After 1918, given the loyal service of Indian troops on the Western Front and in the Middle East and the growth of a nationalist movement towards independence, the time had clearly come for Indianisation of the Indian army leadership. There were concerns as to whether British officers would be willing to serve under Indian officers, and whether the right kind of Indian officer could be found to replace them. As Lord Rawlinson, the Commander in Chief in India in 1919, put it:

> Will we ever get a young educated Indian to lead a charge of veteran Sikhs against a sangar held by Mahsuds and, if he did, would the Sikhs follow him? Will we ever get the sons of landowners of the fighting races, who are brought up to despise the Babu [literate Indians], ... sufficiently educated to be trusted with the lives of men in modern war?[118]

The first two Indian divisions to be raised in 1940, the 4th and 5th, were outstandingly good, serving from 1940 in North and East Africa, then in Tunisia, Italy and Burma through to 1945 and consistently respected by all ranks in the British Army. From 1941 Indian brigades consisted of one British and two Indian battalions, one of which might be a Gurkha unit, which often engendered healthy competition between units and in combat terms proved to be the best combination. Political issues at home were not reported as affecting Indian troops in North Africa. Shortage of British officers and instructors fluent in their Indian soldiers' languages caused difficulties in some of the divisions raised after 1940, until the increasing numbers of ethnic Indian officers eased the problem. Further difficulties were incurred in providing appropriate diet and leisure activities and communication with family despite the pressures of war and ensuring service in the regiment appropriate to their religion, race, caste and language. British officers needed to 'have a thorough knowledge of the peculiar problems that arise ... The younger officers are splendid and do their utmost but they cannot make up in a few years training for the lack of experience and travel among the men's villages and homes.'[119]

The Indian Army commanders of Indian component infantry divisions performed creditably. Messervy was competent at 4th Indian Infantry Division in 1941, if less

117 IWM, J.W. Ramster Diaries S/152130
118 Mason, *A Matter of Honour,* p. 454.
119 TNA WO 201/2644: Report on Indian Troops, 1943.

convincing at 1st and 7th armoured divisions in 1942. In Burma he again proved a capable commander of an infantry division, and later a corps. H.R. Briggs led 5th Indian Division in the summer of 1942, could not be blamed for defeat at Gazala, took the division successfully through the Burma campaign and in post-war Malaya drew up the 'Briggs Plan' which was the foundation of the successful counterinsurgency campaign. Tuker took over 4th Indian Division early in 1942 and was outstanding as a trainer and leader for the rest of the war. Thomas 'Pete' Rees, later to earn an outstanding record in Burma as the ultimate 'fighting' soldier, commanded 10th Indian Division in the desert in June 1942 but was sacked by Gott for querying orders that indeed turned out to be disastrous. Eric Dorman-Smith 'just could not understand Gott's sacking Rees.' He thought Tuker and Rees were 'damn good soldiers', but to the British snobs, 'sepoy generals'.[120]

French Troops

A 2,000 strong unit of the French Foreign legion, the 13th demi-Brigade, had been evacuated to Great Britain in 1940, and from there had joined British forces fighting the Italians in Eritrea. Initial British scepticism was replaced by respect for their performance, and the demi-Brigade then participated in the British invasion of Vichy French held Syria in June 1941, where they encountered their brothers in arms, the 6th Foreign Legion infantry regiment, on the opposite side. After the fighting, a thousand of the latter switched allegiance and joined the demi-Brigade to form the Free French Brigade under General Koenig, who held the 'box' at Bir Hacheim in June 1942 in some of the fiercest combat of the campaign. Despite their military prowess the French contingent was never fully at home in Eighth Army. Some British liked them more than others. Michael Carver as a staff officer with 7th Armoured Division in 1940 attended the 'order group' of a Capitaine Foliot prior to a raid on Italian positions:

> It turned out to be an excellent lunch, gazelle and desert snails featuring on the menu, at the end of which the Capitaine made a long and eloquent speech, followed by the cry: "Maintenant, mes camarades, a Bir Enba!" I asked my neighbour, one of his officers, whether or not we could expect more detailed orders. "Wait for a few hours, until we've all sobered down, and you will get them," was his reply![121]

---

120 JRL GOW 1/11/4, Letter to Connell.
121 Carver, *Out of Step*, p. 60.

Air Marshal Tedder found most of the Free French leaders 'violently anti-British' at this time,[122] and British feeling towards the French tended to reflect generations of hostilities and suspicion. Tuker wrote of 'the modern Frenchman' that 'he's so used to corruption that he suspects all his fellows and us.'[123] The French had their own suspicions of 'perfidious Albion', and Britain's destruction of the French fleet at Oran to prevent its takeover by the Axis was the source of lasting bitterness. Koenig himself was a committed supporter of General de Gaulle whose obduracy and unreliability, as the British saw it, made him a difficult ally at that time. Koenig's Gaullism and British chauvinism were not a good mix. At Bir Hacheim in June 1942 Koenig was determined not to allow the sacrifice of the only active Free French formation and forced its evacuation from the box by refusing to accept resupply. He was described during that battle as 'somewhat hysterical'[124] by his divisional commander Major General Messervy and 'slightly hysterical'[125] by his Corps commander Lieutenant General Norrie. These comments owe as much to conventional British attitudes towards continentals as to Koenig's actual behaviour.

One notes as a matter of interest that the Wehrmacht recruited some 2,000 French Foreign Legionnaires of German nationality from Legion units marooned in Tunisia and Algeria after 1940. They were formed into the 361st Motorised Infantry Regiment of 90th Light Division for active service with the Afrika Korps. Rommel affectionately referred to them as 'my Africans'.

---

122 Air Marshal Lord Tedder, *With Prejudice* (Boston, Massachusetts: Little, Brown & Co., 1966), p. 131.
123 IWM 71/21/2/6: Tuker Papers 25/8/41 DMT's Tour of ME.
124 TNA WO106/2235: Operations 26/5-2/7/42 Report of Court of Enquiry p. 207.
125 TNA WO 201/2871: Norrie report on Operations, May-June 1942, p. 17.

2

Doctrine, Training and Equipment

The 1919 Treaty of Versailles imposed draconian restrictions on the new German Republic's armed forces. Aircraft, submarines, large naval vessels, tanks and heavy artillery were prohibited. The army was restricted to 100,000 men with an enlistment period of twelve years to limit the building up of a trained reserve. Production of much war material was banned and the great German General Staff, seen as the fount of German military efficiency and aggression, was banned. Inevitably, the measures were circumvented to some degree: soldiers were hidden in roles with civilian titles, civilian organisations performed repair, maintenance or transportation roles, German companies could buy foreign arms manufacturers or set up units abroad, and senior German officers could always fulfil the tasks of a general staff under another name. Germany was nonetheless left barely able to defend herself against even the smallest of her neighbours.

The 4,000 officers selected as the founding leaders of the Reichswehr, the German army post-1918, were chosen for their ability and their potential: one foreign observer noted that 'practically every officer from the grade of first lieutenant up has a more or less brilliant war record'.[1] The limited number of openings available each year, and the insecurity of civilian employment, ensured a continuing high standard among each years' 200 new entrants who, despite the restrictions imposed by the Treaty of Versailles, maintained a professionalism honed by annual exercises that looked to a future when Germany would again have an army that was capable of defending its territory. But its initial weakness was brutally illustrated in 1923 when French forces occupied the Ruhr to enforce payment of reparations, and consideration had to be given to instigating a peoples' guerrilla war as possibly more effective in a fight for the integrity of German territory than conventional combat.

Those who joined German cavalry regiments in the 1920s shared some of the outlook and the social and equestrian activities of their British opposite numbers.

---

1   Robert M. Citino, *The Path to Blitzkrieg* (Mechanicsburg, Pennsylvania: Stackpole Books, 2008), p. 133.

Friedrich von Mellenthin, later to distinguish himself in North Africa and on the Eastern Front, regarded the eleven years he spent in a cavalry regiment as the happiest of his life, where he could indulge his love of riding and steeplechasing.[2] Hunting on horseback was widespread until banned by Goering in 1934. Where they differed from their British counterparts was the alacrity with which they took the opportunities offered by mechanisation to assume a leading role in the German army of the future. Hans von Luck in 1930 joined a cavalry regiment in Silesia, but was then transferred unexpectedly to East Prussia, to the 1st Motorized Battalion:

> A bitter disappointment, as the cavalry was the elite force and I loved horses and riding. But we soon realised that the seven motorized battalions in the Reichswehr were to become the nucleus of the later tank force.[3]

In 1945 General Gunther Blumentritt, who had served at the highest levels in the Wehrmacht before and throughout the war, was interrogated on German armoured theory, practice and organization in the 1930s. The transcript (emphases as in the original typescript) provides a good summary of its developement: 'The young officer corps rushed to join the armoured forces, especially the younger type of cavalry officers',[4] a contrast to the British cavalry/Tank Corps schism mentioned earlier. However it was not the rattle of tracks or the scent of engine oil that drew the new recruits so much as the training and doctrine in which they had been educated since they joined the Reichswehr. They were conscious of being in the forefront of a specialist 'operating' army rather than the mass militia, and therefore were to be the decisive component of the mobile defensive battle scenario postulated by Colonel General Hans von Seeckt, Chief of the Army Command from 1920 to 1926, as Germany's only option for survival against the superior numbers that its neighbours could deploy. Young British officers had no similar professional incentive: the British army's role was to maintain the Imperial status quo, and in terms of defence against an existential threat it was second to the Royal Navy and would shortly be third to the RAF. Nor did the British army have anything that might be called a 'doctrine' of warfare, a philosophy underpinning the thinking behind organisation, training and tactics that, being commonly accepted, would help mutual understanding between units and arms.

The cavalry tradition in Germany, dating back to the eighteenth century when it was the decisive arm under Frederick the Great, was even more powerful than in Britain: as Blumentritt implied above, many senior German officers clung on to the mounted arm and did so even after its weakness had been demonstrated in Poland in 1940. As late as 1941, a Wehrmacht cavalry division was among the formations to

---

2   Mellenthin, *Panzer Battles,* p. 33
3   Hans Von Luck, *Panzer Commander (New York: Dell Books, 1989),* p. 13.
4   TNA WO 232/7: Interrogation of Senior German Officers, 1945.

invade Russia, though within three months its commander advised converting it to armour.[5] But young German officers of the 1920s were excited by the opportunity to put into practice through mechanisation their doctrinal principles of mobility, of 'forward leadership', of 'mission command', as fundamental to the German army as 'engage the enemy more closely' was to the Royal Navy. They enthusiastically joined the organisation comprising seven lorried infantry battalions led by Lutz, the Inspector of Motor Transport Troops, with a General Staff trained signals specialist, Lieutenant Colonel Heinz Guderian, as his Chief of Staff. It is impossible to imagine English cavalry officers similarly abandoning their regiments to join an organisation dominated by the British equivalents, the Royal Army Service Corps, and the Royal Signals. Blumentritt's testimony continued:

> The Fuhrer was the real founder of tank armament, which was his favourite weapon... The higher military commanders, who were in the abstract already against war and rearmament, had little understanding for this modern form of arms. Especially, the upper military commander class was by nature distrustful of all forms of technical science ... their sympathies lay in the direction of big cavalry formations with modern equipment. Only the later Field Marshals von Reichenau and von Manstein had progressive views on the subject. Between 1935 and 1938 the Fuhrer fought for his tank armament against the leading military commanders...Colonel Gen Guderian was the Fuhrer's man, who created tank armament for him, both from the technical standpoint as also from that of leadership...The young officer corps rushed to join the armoured forces, especially the younger type of cavalry officers.
>
> Leadership: Idea and spirit was a return to classical standards in the spirit of the great cavalry leaders of olden times. Therefore: speed, mobility, raids, manoeuvrability, freedom of action in large strategic areas, detached from armies on foot.
>
> Training. The far too swift rearmament and the new creation of mobile troops made themselves unpleasantly felt even in the few years. But young and privileged officer corps of this elite force made up for its shortcomings.[6]

There are similarities and differences between the British and German approach to this new form of warfare. The British 'upper military commander class' might be described, in some instances, as having 'little understanding' – but by no means all of them. Milne, Wavell, Pile, Broad, Burnett-Stuart, Lindsay, Hobart and Martel were neither insignificant nor lacking in understanding. There was no movement in favour

---

5   Though horses could provide some mobility in the extreme conditions of the Russian front and both sides reverted to mounted troops in numbers by the close of the war.

6   TNA WO 232/10: Interrogation of senior German officers, Blumentritt Interrogation, December 1945.

of 'big cavalry formations' in the British army and it was the German Army that was the last western European power to send a cavalry division to war.[7] However the younger British cavalry officers did not rush to join the armoured forces as in Germany – they remained in their horsed regiments, accepting tanks and armoured cars as they were issued, but certainly not transferring to join their socially inferior colleagues in the Royal Tank Corps, nor improvising when faced with shortcomings in equipment. Blumentritt's view of the élan and high standard of leadership among the new German formations is confirmed by events. He may have regarded the rapid expansion of the Panzer arm as having unfortunate effects, but their defects went unnoticed by their opponents in the early campaigns. The mechanised formations' shortcomings identified in the Polish campaign amounted to a shortage of medium tanks and the relative ineffectiveness of the mechanised light divisions.[8] Re-equipping the panzer divisions, upgrading the light divisions and massing the panzer corps together rather than using them to support infantry formations brought the panzer arm to a very high level of effectiveness by 1940. German unity of purpose and command in the half dozen years before the outbreak of war contrasts with the situation in Britain. Fully supported by government and under the direction of Lutz's and then Guderian's energy and inspirational leadership, by 1939 a coherent armoured force was equipped in accordance with a mature doctrine derived from a philosophy common to the other arms of the Wehrmacht. It was a doctrine that facilitated understanding and flexibility and it was born from a military tradition quite different to the British army's regimental ethos and imperial duties.

German Military Doctrine

Even after unification in 1870 Germany was still surrounded, as Prussia had been, by potential enemies, almost any two of which in combination could pose a serious threat. The Prussian, and later the German, army was seen in its homeland as an existential necessity just as the Royal Navy was in Britain. It was lavished with resources and also much thought in developing the doctrine under which it trained and would fight. From the mid nineteenth century the German General Staff recognised that a defensive war against greater numbers could be won only if their army was superior in training, leaders and operational skills, and based on aggressive tactics to seize the initiative. A war of attrition was out of the question and decision in battle could only be won through mobility, concentration of forces at the decisive point, the *schwerpunkt*, and ideally a battle of encirclement, a *kesselschlacht*. The series of wars from 1848-70

---

7   In June 1941 1st Cavalry Division advanced with Guderian's 3rd Panzer Gruppe into Russia and operated mounted until September 1941 when its commander requested that it be mechanised. It was reformed as the 24th Panzer Division.

8   TNA WO 232/10: Interrogation of senior German officers, Blumentritt Interrogation, December 1945.

that resulted in the unification of Germany under the Prussian Kaiser validated both the military philosophy of Clausewitz and the training and doctrine of the Imperial German army. Even after defeat in 1918, and despite restrictions on equipment and manning imposed by the Treaty of Versailles, neither military thought nor training were inhibited. The army's leaders followed a doctrine for mobile defensive warfare that made the most of now limited resources, and the Reichsheer of 1919, a professional 'operating' army designed to be backed by a mass army of militia or reservists, proved to be an excellent foundation for the later Wehrmacht. If the German army was to succeed on a strategic or operational level as a mobile, aggressive and flexible force, it would have to act with similar characteristics at the tactical level, and in the 1920s it began to build on its successful stormtroop tactics of 1918. Even before the rise of Hitler or re-equipment with tanks, existing doctrine was refined by von Seeckt into a tactical manual, *Fuhrung und Gefecht der verbundenen Waffen*, or 'Leadership and Combat of the Combined Arms'. Known as *Das F.u.G.*, published in 1921 and 1923, it embodied the principles of German tactical warfare for the next decade. (It should be born in mind that the word 'doctrine' has in German a prescriptive quality, implying a certain orthodoxy in compliance with principles, and it is not a word much used in the German military lexicon.[9] 'Military thought' is a better expression than 'doctrine' for German military philosophy, though the single word will continue to be used for convenience.)

Though highly conservative by nature, Seeckt recognised that faced with the demands of modern war the fighting soldier could not afford to be unthinking. Dr. Otto Gessler, the government minister to whom he answered, described him as having 'an acute intelligence which went straight to the point of things and held fast to realities. He was the enemy of all heroics, all emotionalism and amateurishness in soldiering.'[10] His experience of the Great War on the Eastern Front had been different to that of the British and French in the west. The length of the Eastern front line had made the trench systems of the west impossible and the war of movement in the eastern theatre was in line with the German nineteenth century military tradition of 'operational' warfare, using speed, surprise and aggression of major army units to produce, ideally, a battle or series of battles of encirclement that would destroy or force the surrender of opposing formations. The great size of nineteenth and early twentieth century continental armies made central control next to impossible in these circumstances and therefore delegation of responsibility became essential, ultimately producing a doctrine of '*Aufragstaktik*', usually translated as 'mission command' or 'mission tactics', but perhaps best described as 'independence of the lower

9   Strohn, *The German Army*, p. 14.
10   Karl Demeter, *The German Officer Corps in State and Society 1650–1945 (New York: Frederick A. Praeger, 1965)*, p. 106.

commander.'[11] It allowed, in fact made it the duty of, the lower commander to act on his own initiative in accordance with the overall objective of his senior. Rather than following a prescriptive set of orders, it enabled him to grasp opportunities without the delays that would follow requests for approval of action. Seeckt's methodology was based on aggression and mobility, having seen that better trained, better led and better equipped troops could decisively defeat much larger forces. *Das F.u.G.* was steeped in this spirit, viewing combined arms combat as crucial at the tactical level, employing mobility and firepower rather than mass, and regarding offensive tactical training as essential for success against numerically superior enemies.

Flexibility in the command structure was greatly enhanced by the general staff system that had been a feature of the Prussian army from the nineteenth century, in which the commander's chief of staff had the authority, in fact the duty, to initiate planning and give orders in his own right as well as on behalf of his commander. The team of Hindenburg and Ludendorff in the First World War is a prime example of how well the system could work, Seeckt had performed a similar role for von Mackeson on the Eastern Front, and in North Africa Rommel could absent himself from his headquarters, confident that his chief of staff had the authority to give orders to subordinate units, would execute his wishes, and cope with changes in the situation.

Throughout his tenure as Chief of the Army Command, Seeckt was faced with the insuperable military problem of providing within the terms of the Versailles treaty a defence for Germany with an army limited to 100,000 men. Given the tensions created by the existence of minority populations in Germany and neighbouring countries after the postwar adjustments of national borders, stability could not be taken for granted, and Seeckt's solution to this military problem became the foundation of German tactics and operations. His proposition was that a small army would be easier to supply with the latest equipment, and quicker to mobilise and strike. If Germany's opponents trained and equipped their mass armies with modern technology they would face problems of cost and political will, and without this modernisation their mass army could be outmanoeuvred and crushed. The key for the Reichsheer was mobility and co-operation of all weapons, decisive even for the smallest units, together with an emphasis on increasing infantry firepower through machine guns and mortars. Seeckt was a cavalryman, and cavalry comprised three of the ten divisions that the Reichsheer was permitted, but it was mobility rather than mounted warfare that he saw as paramount. He insisted that despite the complete lack of tanks throughout the 1920s, the use of armour had to be studied, even if only in theory. In his 1925 'Observations' on his command he emphasised that 'the employment and combat of tanks must become a matter of common knowledge throughout the army,' even if only through the use of models in sandtable exercises and dummy tanks in the field.[12]

11   Gerhardt Gross, *The Myth and Reality of German Warfare: Operational Thinking from Moltke,* (Kentucky: Kentucky University, 2016), p. viii.
12   Citino, *The Path to Blitzkrieg,* p. 59.

His comments were taken to heart: they were issued to every officer down to the rank of captain, and the US military attaché in Germany, Colonel A.L.Conger, was told that 'These "Observations" by our chief are our rule and guide for the year's work of training'. Conger himself saw evidence the following year of Seeckt's principles being followed, with dummy or model tanks featuring in every manoeuvre.[13]

It was under Seeckt that the Reichsheer established a motor transport battalion within each of the seven infantry divisions and that Lutz developed them into potentially more than infantry transport. The notion of transport troops acting as combat units was impeded by a somewhat conservative Inspector of Motor Transport, but Lutz took his role in 1926,[14] and began a series of experiments including dummy tanks and wooden artillery and anti-tank guns with the trucks. He emphasised the importance of surprise and established the principles of employing armour in not less than battalion sized units, on independent missions rather than as infantry support but nonetheless combining with the other arms, particularly artillery and anti-tank weapons. Ideas and facilities were sought in other countries. His chief of staff, Guderian, read de Gaulle's and Fuller's works on mechanised warfare and followed the British experimental exercises from 1927 onwards. British manuals based on the Salisbury Plain experiments as well as Brigadier Charles Broad's booklet, the *Purple Primer*, were translated into German and distributed, and 250 copies of an account of the 1932 tank exercises on Salisbury Plain were printed and circulated. By 1929 a few tanks had been built in secret in Germany and some training facilities were provided in Sweden and by the Russians at Kazan. In 1932 Lutz was able to sum up the results of the theoretical and practical work with a number of basic principles. The chief conclusion was to use tanks at the decisive point rather than waste them in a supporting role, and to use them in mass, in at least battalion strength. Surprise, and attack on a broad front with further units following up, would allow the *schwerpunkt* to be switched to take advantage of unexpected opportunities. Tanks were not to be tied down to infantry support but to be themselves supported by all arms in co-operation, including anti-tank guns for use against possible counter attack by armour – the ban on tanks in the Reichsheer forced the German army to appreciate the value of anti-tank weapons even before it was equipped with tanks.

Seeckt's career ended in 1926 in a political storm following an invitation to the heir of the Hohenzollern throne to observe military manoeuvres. It was intended that *Das F.u.G* should not be revised until ten years after first publication so that its tenets would have a chance to be applied consistently through the Reichsheer, but by 1930 it was ready for updating, a task undertaken by the Commander in Chief, Ludwig Beck. The result was a volume named *Truppenführung*, Troop Leadership.

---

13   Citino, *The Path to Blitzkrieg*, p. 60.
14   J.P. Harris & F.N. Toase, *Armoured Warfare* (London: Batsford, 1990), p.54

Truppenführung 'provided a formula for the guidance of officers at every level of combat to produce the appropriate solution at every level.'[15] It is a volume of 1064 paragraphs covering broad principles of warfare, tactical hints and details of procedure, and sets its tone with the first sentences: 'War is an art, a free and creative activity founded on scientific principles. It makes the very highest demands on the human personality.' *Truppenführung* emphasizes the virtues of the attack and pursuit to complete annihilation of the enemy, and in particular the notion of 'forward leadership', which emphasised that the correct place for commanders at almost every level was to be sufficiently close to the front to enable them to assess the situation on the ground and take instant decisions.[16] It dovetailed with other principles of organization and command enshrined in the German Army, including *Auftragstaktik*, 'Mission command', and *Einheitsprinzip*, standardised units capable of being attached and detached without loss of tactical integrity or logistical problems. Efficient wireless communications now made possible the speed, co-ordination and flexibility that was the object of these principles. Speed of decision was rated as more important than a search for the perfect solution, if in doubt the more aggressive course of action was to be favoured, in defence immediate counterattack at the initiative of the local commander up to battalion level was the rule. The speed of German reaction was to become notorious among the British along with the acknowledgement that 'they will always punish your mistakes'. A somewhat rueful description of the effectiveness of German doctrine in this respect comes from Lieutenant General Francis Tuker, one of the better British divisional commanders, who experienced German professionalism outside Tobruk on 15th December 1941. His division lost 1000 men from a battalion and their supporting gunners when the retreating enemy struck back:

> Their counter attacks came in, as did this one, sharp, hard and above all concentrated…we were preparing for an attack and were disposing ourselves for it; but perhaps we were working in the old style of careful detailed staging, instead of the new [German] style of automatic deployment followed by a concentrated stroke at speed at the point selected for outflanking or penetration'.[17]

Concentration of force at a *schwerpunkt* was a feature of German defensive tactics too. Friedrich von Mellenthin, a distinguished staff officer in North Africa for Rommel and on the Russian front for General Hermann Balck and Field Marshal von Manstein, expressed the Wehrmacht's defensive philosophy at a post-war conference:

---

15   Strohn, *The German Army*, p. 186.
16   Bruce Condell & David Zabecki (eds.), *On the German Art of War: Truppenführung* (London: Lynne Reiner Publishers, 2001), pp. 24, 36-38.
17   Tuker, *Approach to Battle*, p.35

You know, in the defence it's the same as in the attack, you must have in your defence also a Schwerpunkt, that means a place where you think there is the most dangerous point for the enemy to come through. At this place you have to concentrate all of your artillery fire, all of your antitank guns, and so on. A defence without a Schwerpunkt is like a man without a character.[18]

German leaders did not merely pay lip service to the precepts in *Das F.u.G* and *Truppenführung*. Their commitment to 'forward leadership', for example, is demonstrated in startling fashion by the front line casualty rate of divisional commanders in North Africa: among German major generals (or higher ranks), there were eighteen casualties, killed, wounded or captured, in North Africa 1941-2 compared to eight British. All but three of the German casualties were incurred while the Afrika Korps was on the attack, commanders up at the front; all the British casualties were incurred while their headquarters were overrun, or on the defensive, or when their forces were static.

German Senior Officer Casualties 1941-42:   Killed 6   Wounded 9   Captured 3

Panzerarmee Afrika HQ
Stumme, GOC Pzarmee   killed 24/10/42
Gause, Army Chief of Staff wounded)
Westphal, Army Ia   wounded) 1/6/42

Afrika Korps commanders
Cruewell   captured 28/5/42
Nehring   wounded 31/8/42
Von Thoma   captured 4/11/42

21st Panzer Division Commanders
Von Ravenstein   captured 28/11/41
Neumann-Silkow   killed 9/12/41
Von Bismarck   wounded 17/7/42, killed 31/8/42
Randow   killed 21/12/42

15th Panzer Division Commanders
Von Prittwitz   killed 10/4/41
Von Esebeck   wounded 25/5/41
Von Vaerst   wounded 26/5/42

---

18   Major General Friedrich von Mellenthin, Record of *Armoured Warfare in World War II*, Conference, Battelle Columbus Laboratories Conference 1979, p. 34.

90th Light Division Commanders
Summerman   killed 10/12/41
Kleeman   wounded 13/7/42 & 8/9/42

Brescia Division
Kirkheim (in temporary command) wounded April 1941

British Senior Officer Casualties: Killed 0   Wounded 4   Captured 4

Western Desert Force Commanders
O'Connor   captured 6/4/41
Neame

2nd Armoured Division Commander
Gambier-Parry   captured 8/4/41

7th Armoured Division Commander
Messervy   captured (& escaped) 27/5/42

2nd NZ Division Commander
Freyberg   wounded 27/6/42

1st Armoured Division Commanders
Lumsden   wounded 31/12/41 & 18/7/42
Gatehouse   wounded 21/7/42

The figures are even more telling if one allows for the greater number of British divisions in the front line during the periods of engagement.[19] One should note in passing that the inferior performance of Eighth Army in this period is sometimes blamed in part on the rate at which British commanders were sacked before they could put into practice the lessons they had learned. It is clear from these figures that the overall turnover of senior commanders in the Afrika Korps was far higher than in Eighth Army, and German performance did not suffer as a result – because, as was recognised at the time by at least one British general, the Germans had a good

19	Number of divisions engaged	German	British
	March–June 1941	1-2	1-2
	Nov–Dec 1941	3	5
	Jan 1942	3	2
	May – July 1942	3-4	5 engaged at any one time, not including reserves
	Sept 1942	4	5
	Oct–Dec 1942	4	8

supply of competent leaders owing to their 'systematic pre-war training and adherence to simple well tried principles which our Army seems to have mostly forgotten.'[20] Though it would have been more accurate to suggest that, rather than forgetting their principles, the British Army had never really developed a commonly understood doctrine on which a set of tactical principles could be based.

The nearest the British Army came to producing a statement of military doctrine was the volume known as Field Services Regulations. FSR III of 1935, intended for 'Higher Formations' and the 'Superior Commander', was an edition heavily revised by the then Major General Archibald Wavell. Wavell had made his reputation as a trainer of troops and devising exercises, including providing opposition for the Experimental Mobile Force in 1927. The imaginative exercises which he devised as a brigade commander, greatly assisted by his brigade major, Eric Dorman-Smith, aimed to simulate the conditions of fatigue, bewilderment and incomplete information encountered in war. A man of broad interests and evident humanity, much admired by his immediate subordinates and contemporaries and one of the more cerebral British soldiers of the period, his view on war in general contrasts starkly with *Truppenführung*'s 'free and creative activity founded on scientific principles'. Writing of 'that very dull business, war'[21] he calls it 'deplorably dull and usually so inefficiently run'[22] and 'a wasteful, boring, muddled affair; and people of fine intelligence either resign themselves to it or fret badly.'[23] He seems to reflect the mindset of a garrison army, maintaining peace, in contrast to the Reichsheer or the Wehrmacht whose mission was to prepare for war. FSR's paragraphs on leadership at the highest level reflect the value he – and the British Army – placed on the personal and humane relationships that a leader should ensure with those to whom he gives orders:

> Besides clear and definite orders, personal touch is an essential factor in conveying a commander's intentions to his subordinates and in inspiring them with confidence and determination. No commander from the highest downward must ever forget that human nature is the ultimate factor on which all his plans, operations and movements depend.

Otherwise, FSR III is concerned with little more than clarifying terms and procedures and identifying hazards in each phase of war. Its tone suggests that provided its recommendations are observed no great harm should ensue and is consistent with Wavell's belief in the value of training, and indeed in the army's confidence in the value of its regular soldiers. The commander is shown as a prescriptive figure who, clearly

20   JRL, Auchinleck Papers GB AUC133/742, Letter 7/3/42 to Brooke from Galloway, DCGS 8th Army
21   Wavell to Dorman-Smith Feb 1941, quoted in Corelli Barnett, *The Desert Generals*.
22   Quoted in Lavinia Graecen, *Chink: A Biography* (London: Macmillan, 1989), p. 167.
23   Quoted in Barrie Pitt, *The Crucible of War, The Western Desert 1941* (London: Jonathan Cape, 1980) p. 3.

explaining his intentions, will allot his subordinates definite tasks, and although he should 'then allow them liberty of action in carrying out these tasks', the aim is to avoid excessive centralisation and micromanagement from the commander rather than to suggest that subordinates have a responsibility to take decisions in the light of the commander's objective. It was perhaps British distrust of intellectualism and abstract ideas that made the notion of 'doctrine' less acceptable than a hierarchical and autocratic command system, leavened by a degree of freedom of choice which could be justified historically by the British tradition of individualism and 'muddling through'. As Milne told his audience at the 1927 Staff Conference, 'The interpretation [of FSR] as you get on in the service, especially as regards senior officers of the General Staff, must be left to you to a great extent'. This was not likely to lead to either consistency of training through the army, or reliable transmission of orders through the chain of command. Nor in practice did it allow individuality and initiative to flourish. Early in 1942, Rommel's Panzerarmee headquarters summarised the British command's performance in the previous winter's fighting:

> Their orders were schematic and went into the smallest detail. The middle and lower command were consequently allowed little freedom of movement. The higher command usually adapted only slowly to the changing situation resulting from the flux of battle.[24]

In view of Wavell's influence pre-war and his later role as Commander in Chief in the Middle East, his views on training, leadership and tactical development in the 1930s are significant. In FSR III he lists and defines the 'principles of war' but his talks and publications throughout the 1930s discount their importance, describing them as 'all simply common sense, and... all instinctive to the properly-trained soldier'.[25] His advice to students of military history was, 'Don't read outlines on strategy or the principles of war. Read biographies, memoirs, historical novels ... get at the flesh and blood of it, not the skeleton.'[26] The key was training, infantry training in particular, to bring out the 'qualities of the good soldier, by the development of which we make the man war-worthy – fit for any war'. Unlike *Truppenführung*, Wavell's FSR III does not attempt to look for a philosophy that could be inculcated into the army to provide common understanding of a tactical method that would remain valid despite technical developments. His readership would be likely to conclude that the army as it stood, built around the regimental system commanded by officers with, ideally, a somewhat broader education and more modern outlook and led by alert and enlightened brigade and divisional commanders, would amply suffice for at least the

24   Behrendt, *Rommel's Intelligence*, p. 141.
25   John Connell, *Wavell: Scholar and Soldier* (London: Collins, 1964), pp.161-62.
26   General Sir Archibald Wavell, *Generals and Generalship: The Lees-Knowles Lectures 1939* (London: The Times Publishing Company, 1941), p. 18.

medium term. Looking at the immediate future, Wavell's discussion of armoured forces covers no more than the then state of development in Great Britain and treats it in the most general terms. Tank brigades or other mechanised forces were deemed unsuitable for attacking strongly defended localities and generally were to be used to attack the enemy's weaknesses rather than his strength. Their targets should be the enemy's tanks, reserves in movement and rear positions such as gun batteries, headquarters or communications:

> When the attack is aimed at penetrating the enemy front, it will not be normally possible to employ armoured and mobile forces until the main attack has succeeded in breaking down organised resistance and creating conditions favourable to their action.[27]

This was to equate the role of mechanised forces with the traditional exploitative role of cavalry rather than to build on the experience of the last months of war on the Western Front in 1918, when tanks, artillery and infantry had combined with air power to break through German lines. There is no recognition that the primitive state of early 1930s armoured vehicles would develop, most likely in directions that would improve their capabilities sufficiently to change the nature of modern war.

British Doctrinal Development

British use of armoured vehicles had proved decisive in breaking through German defences and defeating the German army at the Battle of Amiens, 8 August 1918 – 'the black day for the German Army', as Ludendorff called it – when a mass of tanks combined with infantry, artillery, and air attack to shatter German defences and stir the imagination of those involved in planning the next stage. Brigadier J.F.C. Fuller in particular, the chief of staff of the Tank Corps, was struck by the possibilities of using large numbers of the next generation of faster, more reliable tanks to finish the war with a decisive blow. Working on the ideas of his assistant, Major Giffard le Quesne Martel, a Royal Engineer involved with the first British use of tanks on the Somme and at Cambrai, his plan called for 10,500 British, French and American tanks to break through German lines in 1919. The intention was to use speed and surprise to disrupt German rear headquarters and command structure and to disintegrate their army rather than to destroy it in combat. Even if the war had not ended that November, the chance of his 'Plan 1919' ever being enacted was small, for the new British tank model on which it largely depended, the unprecedently speedy 'Medium D', was at the concept stage in the summer of 1918 and with total British tank production for the war only 2636 it is unlikely that numbers could have been

---

27 *Army Council, War Office, Field Service Regulations*, vol. III: *Operations: Higher Formations, 1935*, issued by Army Council, 31 December 1935 (HMSO: London, 1936), p. 46.

great enough by the following summer for the plan to be resourced.[28] But Fuller's vision struck a chord with those who later wished at all costs to avoid a repeat of the Great War experience and saw a strategy similar to Plan 1919 as the means to do it. Fuller was of a high intellectual order, described by a fellow staff officer as

> a totally unconventional soldier, prolific in ideas, fluent in expression, at daggers drawn with received opinion, authority and tradition … neither an administrator nor probably a good commander, but just what a staff officer should be, evolving sound ideas and leaving their execution to others. He was well up in Napoleonic lore, and had all the maxims at his finger ends.'[29]

His wartime deputy, le Quesne Martel, was pugnacious and direct, the only one of the early British enthusiasts for mechanisation to show a real grasp of the technicalities and, later, the only one of them to command a formation in action in the Second World War. Although he had visions of tanks deployed in fleets naval fashion, a notion further developed by Fuller, he appreciated that armour could only properly function if accompanied by artillery, infantry and engineers in mutually supporting roles. At Staff College in 1920 he renewed his relationship with Fuller and then at the War Office continued his involvement with armoured vehicles, setting out his ideas for a heavy tank to break through enemy lines and a lighter faster 'cavalry' tank to exploit the openings, together with a small inconspicuous machine to give direct support to infantry. He built half a dozen of the latter with the help of a neighbouring garage and after demonstrating them to great acclaim in 1925, they became the inspiration for the later Bren gun carrier that proved to be the most numerous British armoured vehicle ever produced.

Through an essay on a New Model Army built around armour that he delivered to the Royal United Services Institute, a highly respected independent defence research body, Fuller established a relationship with another intellectual and visionary, Captain Basil Liddell Hart. Hart, disabled by gas on the Somme and appalled by the deadlock of trench warfare, was looking to develop an alternative to the attritional warfare and frontal attacks of 1914-18. Fuller and Liddell Hart were to work together closely for the next dozen years. On the strength of his own talk at the RUSI in 1923 on an 'expanding torrent' system of attack, Liddell Hart was asked to write the new official Infantry Training Pamphlet and secured a post as military correspondent for the Morning Post, later moving to highly influential positions with the Daily Telegraph and the Times.

In 1923 the Royal Tank Corps was established as a separate arm, giving it the freedom to explore new methods of operation rather than remain as an auxiliary to the

---

28   Richard Ogorkiewicz, *Tanks: 100 Years of Evolution* (Oxford: Osprey Publishing, 2008), p. 50
29   Trythall, *'Boney' Fuller*, p. 50.

infantry or cavalry. At this time Vickers produced their 'Medium' tank – recognisably modern in that it had a turret housing the crew and gun, a range of 100 miles and a speed of 20 mph – and Colonel Lindsay, the Inspector of the RTC, submitted to Field Marshal Milne, the new Chief of the Imperial General Staff, a proposal for an Experimental Mechanical Force to explore the possibilities of mechanised warfare. With Fuller in situ from 1926 as Milne's Military Assistant (thanks to Liddell Hart's recommendation), the proposal took shape the following year as the Experimental Mechanised Force (EMF). It consisted of a battalion of 48 Vickers Medium tanks, a machine gun battalion in cross country lorries, a regiment of artillery including some self-propelled guns, a company of engineers and appropriate signallers. Martel was positive about the set-up, writing that 'co-operation between all arms took place at every stage'.[30] But by now Liddell Hart and Fuller's crusade to mechanise the army and reform it on their new model, had begun to alarm the more conservative elements, who were concerned for the future of their regiments. Even those in the cavalry who accepted that mounted action was a thing of the past feared that they might be converted to 'tank marines', as Fuller put it, mechanised infantry in modern parlance. Artillery officers suspected that once field guns were mounted on tracked vehicles, and there was a battery of these included in the EMF, their own regiments might be dissolved and come under command of the Royal Tank Corps. The infantry felt that their regimental traditions, a key element of their commitment to the service, were similarly being ignored. It was clear to many outside the RTC that if the Tank Corps dominated the army as Fuller and Liddell Hart forecast, there might be implications for their careers, since Tank Corps officers would have a head start in promotion to command the new formations. Thus when Milne held a Staff Conference at Camberley in January 1927, though he gave time for the prophets of mechanisation such as Lindsay, Martel and Fuller to address the audience of colonels and generals, he was obliged to reassure their listeners that change in the army did not mean that they or their regiments would become obsolete as a result, saying that the 'doctrine that infantry cannot make progress without tanks...is entirely fatal to the spirit of the Army'[31] and that he had 'read some articles by some officers who imagine that the Tank Corps is going to swallow up the whole of the army. I do not think the Tank Corps will get the rapid promotion in that respect that they imagine.'[32]

Milne's efforts to negotiate a path between the different concerns were made no easier when Fuller first accepted command of the Experimental Mechanical Force for the exercises of 1927, and then refused it on the grounds that he would also be burdened with command of the garrison where it was to be based. Unfortunately, under pressure from journalists like Liddell Hart to be seen as a modernizer, the Secretary of State for War had already announced and taken the credit for Fuller's

---

30   Martel, *Our Armoured Forces*, p. 42.
31   TNA WO 279.57: Staff Conference at Camberley, 17-20 Jan 1927, p. 26.
32   TNA WO 279.57: Staff Conference, p. 88.

appointment in the House of Commons. Fuller's refusal was, therefore, as Fuller himself put it, 'like an exploding bomb – the War Office was upheaved',[33] all the more since Liddell Hart then wrote for the Times a commentary on the event highly critical of the Army. Fuller's immediate superior, Lieutenant General Ironside, did his best to save Fuller's career and secured his promotion to brigadier and then to major general. However Fuller never properly recovered from the contretemps and he 'was consigned, politely but effectively, to the military outer darkness',[34] placed on half pay in 1930 and finally resigned in 1933 after refusing a posting to Bombay. Like Fuller, Liddell Hart too showed a reluctance to take responsibility. The GOC British troops in Egypt, in friendly but "put up or shut up" terms, had offered him the opportunity not just to observe but to command a mechanised column in a four-day exercise. Despite describing himself in a letter to his father as 'seeking to be prepared' to 'grasp the reins in a future crisis' to 'check the stampede and avert endless tragedy',[35] Liddell Hart nonetheless pleaded that at 37 he was too old for the role, perhaps because he feared losing his credibility as a critic of military affairs, and his self proclaimed status as 'the best known military writer in the world'[36], if he failed. This refusal can have done little for his standing in senior military circles.

In the exercises of 1927, even under its somewhat pedestrian substitute commander, the EMF outmanoeuvred & paralysed its opponents, the 3rd Infantry Division and the 2nd Cavalry Brigade under Lieutenant General Burnett-Stuart. But it lacked the inspirational leadership that Fuller might have provided. There was useful progress by Charles Broad and Lindsay in developing wireless communications to allow a single individual to control a formation on the move, but no developement of doctrine or tactics. The difficulty that tanks found in working with the other arms unless they too were in tracked armoured vehicles became apparent. But with more logic than imagination it was decided to therefore ignore the possibilities of combining tanks, infantry and artillery in armoured formations, and to adjust the role of tanks to the separate roles of reconnaissance, supporting infantry divisions, or deep mobile manoeuvres of tank only formations. Whether Fuller himself would have taken a longer view and worked towards combination of arms and obtaining cross country transport for supporting arms is impossible to say.

After the EMF's first training season, Milne's summary, drafted by Broad and drawing on Liddell Hart's and Fuller's writings, spoke of the petrol engine facilitating 'strategical mobility' as in the days of the Parthians and Mongols, with an armoured force 'that can go long distances and carry out big turning movements' independently of cavalry and infantry divisions. The emphasis, under the influence of Percy

---

33   Quoted in Alex Danchev, *Alchemist of War: The Life of Basil Liddell Hart* (London: Orion Books Ltd, 1999) p. 149.
34   Trythall, *'Boney' Fuller*, p. 145.
35   Danchev, *Alchemist of War*, p. 166.
36   Danchev, *Alchemist of War*, p. 151.

Hobart and Broad, was now on tank-only units, giving armour a decisive role. But Milne's view was that while experimentation was valid, 'we have to act cautiously so as not to upset the tradition, the *esprit de corps* and the feeling of the army as a whole'. In January 1929 he proposed organizing four brigades, one each of cavalry, light armoured vehicles, medium tanks, and infantry, which once they were 'properly worked out and equipped...it will be the task of our successors to bring them together and form them into higher organisations'.[37] This had more than a hint of kicking the awkward issue of the army's mechanisation into the long grass to avoid confronting the vested interests of traditional units, and indeed nothing came of it. Milne's policy of 'gradualness', working within the possibilities, was not helped by the intemperance of the progressive element, whose radical views at a time when there was no chance at all of their reforms being funded, tended to close the debate as far as the bulk of the army was concerned. Broad in March 1928 had suggested funding two armoured divisions 'by scrapping useless things … the horses and everything connected with them, schools, veterinary services etc.' and wrote that he and his colleagues must 'harden our hearts and create one Armoured Corps to contain all units which man armoured cars and fighting tanks of all kinds'. [38] Lindsay argued that a new Corps 'unhampered by the old and useless part of tradition' would make a New Idea 'go' far quicker than an old one and, in contradiction of Liddell Hart's view that a cavalryman could command an armoured force, described the cavalry as 'supremely ignorant ' of mechanical matters. His reforms involved converting four regiments of cavalry and sixteen battalions of infantry to mechanised duties and would have generated opposition on a commensurate scale. The depth of the opposition to mechanisation can be judged by a letter from Montgomery-Massingberd, GOC of Southern Command to the War Office in 1930:

> I am of the opinion that constant traveling in motor cars and tanks is largely the cause of loss of eye for ground. There is no doubt that the officer who is constantly riding about on a horse cultivates the eye for ground automatically. It is for this very reason that I have been very opposed to the taking away of horses from Tank battalions, and I should very much like to see them replaced.[39]

The army's first attempt to formulate doctrine for armoured warfare appeared in Broad's 1929 booklet 'Mechanised and Armoured Formations', better known from its unusually vivid cover as 'The Purple Primer'. It ignored the question of operations 'against hostile armoured formations' with 'considerable bodies of tanks on both sides' on the grounds that the subject was purely theoretical as such formations did not currently exist. Instead it advocated small, slow, heavily armoured but cheap tanks

---

37   Quoted in Carver, *Apostles of Mobility*, p. 48.
38   Kenneth Macksey, *The Tank Pioneers* (London: Jane's, 1981) p. 81.
39   Lewin, *Man of Armour*, p. 75.

to support infantry, and quite separate brigades of fast lightly armoured tanks, up to half of them armed with a weapon heavier than a machine gun, operating in open ground, using speed to achieve surprise while conducting raids of at most brigade strength, presuming that 'more frequent demands will be made on mobility, i.e. power to manoeuvre, than on the actual act of battle.' The influence of Liddell Hart is here unmistakable, as is that of Fuller in advocating large numbers of fast-moving light machines. 'Surprise should result from freedom of manoeuvre', since time and place of attack would be at the attacker's choice, but preference was for surrounding and cutting off an enemy from his supplies 'rather than to attempt a quick decision by attacks, the success of which is doubtful.' Broad's treatment of an assault on the enemy's main line of defence envisaged a breakthrough phase, establishing a breach wide enough to enable supplies to reach exploiting troops, and an exploitation phase. Mobile divisions should be reserved for this second task, distinct from those taking part in the initial battle, the objective being to cause a general collapse of the whole front by attacks on the rear of the position, interrupting enemy supply and disrupting their command. 'The resultant chaos should create opportunities for decisive operations under conditions of mobile warfare.'

Frederick Pile in that year was commanding a regiment of light tanks in the exercises and had evolved a method of advancing in bounds with co-operation of all arms at every stage. It had completely surprised the opposition and baffled the directing staff who 'said it was very dangerous and was not war,' and after two years of trials 'attention was changed to armoured forces as opposed to mechanised forces. All-armoured forces were designed to pass through enemy lines and fight behind them.'[40] Pile's view was that this shift away from combined arms was sponsored by the rising star in the RTC, Colonel Percy 'Patrick' Hobart, and was supported by Broad.

Broad's thinking in the Purple Primer is echoed in Liddell Hart's 'The British Way in Warfare', published in 1932, which speaks of a 'close fighting part, composed of semi-mechanised infantry', and a 'fighting part', composed entirely of armoured fighting vehicles. While the infantry cleared urban areas, entrenched positions and rough terrain and occupied strategic points, 'the mobile fighting units would manoeuvre widely to turn the enemy's flanks and attack his lines of supply'. Faced with 'a well-prepared position bristling with anti-tank guns, their tactics will probably be to harass the inert foe by fire while they cut off his supplies', forcing surrender or a hazardous retreat. His emphasis is consistently on attacking the enemy supplies, transport, and communication, and he condemns the 'customary attacks on the fighting troops' by mobile arms during exercises as 'merely spectacular illusions, mirages in the peace-time military desert.' His conclusion is that manoeuvre rather than combat is the tactic that will produce decisive results.

Broad himself was given command of the Experimental Tank Brigade that in 1931 superseded the EMF. As an all RTC formation it had no artillery or infantry

40   Pile, *Ack Ack*, p. 28.

components and its main achievement was to at last convincingly demonstrate the possibilities opened up by wireless voice control for battalion and company commanders, in particular in controlling passage through an enemy's lines and operating in his rear. Broad described it as 'the beginning of the realization of all our dreams'.[41] The emphasis had changed from a mechanised mixed force that included infantry and artillery to an armoured, mostly tank, force under the influence of Hobart whose views were now supported by Broad.[42] One sign of this shift is that Broad did not mention any requirement for self propelled artillery in the 1931 second edition of the Purple Primer, though it had been specified in 1929. A battery of five 18-pdr self-propelled 'Birch guns', the brainchild of the Master General of the Ordnance, Major General Sir Noel Birch, had been included in the mechanised artillery regiment of the EMF, but they were then discarded and did not feature in the 1930 exercises.

The Experimental Tank Brigade achieved permanent status in 1933 and became 1st Army Tank Brigade under Hobart himself from 1934-6, and its mixed battalions of three companies of medium and one of light tanks with minimal supporting troops became the pattern for the next few years. Lindsay in the meantime had been given command of the 7th Experimental Infantry Brigade and Hobart suggested that for the exercises in 1934 the two brigades should combine as a Mobile Division. Unfortunately Lindsay was diverted by family and local duties from full concentration on training up his brigade and his brigade major, 'a member of the Rifle Brigade who let it be known that he neither liked nor trusted Hobart and who also found it hard to communicate with Hobart's Brigade Major', failed to make up for Lindsay's shortcomings.[43] Furthermore the current CIGS, Burnett-Stuart, was intent on an 'infantry revival'. To avoid a repetition of the defeat that his conventional formations had suffered in the exercise of 1927, he imposed impossible conditions on the mechanised forces for the exercise of 1934, changing terms of engagement and enforcing delays on Hobart's tanks. When Lindsay's administrative and signals arrangements also proved inadequate, the Mobile Division was deemed to have failed and Lindsay was publicly held to be at fault by Burnett-Stuart. Press and political interest in the exercise was considerable: Lindsay recorded that 'Boney Fuller had a scathing article in the Evening Standard that could only be described as a personal attack on me.'[44] Instead of the promotion to command a division which a successful exercise should have brought, Lindsay was sidelined in an appointment to the Presidency and Assam District in India where his career faded out. Hobart continued in command of 1st Army Tank Brigade, and his 'tank heavy' policy remained standard practice.

Inevitably, lack of clarity over the role of armour affected procurement of tanks. The only tanks built in quantity in the 1920s had been the Vickers Medium model,

41   Macksey, The Tank Pioneers, letter from Broad to Lindsay, p. 88.
42   Martel, Our Armoured Forces, p. 42.
43   Macksey, The Tank Pioneers, p. 131.
44   Quoted in Macksey, The Tank Pioneers, p. 133.

of which 166 were completed by 1923. No British tanks armed with anything heavier than a machine gun were built between 1923 and 1936 except for half a dozen prototypes some of which showed potential but were considered too expensive to put into production in the financial climate of the time. The battalions of the RTC remained equipped with the Vickers Medium and since the horsed cavalry regiments now had no role but reconnaissance, it was with light tanks that they were equipped as they gradually mechanised. As the European political situation deteriorated after 1933, the Tank Brigade was put on permanent footing with one of its four battalions assigned to the role of infantry support, so an attempt had to be made to provide suitable tanks both for infantry support and the exploitation and harassing roles envisaged by the prophets and their disciples. John Carden, the garage owner who had been drawn into tank design by Martel and whose talent for designing light tanks had been rewarded by a knighthood and his recruitment as a design engineer by Vickers, produced in 1936 the A9, a medium sized tank fast enough to take on an exploitative role. It was armed with a 2-pdr gun in a central turret to deal with enemy armour and two auxiliary machine gun turrets to assist the infantry or devastate the enemy rear areas after the breakthrough. Given the size needed for a six-man crew and the lack of powerful British engines, compromise had to be made in the weight of armour it carried. As built, it was vulnerable to anything more than rifle fire and was clearly unsatisfactory. His modified version, the A10, doubled the armour thickness, but despite removing the twin machine gun turrets the extra weight halved the tank's speed, and without the secondary turrets it had little potential against anything but opposing armoured vehicles. An infantry tank, the A11, small, inexpensive, and heavily armoured as suggested by Broad in 'The Purple Primer', was built to a price, recognised as unsatisfactory and had only a limited production run but did see action in France in 1940. A much- improved infantry tank, the heavily armoured A12 also known as the 'Matilda', began production late in 1939. Meanwhile Martel, now in the War Office in charge of tank design and development, had in 1936 visited Russia with Major General Archibald Wavell as an official observer of the Red Army's summer manoeuvres. He was greatly impressed by the numbers and deployment of Soviet tanks, many developed from Vickers designs, and also of the Russian development of a tank designed by an American engineer, Walter Christie. On return to Britain he broke most Whitehall procedures and circumvented US restrictions on arms exports to purchase the last remaining prototype of Christie's chassis, which became the basis of British medium tank design in the 1940s. Using a modified Christie suspension system and Christie's choice of an elderly but powerful airship engine, Nuffield was persuaded to produce the A13 tank, which came into service just as war began and was reasonably competitive with the German opposition until late 1941. These models, A9, A10 and A13, were classified as 'cruisers', better suited by speed and relatively light armour to an exploitative cavalry role than to infantry support or assault. Their common defect, which might have been avoided had a doctrine been thought through and tested on exercises, was their 2-pdr gun. Though an excellent antitank weapon when introduced, it fired only solid shot, and without high explosive shells was of limited use against 'soft' targets such as anti-tank guns and infantry, a problem that surfaced in North Africa. Britain was the only country to make this serious mistake. In France, the Char 2B featured a high velocity anti-tank weapon in a turret, and a larger calibre gun mounted in the hull to fire high explosive, while Germany, Russia and Italy chose dual purpose guns as their tanks' main armament.

In 1938 as political crises developed on the Continent, the first British based armoured division was raised, christened the Mobile Division. It consisted of a Tank Brigade of medium and light tanks and two cavalry brigades each of three regiments of light tanks. Its establishment of two artillery regiments and two infantry battalions came up against the 'all tank' philosophy and at the end of the year these supporting troops were reduced by half. Given the lack of any doctrine for the employment of armour, the view in the War Office was that the Mobile Division would be the old cavalry division in modern form, requiring fast light and medium tanks, while infantry divisions would need to be supported by heavily armoured tanks, independent of the Mobile Division, for their assault role.[45] Design and production of armour therefore continued along these lines, and training for cavalry and infantry support roles proceeded independently. Cavalry regiments were equipped exclusively with light and cruiser tanks and all infantry tanks were manned by the Royal Tank Corps, on the basis that the manning of heavy tanks for infantry co-operation was in keeping with the past history of the RTC and crewing the faster tanks with cavalry was in line with theirs. If this made sense in terms of fostering regimental tradition, the disadvantages of a cleavage between the two were ignored.

The first commander of the Mobile Division was Major General Alan Brooke who brought with him from his previous role as Director of Military Training his GSO1, Vyvyan Pope. Rather than subscribing to the revolutionary teaching of the prophets of mechanisation, he believed in the sound principles of warfare that had eventually proved successful on the Western Front, now potentially enhanced by the opportunities from newly restored mobility on the battlefield. Much of his period in command was taken up with the basic training of the formation, and he only held one divisional exercise, but he laid down a basic doctrine: the division must be used as a division and never split up, it should not be used piecemeal to support a break-in by the infantry, and after the break-in its role was to go deep and wide and keep the battle mobile. Brooke was appointed to the new post of Anti- Aircraft Command at the end of 1938, then became GOC of Southern Command in March 1939 where Pope was already in place as Brigadier General Staff, or BGS, the principle staff officer. Their partnership continued after the outbreak of war when they took II Corps to France as part of the British Expeditionary Force.

In April 1939, the RTC was renamed the Royal Tank Regiment and brought under a new organization, the Royal Armoured Corps headed by Martel, together with the regiments of the cavalry and yeomanry. The intention was to centralise training policy

---

45   Martel, *Our Armoured Forces*, p. 48.

'and gain efficiency and a common doctrine', as Martel recorded, though 'the cavalry units were to retain their identity and their great traditions'.[46] However the cavalry continued to select their own officers in order to keep their individual identity and regimental idiosyncrasies, and the common doctrine never materialised. While some RTR units were included in the Mobile Division and in the later armoured divisions and were therefore trained in common with their cavalry colleagues, there were no cavalry units in the Army Tank Brigades that supported the infantry, and therefore no infantry cooperation training at all for cavalry units. Indeed, there was no more a common doctrine in the Royal Armoured Corps than there had been when cavalry and RTC regiments had been separately organised.

In 1938, as war loomed once again, Field Marshall 'Tiny' Ironside, the Chief of the Imperial General Staff, confided to his diary his despair at the situation his country now found itself in: not only was there no army to send abroad but no tactical doctrine around which to build and train.[47] Instead, there was a collection of regiments just commencing a programme that would bring them up from 1918 equipment and organisation, a handful of tanks, and no army air element nor any means of cooperating with the RAF. The long term institutional weaknesses of the 1930s British Army were always going to put it at a disadvantage against its future opponents. Its primary role as an imperial gendarmerie had made training at brigade and divisional level before 1939 almost impossible; the parochialism of the regimental system inhibited cooperation between the arms; the social ethos of the army rarely encouraged professionalism or deep military thinking; inadequate funding throughout the 1930s precluded re-equipping with modern equipment; and in a period of radical military developments the army's limited resources had made it impossible to test or evaluate military theory.

Armour in Action 1936-40

There was little opportunity for the British military to glean lessons from the fighting that preceded actual involvement in the Second World War. The strict neutrality of the British government and absence of British observers prevented them drawing worthwhile conclusions from the mechanised operations of the Spanish Civil War. In Germany Hitler and leading military figures enthusiastically supported Franco and the Nationalists, though German participation was limited to air support, supplemented by army training teams and equipment including about 100 Mk I tanks armed only with machine guns. German training units rather than ground combat units were shipped to Franco's forces, though their commander, von Thoma, claimed he participated in 192 tank actions. Soviet armour supplied to the Republicans outclassed both the German and the more significant number of Italian tanks on the

---

46   Martel, *Our Armoured Forces*, p. 51.
47   McCleod & Kelly (eds.), *The Ironside Diaries*, p. 60.

Nationalist side and the vulnerability of both sides' equipment to anti-tank guns did not encourage the notion of armour as the decisive weapon. On only one occasion, at Brunete in 1937, were a significant number of medium tanks armed with anything heavier than machine guns deployed, when 130 Republican tanks went into in action and, dispersed rather than concentrated, suffered heavy losses.[48] Given tanks' technical limitations at the time, an infantry support role seemed their most likely immediate role. However the German doctrine of concentration and of all arms combination coloured the views of von Thoma and other German observers. They argued that the tanks had fought in packets in support of infantry and in numbers too small to be decisive, but that given coming technical developments tanks in mass could indeed play a decisive role provided they included gun-armed tanks and were accompanied by supporting arms, including mobile anti-tank guns.[49]

The 1939 Polish campaign was over so quickly, and so little information of value came through to the War Office, that no worthwhile lessons could be learnt in Britain. From Poland the German high command came away well aware of the deficiencies of their own arms. Rather than look for aspects of the campaign that validated existing doctrine and tactics, the Wehrmacht's reporting system was critical and honest at both the tactical and operational level. It was clear that cavalry units were of no value and incapable of co-operating with mechanised formations, that the infantry divisions, little changed from 1918, needed upgrading and retraining to a higher plane, that the reserve units needed to be raised to the standards of the regular army and that the armoured divisions needed a higher proportion of infantry and artillery. After Poland panzer divisions had their tank component reduced from a nominal 400 per division to around 200 (and further reduced after 1940 to 100 medium plus a number of lighter tanks) while retaining roughly the same numbers of supporting arms, recognizing the absolute necessity for tank units to be backed in strength by infantry and artillery. And the value of concentrating panzer divisions for an operationally decisive blow on a single axis of attack, rather than separating them and allocating them in support of infantry corps, became clear. This lesson was put into practice in France in 1940 with devastating effect. For the attack on France in May 1940, nine of the ten panzer divisions were concentrated on the main thrust through the Ardennes leaving a single panzer division to drive through Holland and Belgium as a diversion.

In April 1940 Pope had been appointed Inspector of the Royal Armoured Corps, and then nominated to join the BEF as Advisor on armoured vehicles. The German attack on 10th May came before he could reach France but he crossed the Channel immediately on hearing the news to find that there was not much armour for him to advise on, only a number of reconnaissance regiments with light tanks and armoured cars, and the 1st Army Tank Brigade. The Brigade consisted of the 4th and 7th RTR

---

48   Ogorkiewicz, *Tanks: 100 Years of Evolution*, p. 109.
49   T.L. Jentz (ed.), *Panzertruppen*, (Atglen, Pennsylvania: Schiffer Military History, 1996), p. 46.

equipped with the unsatisfactory Mk I infantry tank and a smaller number of Matildas. They were under the command of I Corps and since he could only advise and not order, he was unable to change the plan for these to move into Belgium in support of the infantry divisions to meet the Germans. As news came of the German breakthrough in the Ardennes, the advance into Belgium to meet the Germans was reversed and the tanks motored back to France. By the 20th May they were back at their start point having covered some 120 miles on their tracks and lost 25 percent of their number through breakdown, the brigade being reduced to 16 Matildas and 58 Mk Is. At this point Pope was told that the Tank Brigade with two infantry divisions was to counter attack the German spearhead at Arras, then contact French troops in the locality and restore a defensive position along the River Scarpe. In the event French co-operation barely materialised and the urgency of the situation meant that the attack went ahead with the only available infantry, two very tired battalions in need of food and rest, under Martel's 50th Northumbrian Division. Time was running short, so before the infantry could be made ready the Tank Brigade was sent off, its support reduced to a single battery of artillery without wireless communication. Even so, the shock of a counterattack led by British tanks that were impervious to the anti-tank guns of Rommel's 7th Panzer Division was enough to halt the German advance. Rommel had been leading his division from the front – his aide de camp was killed alongside him – and he personally organised the defence as his panicky troops retreated:

> The crew of a howitzer battery, some distance away, now left their guns, swept along by the retreating infantry. With Most's help, I brought every available gun into action at top speed against the tanks. Every gun, both anti-tank and anti-aircraft, was ordered to open rapid fire immediately and I personally gave each gun its target. With the enemy tanks so perilously close, only rapid fire from every gun could save the situation. We ran from gun to gun. The objections of gun commanders that the range was still too great to engage the tanks effectively, were overruled. All I cared about was to hit the enemy tanks by heavy gunfire.[50]

The British armour advanced some miles destroying a great deal of enemy transport and literally running over German anti-tank guns. Some distance behind the armour, the infantry mopped up surviving Germans, eliminating pockets of resistance and collecting several hundred prisoners in the wake of the tanks. But there had never been time to properly co-ordinate their actions with the supporting battery and infantry, which were therefore not available to help overcome Rommel's improvised defence. As the armour moved on, German field artillery and anti-aircraft guns began to take a toll, the Luftwaffe made its presence felt, casualties mounted, and it was clear that the Tank Brigade would not reach its objectives. Early in the evening the tanks began to withdraw, covered to some degree by a French armoured unit.

50   B.H. Liddell Hart (ed.), *The Rommel Papers* (London: Collins, 1953), p. 32.

The counter attack at Arras has gone down in legend as instrumental in halting the advance of the Panzers and thereby giving the BEF time to organise its defence at Dunkirk. Dramatic though the event was, leading German forces had already reached their objective of the Channel coast and German orders to halt had been issued (and disobeyed) before the attack took place. But the attack does illustrate the lack of inter arms training and limited capacity for armoured warfare in the pre-war British Army, and the lesson was not lost on Pope. Convinced that he and the bulk of the BEF were unlikely to return to England, he summarised the performance of British armoured forces during the campaign and had the document delivered to the War Office on 26 May, the day before the Dunkirk evacuation began. Besides mentioning British tanks' inadequate armour (referring here to light tanks and cruisers rather than the infantry tanks), their very poor reliability – 75 percent of losses were due to breakdown – and the pressing need for a better gun, his principle conclusion 'as a result of bitter experience' was that armour must be concentrated: 'there must be a Commander RAC in the field with an adequate staff to enable him to command, and he must control all movements of RAC troops as directed by the General Staff. Unless this is done we shall continue to fritter away our tanks.'[51]

Britain's 1st Armoured Division was not despatched to France until the German invasion had started, and even then in piecemeal fashion. In the chaotic response to the attack, the division's Support Group was separated from the armoured brigades and with a single tank regiment was despatched to Calais as the only reserve available to forestall the German advance on the Channel Ports. It was destroyed there. Meanwhile 1st and 2nd Armoured Brigades were shipped to Cherbourg to bolster the French defensive line on the Somme. Here, lacking their divisional infantry and artillery and unsupported by French units with which they had never had the chance to train or liaise, they were ground down in a series of ineffective counter attacks, and the remnants were evacuated from Cherbourg.

The Bartholomew Report[52] of July 1940 did attempt to draw lessons from the campaign in France. Limited in its depth by the haste with which it was produced, it reviewed what could be learnt from the defeat and concentrated on the experience of the retreat, the use of terrain in defence and the importance of counterattack. Perhaps inevitably, it was determinedly positive in tone: 'The British soldier is at least as good as the German...The key to success against the German is to hit him hard and to hit him hard at every opportunity – it is the only means of conducting a successful defence'. Similar to the German principle of immediate counterattack but, gung-ho rather than coolly professional, it was not expressed in terms that invited translation into doctrine and was not to be featured as a central tenet in training guidelines. The Report contained a nugget of wisdom in its perception that 'The greatest effect against enemy tanks will be obtained when they have been divorced from their supporting

51 Lewin, *Man of Armour*, p. 123.
52 TNA WO32/9581: Bartholomew Report.

troops' but failed to observe that if German armour was at its most effective when working closely with supporting troops, British armour would also benefit from being so accompanied. There is no reason to suppose that the Report was widely circulated in the only remaining active front, the Middle East, for its most far reaching conclusion, that the "brigade group" of three battalions plus a regiment of artillery and supporting troops should replace the division as the lowest self-contained fighting formation, took another year to reach North Africa. This recommendation is similar to a 1934 appreciation from the British Military Attaché in Berlin which mentions how the Germans on exercises 'make very great use of the so-called "reinforced infantry regiment" or "Brigade Group", the smallest formation that can fight a short independent action' and describes it as 'the best medium for teaching commanders & staff officers the co-operation of all arms'.[53] Bartholomew also refers to its training value but neither the military attaché nor Bartholomew noted that in German doctrine the 'short independent action' meant the immediate counterattack on an enemy penetration, and that a reinforced regiment was by no means the standard German deployment. It is possible that the Bartholomew Committee had been impressed by the use in France by the BEF of ad hoc formations of mixed arms that were deployed independently as cover against German breakthroughs. The brigade group principle did coincide with the fashion among military theorists for decentralisation and flexibility, and in principle it would allow more initiative to brigade and battalion commanders to 'hit him hard at every opportunity'. At all events, Bartholomew concluded that 'The tactical handling of the division should be based on these self-contained groups, which will be normal [sic] both for training and fighting.' This was despite the appearance of Vyvyan Pope before the committee on 17th June when he argued against the tendency

> to form penny packets of brigade groups containing all arms and tanks and to scatter them broadcast. I made it very clear that I could not subscribe to any doctrine of that kind, that our experience had shown that distribution of armoured forces led to defeat in detail since it was not possible to ensure that adequate numbers could be placed in the right place at the right time, and that in defence armoured troops should be held concentrated in reserve ready to strike when required.[54]

It was a year before the prescription of brigade groups filtered through to British forces in North Africa, but it did then take root in the absence of any other official doctrine. It was also by then in the absence of Pope, killed in an air crash. Bartholomew makes no mention of 1st Tank Brigade's fight at Arras or the short campaign by elements of

---

53   TNA, WO190/283: Appreciation of the Military attaché, Berlin on the views of German General Staff on Future War, 26 November 1934.
54   Lewin, *Man of Armour*, pp. 127-8.

1st Armoured Division from the Somme back to Cherbourg and makes no suggestions for doctrine that could be useful for armoured forces. An accurate perspective into German doctrine did not appear in an Army Training Manual until May 1942, and it reads more as the conclusion from an officer's private studies than the result of analysing events. The paragraph outlines the German conception of command as described in the memoirs of an unspecified First World War German general:

> The commander tells the junior the things he cannot know for himself, the general situation, the objective, the execution. The junior's job is to carry out his orders in accordance with the situation as he finds it on the spot.[55]

This insight into *Aufragstaktik* does not seem to have been widely grasped by British leaders, though the pamphlet was intended for distribution to every battalion officer.

The major point made by Pope after Dunkirk was the need for a RAC Group Commander attached to each Corps. His view was that brigade, divisional and corps commanders demanded help from tanks as an instant answer to their immediate difficulty, and he was anxious to stop armour being dispersed on fire-fighting missions. It was the absence of any armoured doctrine that allowed worried formation commanders to see the role of armour as a rescue service for them. But the suggestion that senior commanders needed supervision, inevitably by someone with a specialist RTR or at least cavalry background, was not going to please senior officers of other arms. The eventual outcome, the formation of Armoured Group HQs, with an advisory rather than a command role, created all the problems of divided command that one might expect from a supervisory group. The first Armoured Group HQs were formed in August 1941 and they did not prove popular. Major General Creagh was posted to such a Group in Northern Command early in 1942 after leading 7th Armoured Division in North Africa. But the GOC of Northern Command deliberately ignored him in favour of a staff officer when debriefing after an exercise and made it clear that his presence was redundant. Creagh had disagreed with the Corps solution to the exercise and found in that antagonistic atmosphere, 'it was difficult to bring out my point of view without criticising the corps plans which was not my function ... I feel in the back of my mind he is one of those people who regard Group as part of an RAC racket.'[56]

Pope himself was despatched to the Middle East to take on the Group role.[57] Once there, he was quickly appointed to command rather than to advise the Armoured Corps, which avoided any problem of divided responsibility. After his early and unfortunate

---

55   TNA WO231/260: 'Demands of Modern War', Army Training Manual No. 43, May 1942.

56   Liddell Hart Centre for Military Archives, Creagh Papers, Letter to Martel, 9 January 1942.

57   Richard Doherty, *British Armoured Divisions and their Commanders 1939–1945* (Barnsley: Pen & Sword, 2013), p. 56.

death in an aircrash there was more pressure from London for the appointment of a senior officer to take on the supervision of armoured forces in North Africa. This was resisted by the Commander in Chief in the Middle East, Lieutenant General Claude Auchinleck, who was reluctant to accept anyone with more authority than a brigadier in the post. Only in March 1942 was a major general, Richard McCreery, appointed with responsibility for AFVs in the Middle East. His falling out with Auchinleck and consequent dismissal, shortly before Auchinleck's own dismissal in the 'Cairo Purge' of August 1942, repays examination. It shines a glimmer on the cross currents of institutional flaws, social divisions and lack of common doctrine or training.

3

Auchinleck's Men

North Africa before Auchinleck, 1938-41

The opening of the Suez Canal in 1869 had vastly improved communications to India and to the British colonies in East Africa, the Far East and Australasia, and made the stability of Egypt crucially important to Britain. The country was never a colony of the Empire, but became a 'protectorate', self-governing under a King installed by the British when the ruling Ottomans sided with Germany in the First World War. A treaty in 1936 gave Britain the right to station troops in Egypt for the defence of the Canal, which was becoming even more important as Japan's aggression mounted in the Far East and Mussolini's ambitions in Africa became clear. With a naval base at Gibraltar at the entrance to the Mediterranean, another in the central Mediterranean at Malta, and a third at the great Egyptian port of Alexandria, Britain was secure in the Mediterranean as long as France remained an ally. But the defeat of France by Germany in 1940 removed the French navy as a partner and without that help the British Mediterranean fleet would struggle to dominate the Italian navy. Mussolini saw an opportunity to take over Egypt and unite Italy's colony of Libya with the East African empire that he was establishing in Abyssinia and Eritrea. In June 1940 he declared war on Britain. An oddity of the situation was that although British troops in Egypt were now engaged in hostilities with Italian forces on the Libyan border, Egypt itself was not at war with the Axis and was therefore free from attack on its cities and installations, other than British military facilities and of course the Suez Canal which was British owned.

Even before the outbreak of war, the threat from the Italian Army in Libya had in 1938 prompted the creation of a Mobile Force in Egypt under Major General Hobart, now the leading serving British proponent of armoured warfare. Raised from existing tank, cavalry, infantry and artillery units in Egypt and equipped with a motley collection of obsolete tanks and trucks, it earned the soubriquet 'The Mobile Farce' before it was renamed 7th Armoured Division. But Hobart's energy and drive created

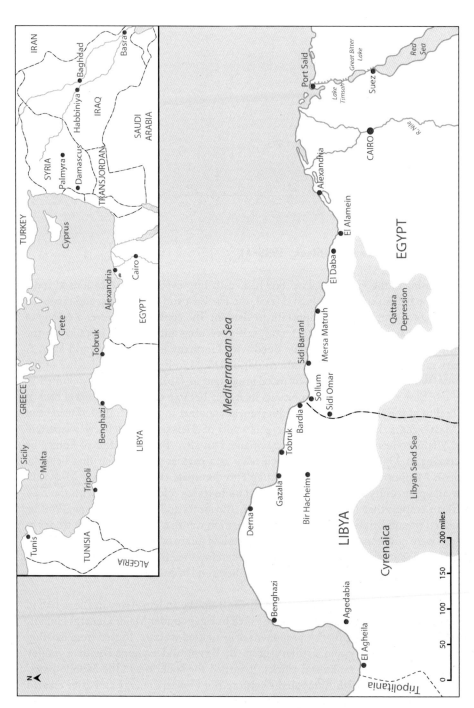

1. North African coastline and Mediterranean Theatre of War

a formation exceptionally well trained in all the basics of wireless communication, command techniques, maintenance, desert navigation and gunnery. In the absence of any official doctrine for handling armoured forces, he prescribed his own philosophy of mobility as a force multiplier, believing like Fuller that a powerful tank formation could penetrate enemy lines, destroy their headquarters and communications and paralyse any counter moves. Fuller's naval analogy of tank fleets comprising heavy battle tanks, medium cruiser tanks and light reconnaissance tanks manoeuvring for a decisive encounter appeared to suit perfectly the open spaces of the North African desert, and for his 1939 training season Hobart accordingly decided to concentrate on dispersion, flexibility and mobility rather than assault tactics on defended positions.[1] A battalion of infantry supported by a battery of artillery could play the role of 'tank marines' to protect the tanks as necessary when undergoing repairs or refuelling, and would be organised into a Pivot Group, providing the 'pivots of manoeuvre round and between which naval strategy and tactics will be applied to land operations' as advocated in Fuller's RUSI Gold Medal prize essay of 1919.[2]

It did however go against the British military experience of the last months of the Great War, when success on the battlefield had been achieved by a sophisticated artillery command structure with combined tank and infantry assault on a large scale supported by ground attack aircraft. It also ran counter to the experiments with mechanised forces of the 1920s and early 1930s when tank regiments had operated in combination with artillery and infantry. General Maitland Wilson, commander of British troops in Egypt, was a firm believer in all arms cooperation. Hobart thought the mobility and firepower of tanks would be hampered by the unarmoured wheeled vehicles of the other arms. He was not one to compromise or take the views of his superiors into account – he believed that the secret of success in the army was to be 'sufficiently insubordinate' – and, making himself intolerable to Wilson, he was sacked.[3] His legacy of tank heavy formations, dispersal, and Pivot Groups, renamed Support Groups in line with British practice, lived on. His replacement, O'Moore Creagh, believed in some mixture of arms, but as Corelli Barnett noted after interviewing him, 'this went not much further than moving from a Light and a Heavy Brigade to mixing light and medium tanks in the same brigade.'[4]

In September 1940, the Italian army in Libya moved some 75 miles into Egypt, harassed by what became known as Jock columns, mixed groups of armoured cars, artillery and a company of infantry whose major concern was to conserve the feeble tank strength of

---

1   Liddell Hart Centre of Military Archives, 15/11/8/1 Armoured Division Training report, May 1939.
2   *RUSI Journal*, Vol. 65, J.F.C. Fuller 1919 Gold Medal Prize Essay, p. 250.
3   Carver, *Out of Step*, p. 33. Dorman-Smith believed there was more to his sacking than was made public: he revealed another reason (there is no copy of this letter in the file) to Hobart's biographer, Kenneth Macksey, who replied ' I will treat it with the discretion that it deserves.' JRL, GOW/1/4/2, letter 6/7/65.
4   Liddell Hart Centre for Military Archives, Creagh Papers.

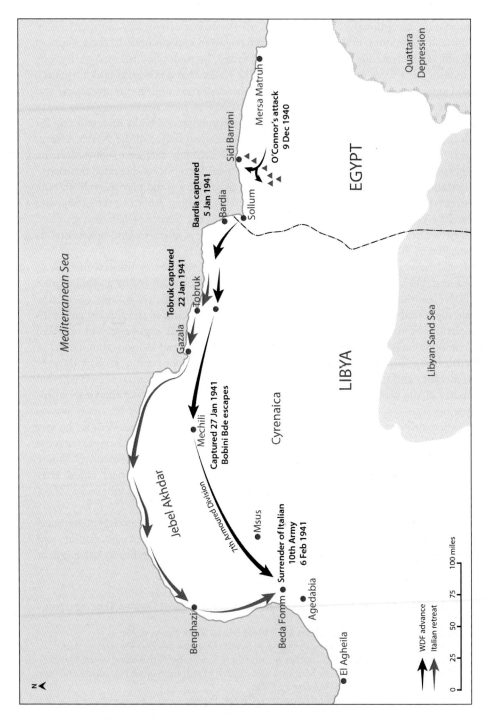

2. O'Connor's Campaign, 1940–41

7th Armoured Division, Britain's only operational formation in Egypt. The threat to the Suez Canal prompted Churchill to send reinforcements of modern armour despite the danger of invasion at home, making it possible in December to mount Operation Compass, an attack under Lieutenant General O'Connor to remove Italian offensive capability by destroying their advanced forces. The initial assault was carried out not by 7th Armoured Division, whose role was to bypass enemy forward positions and block lines of retreat or reinforcement, but by the newly arrived 4th Indian Division led by a battalion of Matilda tanks, slow heavily armoured AFVs impervious to the anti-tank weapons of the day. This was successful beyond expectations, so much so that it could be exploited by mopping up the Italian garrisons along the Egyptian and Libyan coast. While 7th Armoured Division held off weak Italian mobile forces, the Matildas and infantry eliminated in turn each Italian encampment and town until with the fall of Tobruk the Italian command abandoned its attempt to hold eastern Libya and began a retreat, intending to make a stand at the only available defensive position 350 miles further west at Agedabia.

4. A13 Cruiser tank and A12 Matilda infantry tank in November 1940 The instruments of victory against the Italian Tenth Army in 1940-41. (Imperial War Museum E5366)

By now – mid January 1941 – the Matildas were worn out, the Italians had brought up a brigade of modern M13 tanks, a reasonable match for the cruisers of 7th Armoured Division, and O'Connor ordered an attack on them at Mechili. To the mortification of the commander of 7th Armoured Division, and the extreme annoyance of O'Connor, the attack miscarried, the Babini Brigade escaped to cover the retreat of the Italian army, and O'Connor was faced with the prospect of a long pursuit through difficult country.[5] He chose the alternative of a logistically risky dash across 200 miles of unmapped desert to intercept the Italians and hold them long enough for the main body of pursuers to overtake them. After a 36 hour journey, a single battalion with some armoured cars and artillery reached the Italian line of retreat near Beda Fomm 30 minutes before the leading Italian elements arrived and held them until tank reinforcements could consolidate the road block. Together they forced the surrender of the entire Italian 10th Army early in February 1941. 30,000 British troops had eliminated an army of 135,000 men.

5. O'Connor, left, & Harding, right, in Libya, 1941: 'Both diminutive in stature, lively, quick and clear in thought and decisions, bold and impatient of delay: they were like two cheerful, chirping, active little birds'. Major General O'Moore Creagh is in the centre. (Orion Publishing Group)

5   'O'Connor was in a flaming rage – not in the least like his normal mood: "Those bloody fools at Mechili have let the Italians slip through at night, although they could hear the tanks perfectly well. I am going down to Mechili at dawn tomorrow to drive them on!'. Air Marshal Lord Tedder, *With Prejudice*, p. 58.

This first success for British arms should have provided lessons for the army as a whole, and 7th Armoured Division's War Diaries and a training pamphlet, 'Lessons of Cyrenaica', contain some valid conclusions.[6] Overall, British units were credited with superior manoeuvring, fire skills and fire discipline – true enough, thanks to the Italian practice of operating tanks in penny packets and then having forced on them the disadvantage of attacking British defensive positions at Beda Fomm. One conclusion in particular – 'The proper place for a commander is near the point of decision' – has O'Connor's stamp and could be taken from *Truppenführung* itself, but there are no signs that it was generally adopted in practice. There was a re-assessment of the 'tank only' doctrine that had been Hobart's legacy: it was now appreciated that 'the fear that the presence of artillery units would "cramp the style" of the armoured fighting vehicle is groundless ... Mechanised units for dismounted action are an essential component of all higher armoured formations.

Brigadier Caunter, the leader of 4th Armoured Brigade at Mechili, acknowledged this when he put at least part of the blame for his failure to destroy Babini's Brigade on the lack of infantry under his command. The major failing of British forces was perceived to be their appalling wireless security:

> Many damning records exist of intercepted conversations and messages, which show complete lack of forethought and common sense by the originators. Had we been fighting the Germans the consequences would have been grave.[7]

It is difficult to tell how widely these conclusions were circulated – there is a suggestion that the pamphlet was not distributed until the following year. O'Connor did issue an Order of the Day in February, as he and 7th Armoured Division returned to Cairo, in which he emphasized 'mobility' as the key to his destruction of the Italian 10th Army, true enough in the sense that Italian movement had been neutralised by 7th Armoured Division.[8] But it was not the case that mobility in itself had been a weapon as Fuller and Liddell Hart had envisaged – contrary to propaganda at the time and legend ever since, the Italian army did not collapse, demoralised and confused by a plethora of outflanking and encircling columns of armour, without resistance. It had been six weeks into the campaign before the fall of Tobruk set the Italian army in retreat and O'Connor also acknowledged 'hard fighting' in the assault on Bardia and at Beda Fomm.[9] But with the dispersal of 7th Armoured Division after the victory, some components being sent to Greece, others on well-deserved leave during the February-March lull, lessons from the campaign do not seem to have been absorbed,

6   TNA WO 201/2586: Middle East Training Pamphlet No. 10, Lessons of Cyrenaica
     Campaign December 1940—February 1941
7   TNA WO 169/1185: Sp. Gp War Diary.
8   Order of the Day, February 1941, copy in possession of author.
9   Order of the Day, February 1941.

and faith in manoeuvre and dispersion, and the use of tank heavy formations while infantry and artillery worked separately from armour, persisted. O'Connor's capture before he could make a full report on 'Compass' deprived 7th Armoured Division of a valuable commentary.

6. Italian M13 tanks captured at Beda Fomm, February 1941. (Imperial War Museum 0023-B6)

The Italian disaster forced the Axis to reinforce with German troops, under Rommel, and their arrival coincided with the stripping of O'Connor's corps to make up an expeditionary force to assist Greece, already at war with Italy and under threat from Germany. Only two British tank regiments, one equipped with captured Italian M13 tanks and manned with inexperienced crews and commanders fresh from England, remained in the desert. When Rommel attacked in March 1941 in overwhelming numbers – 78 medium tanks against 28 British, the British crewed M13s all breaking down or running out of fuel – his divergent thrusts scattered the opposition, overran supply dumps and captured the divisional commander, the corps commander and O'Connor himself. O'Connor's BGS Brigadier Harding, acting in true chief of staff fashion, escaped to organise the defence of Tobruk, which Rommel bypassed on a drive to Egypt until he halted on the Libyan/Egyptian frontier for lack of supplies. He failed to take Tobruk in a series of costly assaults, simultaneously skirmishing on the frontier as the British tried to retake key features.

7. Rommel with his then Chief of Staff Fritz Bayerlein, 2nd June 1942. (Imperial War Museum 5628)

Reinforcements of tanks and men reached the British in May 1941 enabling Wavell to mount Operation Battleaxe, with 4th Indian Division under Major General Messervy supported by Matildas attacking Axis fixed defences on the path to Tobruk while 7th Armoured Division under Creagh outflanked the enemy and cut off reinforcements. Enemy defences cleared, a joint move on Tobruk would proceed. The operation bore some resemblance in principle to the attack on the Italian forward defences five months earlier, perhaps not surprising since the commanders lacked only O'Connor from that team, but Rommel was fully alerted by the earlier skirmishing on the frontier and had experienced attack by Matildas in France the previous year and at Tobruk more recently. He now emplaced 88mm guns specifically to counter them at the key point of Halfaya Pass where the only metalled road wound its way up a 600 foot escarpment. Lacking artillery to suppress the 88s, many Matildas were destroyed, while the outflanking movement came to grief on German anti-tank defences that also could only be suppressed by artillery, unavailable in quantity since it had been

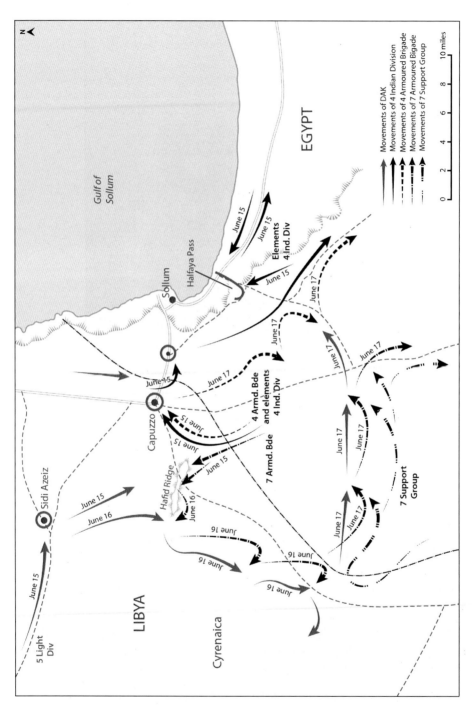

3. Operation Battleaxe

concentrated in 7th Armoured Division's Support Group and given a detached role guarding the open flank of the operation. The attack nonetheless caused alarm at Rommel's HQ[10] when Capuzzo was captured and the Germans feared a breakthrough to Bardia, their supply centre, but the situation was 'saved by one 88mm gun which had been lying derelict with a broken tractor'.[11] At this point there was still some hope of success, but lack of direction from Lieutenant General Beresford-Peirse, who was commanding the operation by wireless 60 miles from the front, and dissension between 7th Armoured Division and 4th Indian Division over whether the remaining Matildas should continue in support of the infantry or be concentrated with the cruisers to face the enemy armour, resulted in Beresford-Peirse and Wavell both flying up to 7th Armoured Division headquarters on 17 June. By then Messervy had already ordered his own division and the remaining Matildas to withdraw from Capuzzo. Major 'Pip' Roberts, GSO2 of 7th Armoured, was able to observe his commander in chief's famously taciturn manner and 'expressionless, poker face'[12] when Creagh briefed the visitors:

> 'The great men said little though Wavell did grunt a few times, and then at the end said, "Well, you've got a lot of 25-pounders, if you can't stop them I don't know who can." He and Beresford-Peirse then boarded their Lysander and flew away … no order was given, nor suggestions made, nor even helpful advice tendered.'[13]

With 4th Indian Division already withdrawing, Creagh could only follow suit. Poor intelligence had underestimated the numbers of German tanks and their supplies, and abysmal wireless procedure that revealed British plans and confusion to the Germans had played a major part in the defeat. Though casualties were relatively light, losses of equipment, including about 100 tanks, were heavy. It was clear that new personnel and fresh ideas were needed. Wavell was replaced as C-in-C Middle East by Lieutenant General Claude Auchinleck and there followed a lengthy pause to rebuild the army and appoint new blood to command it.

'Battleaxe' demonstrates that the lessons of the victory over the Italians had not been absorbed: rather than being at 'the point of decision', Beresford-Peirse had conducted the battle 60 miles from the front, in order to liaise with the RAF, who in the event had no effect on the battle; 7th Armoured Division attacked the main German position on Hafid ridge with inadequate artillery support and without the 'mechanised unit for

10   Hans-Albrecht Schraepler (ed.), *At Rommel's Side* (Barnsley: Frontline Books, 2009), p. 117.
11   Bruce I. Gudmunsson (ed.), *Inside the Afrika Korps: The Crusader Battles 1941–2* (London: Greenhill Books 1999), p. 309.
12   Lieutenant-General Sir Brian Horrocks, quoted in Victoria Schofield, *Wavell: Soldier and Statesman* (London: John Murray, 2006), p. 110.
13   Roberts, *Desert to Baltic*, p. 50.

dismounted action' as recommended in the 'Lessons from Cyrenaica' pamphlet that, working with artillery and armour, might have overwhelmed the German *pakfront*; and abysmal wireless procedure was a major contribution to defeat.[14] Even after 'Battleaxe', preconceptions and existing practices continued, and appropriate conclusions were not drawn from observing German tactics. These were reported accurately enough – up to 70 tanks moving in much closer formation than British units and clearly responding in unison to orders by wireless – but, failing to recognise battle drills for what they were, chauvinism and complacency are evident in the British report:

> The enemy tactics are rigid and rather stereotyped. Envelopment is the main theme … In the defensive battle his policy is to draw our tanks on to his guns and then to counter attack with his tanks after we had disclosed our intentions… [The enemy] is slow to adjust to altered circumstances. It is this weakness that we must exploit by manoeuvre…In principle touch must be kept with the head of his advance and counter attack from a flank … A quick wit, a close watch on his movements and good communications are the answer.[15]

Among the regiments themselves, although it was clear that British manoeuvring and fire skills did not achieve superiority in attack against Germans as they had in defence against Italian armour at Beda Fomm, the tank units themselves did not feel they had been outfought by German tanks. They came away with faith in their Crusaders' 2-pdr guns and the prospect of new American Stuart tanks.[16]

The 7th Armoured Division's commander's major complaint was that with only two regiments of cruisers he had no reserve during his initial assault on Hafid ridge, thus restricting his opportunity for manoeuvre. The Support Group, which could have acted either as a reserve or to pin German defences, was not available having

---

14   Liddell Hart (ed.), *The Rommel Papers*, p. 145.
15   TNA WO201/25483. An Intelligence report on likely enemy actions in April had similarly been misled by a stereotyped view of the German character when assessing the likelihood of Rommel attacking: 'It would not be in accordance with German tradition to undertake without careful preparation and study anything so foolhardy.'
16   Contemporary sources are unanimous in their satisfaction with the 2 pdr gun at this time. 7 Support Group Intelligence Summary (TNA WO169/144) of 17.4.41 after an engagement with 90 Mk III and IV tanks reported that 'All prob incl[uding] MkIV vulnerable to 2-pdrs'. Major General Tuker's Report Para 8 (IWM, 71/21/2/6) observed 'The 2pdr is capable of knocking out any Italian or German tank in Mid-East now', and in Para 9 considered the Stuart 'a really first class AFV… Mid-East say it's the best thing of its sort they've struck.' 7th Armoured Division Intelligence report of 5.6.41 (TNA WO169.1185 7 Sp Grp) described a test firing by the 2-pdr against a German Mk IV achieving penetration of 20 & 40mm armour at 1200 yds, and of the thick double frontal armour at 500 yds. And as late as November 1941 2pdrs in the well trained New Zealand Division, carried portee on unarmoured trucks, destroyed numerous German tanks. See *Pitt, The Crucible of War*, p. 127.

8. Remains of Panzer Mark IV destroyed at Tobruk, April 1941. Fitted with additional armour plating, it may have been tests on this type of improvised post production armour that provided Eighth Army with an optimistic view of the 2-pdr tank gun. (The Tank Museum Bovington 5549-A2)

been deployed to provide flank protection at too great a distance for its artillery to support the armour and, having been split into four Jock columns to try to emulate the previous year's success against the Italians, was unable to concentrate rapidly enough when a worthwhile target was located. Its wireless communications were so poor that for two of the three days of the battle it was out of touch with both 7th Armoured Brigade and 7th Armoured Division. It was of course clear that the inferior speed of Matildas made their participation in rapid manoeuvre impossible, so they were definitively consigned to the infantry support role, even though their value in a firefight with German armour could have been decisive if a tactical plan had been devised that included them.[17] As foreseen in the spring poor wireless procedure revealed British plans and discord between commanders to the enemy, but little was done to rectify this failing.

The Support Group war diary, presumably reflecting the view of their commander Brigadier Gott, recognised that separating artillery from the armoured brigades had weakened the assault by tanks on a defensive position for which 'maximum artillery

17   TNA WO201/357: The Germans also recognised their value and whenever possible recovered Matildas for their own use.

9. 'Strafer' Gott, as a brigadier in April 1941. (Imperial War Museum E00 2623)

support was necessary' but Gott made no proposals after 'Battleaxe' for his artillery to coordinate its action more closely with armoured brigades. In the future when involved against enemy armour the artillery was instructed to harass the enemy as they formed up, but 'intervention in a tank v tank battle is not their role' since tank regiment commanders would be too occupied to give the necessary orders.[18] The guns should support to the best of their ability, withdrawing as the situation demanded. He did suggest they had something to learn from the German ability to take up defensive positions in the desert and draw or force enemy tanks on to their guns, a policy that would be adopted the following year. He questioned 'the column system' under which his Support Group had been divided into four, but otherwise blamed his failure to inflict serious damage on the Afrika Korps on a shortage of armoured cars to locate targets for his artillery. The ineffectiveness of the Support Group's attempts to harass German outflanking moves went unremarked.[19] The idea of increasing the hitting power of columns by including a few tanks was mentioned but was clearly impractical, given the unreliability of the cruisers and the justified prejudice against

18   Liddle Hart Centre for Military Archives, Creagh Papers, Notes on the Last Operations.
19   TNA WO169/1185: 7 Sp. Grp War Diary 21/6/41 Summary of 'Battleaxe'.

10. Matilda recaptured after service with the Afrika Korps. (The Tank Museum Bovington 2476-D2)

11. Crusader tanks. (Imperial War Museum E6724)

'penny packets' of armour, and the idea of combining artillery and tank units appears not to have crossed anyone's mind.

O'Moore Creagh was succeeded by Gott in command of 7th Armoured Division in September 1941, but there was no change in the division's tactical philosophy. Despite the 'Lessons of Cyrenaica' pamphlet's emphasis on the need of artillery and infantry support for armour, a subsequent paper, 'Organisation of 7th Armd Div', undated and unsigned though clearly written before Gott took command, reverts to the Hobartian view: it comments 'Like crabbed age and youth, unarmoured and armoured vehicles do not go well together', even less so in the desert, and suggests that divisional infantry be concentrated in the Support Group.[20] It rejects a proposed reorganisation along the lines of the Brigade Group structure current in Great Britain whereby each armoured brigade was allocated its own infantry battalion and artillery regiment. As a result, in November the division's two armoured brigades went into action with only one infantry company and one field battery each, sufficient for no more than local protection at night when replenishing. The bulk of the division's infantry and artillery was again concentrated in the Support Group, whose role was once more to form Jock columns, to occupy country unsuitable for tanks or to form a pivot on the flank of armoured brigades as appropriate, working in conjunction with armour rather than being integrated with it on the German model. Both 2-pdr anti-tank guns and 25-pdr field guns (which were quite effective against enemy armour) were regarded as infantry equipment within the Support Group, and thus were once again unavailable to add firepower to the armoured regiments in the way that German artillery and anti-tank guns supported the tanks of the Afrika Korps.

In contrast to the British command, the Afrika Korps was quick to seek lessons from the summer fighting. 'Battleaxe' and the German failures to take Tobruk had alarmed Rommel and the Afrika Korps more than British commanders realised. The ferocity of the fighting at Tobruk had shaken German morale as well as inflicting losses.[21] For a period, 'Battleaxe' had looked very threatening to the Germans: an unposed photograph shows a relieved Rommel celebrating with the German hero of Halfaya Pass, Hauptmann Bach, a former pastor who had held his positions against all attacks.[22] Others had not performed so well: Rommel sacked Streich,

---

20   Liddell Hart Centre for Military Archives, Creagh Papers, Organisation of 7th Armd Div.
21   Schraepler, *At Rommel's Side*, p. 84. Letter 19th April. Maj Gen Streich, and his 'inefficient panzer commander…the troops have strong nerves no longer… they did not have the nerve, apart from making serious tactical mistake, to stand it all, especially Olbrich, commander of the panzer regiment.' Tedder, *With Prejudice*, p.72. Tedder's diary entry remarked on enemy prisoners 'in a poor state, many of them sobbing their hearts out'.
22   TNA WO201/2769 Intelligence Report Enemy Ops Apr-June 1941. Also Schraepler p.118 Letter 17 June: [T]hese days of combat which asked of them so much effort and extraordinary performance …. The past days had been extremely tough, at times literally very hot … This battle, which is essential for strategic and operational reasons, is a more remarkable achievement than the conquest of Cyrenaica. If we had failed here, we should have folded.'

the commander of 5th Light Division, as no doubt he would have Olbricht, the commander of 5th Panzer Regiment, had the latter not been killed. Furthermore he replaced his chief of staff, van den Borne, with an armour specialist, Cruewell.[23] He also embarked on extensive retraining of his troops. The Italian garrison of Capuzzo had quickly succumbed to the British attack, so Rommel's Italian divisions underwent further training by German officers and they were entrenched in a series of battalion strongpoints stretching 40 kilometres south from the coast. These would force any attempt to relieve Tobruk into a wide detour during which it would be vulnerable to a counterstroke.[24] Each strongpoint was centred on a section of 88mm guns, was within supporting distance of the next, and the line was strengthened with a few independent companies of German troops. Rommel and his divisional commanders personally supervised construction of positions down to platoon level. Sections of infantry provided cover for heavy weapons – machine guns, anti-tank guns or mortars – in a system of all round defence where a company covered an area perhaps 800 metres square. If attacked, these positions were to be regarded not simply as defensive posts but as jumping off points for an armoured counterattack. Armoured tactics were also refined. The tank regiments in 15th Panzer and 21st Panzer divisions (on August 5th Light Division was upgraded to a panzer division and given the number '21') were now to be supported by other arms even when in action against enemy armour, whereas previously infantry and artillery had only joined armour in attack against mixed formations of all weapons. 88mm guns were recognised as the most important support weapon and moved with the tank regiment which would also be covered by motorized field artillery to suppress enemy antitank guns and artillery observers. 'Almost all armoured units were accompanied by 88mm flak guns, often just one, in the anti-tank role. The weapon's range, its ability to open fire early and its accuracy generally forced enemy tanks onto the defensive and into acts of desperation.'[25]

Antitank units would cover the flanks of panzer formations to hold off enemy outflanking moves. Infantry in trucks or halftracks kept as near as possible to armoured battle groups for protection and rapid deployment. The divisional headquarters now travelled with the armoured formations and by listening in to the tank units' wireless did not have to wait for situation reports. The proximity of the divisional general to his armour, artillery and infantry commanders would allow quick, short orders to be delivered verbally in person, speeding reactions to changes in the situation. The divisional supply echelon also travelled with the column to facilitate the resupply of fighting units.[26] The panzer regiments retained the tactics

23   Olbricht's diary was captured by the British and confirms Schraepler's comments.
24   Gudmundsson, *Inside the Afrika Korps*, p. 40.
25   Herman Buschleb, *Operation Crusader: Tank Warfare in the Desert, Tobruk 1941* (Philadelphia & Oxford: Casemate Publishers, 2019), p .22.
26   Gudmundsson, *Inside the Afrika Korps*, p. 45.

which had been commented on by 7th Armoured Division during Battleaxe: a cautious advance in mass supported by high explosive shelling from Mk IV tanks and artillery to disrupt British defences from beyond the range of British antitank guns. Following these changes in command and control there were no further British comments on German rigidity and inflexibility.

Auchinleck in Command

Despite the victory over Italian troops in Libya, Wavell's period in command was a time of severe difficulty, and his restrained, undemonstrative personality could not have been more out of tune with Churchill's desire for action and need for communication. Rommel's defeat of British forces in April and his advance to Tobruk dispersed the optimism that followed Beda Fomm. The attempt to assist Greece against the Axis ended in defeat and serious losses with the evacuation of the British force that had been sent to help the Greeks. In May, a further defeat in Crete, where Churchill's access to Ultra sourced intelligence had given him every reason to hope for a victory, was a serious blow to prestige. In Iraq, a nationalist revolt threatened the security of British oil supplies. If they had been lost both the British army in Egypt and the Royal Navy in the Mediterranean and the East would have been immobilised. In Syria, a Vichy French government provided an entry point for Nazi influence into Persia and Iraq and a major military effort was required to overthrow it. In Persia itself the threat of German penetration through Turkey could not be ignored, and Turkey had to be encouraged to at least maintain neutrality, despite weakening British prestige. The failure of 'Battleaxe', for which Churchill had accepted the extraordinary risk of sending a convoy of Britain's precious tanks through an enemy dominated Mediterranean, was the last straw, and he replaced Wavell with Lieutenant General Claude Auchinleck as Commander in Chief in the Middle East.

Auchinleck was a well-respected figure, 'an unaffected, almost naive man beneath his shyness',[27] marked out before the war together with Harold Alexander as a candidate for high command, an able administrator and a 'soldier's soldier'. He had led a brigade on the North West Frontier, taken command of the British intervention in Norway in 1940, held key sectors of Britain's defences after Dunkirk as a Corps and Army commander, then returned to India in January 1941 as Commander in Chief in India to face the growing danger from Japan. His positive response in providing Indian troops after calls for assistance from the Middle East positioned him as the prime candidate to replace Wavell following the setbacks against Rommel. As the new Commander in Chief in the Middle East from July 1941 his responsibilities extended beyond the conflict in Libya and Egypt, though the overall situation was not at the same level of imminent disaster that it had been under Wavell.

27   Graecen, *Chink,* p. 141.

As the man also responsible for the only active land front against Germany, Auchinleck needed to be in constant touch with London and was always under scrutiny from Churchill and the Chief of the Imperial General Staff, Field Marshall Sir John Dill. He was also involved with the naval and air aspects of the theatre, and with the political situation within Egypt as well. With all his responsibilities, he was therefore not involved in the detailed planning of the new offensive against Rommel and his participation was limited to selecting the commanders, overseeing the general outline of the operation and negotiating a start date with London – in practice, resisting Churchill's demands for immediate action. But his fortunes as Commander in Chief were dependent on success in the desert, and therefore on the men who served under him in Eighth Army, whether already in post, selected for him by the War Office, or his own choices.

Auchinleck's three senior commanders in the autumn of 1941 were all newcomers to the desert. Rommel's first offensive had eliminated some experienced senior officers and the failure of Operation Battleaxe resulted in the removal of most of the rest. Churchill's preference for Eighth Army Commander had been 'Jumbo' Maitland Wilson who had commanded the expedition to Greece but Auchinleck selected Alan Cunningham who had made his name in an efficient and highly mobile campaign against the Italians in Abyssinia. Cunningham's immediate subordinates were Lieutenant General Godwin-Austen who had also impressed in East Africa and was appointed to command the bulk of the infantry in XIII Corps, and Vyvyan Pope, the energetic one armed Royal Tank Regiment veteran who had been Gort's advisor on armoured warfare in France in 1940, and was sent from England to command the armoured formations of the newly formed XXX Corps. Soon after taking up his post Pope was unfortunately killed in an air crash together with Brigadier Russell, almost the last senior survivor of O'Connor's victorious team. He was replaced by Willoughby Norrie, a cavalry officer of great charm who had not yet seen action in the war. Thus the Army commander and both Corps commanders, though highly rated, all lacked experience of war in the desert or indeed of commanding troops against Germans since 1918. But with strength by November 1941 triple that of June, and with frontline experience gained by commanders at divisional level during the summer, there was reason for confidence in the outcome of the new offensive.

Of Auchinleck's three infantry division commanders, Freyberg and his 2nd New Zealand Division had emerged with credit from the tough campaign in Greece and Crete, but had no experience of desert or armour. To remedy this Freyberg put his men through a six week programme to train for the specialised type of fighting that had developed in the desert, practising assaults on heavily defended positions with live artillery support and mocked up tanks. Later, they concluded that this additional training had made all the difference between success and costly failure.

Brink and his 1st South African Division on the other hand had experienced more manoeuvre than battle in their campaign in Abyssinia. They were accustomed to a lavish scale of transport not all of which had arrived when the offensive opened, much equipment being issued only just before the battle, and in some cases training was

12. New Zealander 2-pdr Portee and a wrecked Panzer Mk III, December 1941 (Imperial War Museum E12792)

incomplete.[28] And though most of the South African fighting units were to prove robust enough, fragile political support at home for the war inclined their senior officers to caution.[29] Like Freyberg, Brink had the right of appeal to his government if he felt his division was being unduly put at risk.[30]

Messervy still headed 4th Indian Division. He had been a dynamic and aggressive commander of a mobile column against the Italians in Abyssinia in 1940 and a competent brigade commander in 5th Indian Division at the hard fought battle of Keren in Eritrea. He then took over 4th Indian Division for Operation Battleaxe in June 1941. His refusal to allow his division be deprived of the protection of an armoured brigade sealed the fate of that operation by preventing the concentration of British tanks, though this was not at the time judged to be the prime cause of failure.

28   Dunn, *Sword and Wig*, p. 38.
29   JRL GB133AUC156. Nevertheless, Galloway, BGS XIII Corps, thought that compared to the Australians and New Zealanders "they were and are brittle', CAC, GLWY1/6.
30   Churchill was obliged to personally assure the New Zealand government in October 1941 that their troops would have adequate air support in the coming offensive. Playfair, *Official History*, vol. iii, p. 15.

His biography leaves an impression of vanity and self-satisfaction,[31] but he did later demonstrate competence under Slim in Burma.

Auchinleck's main striking force, 7th Armoured Division, was now under 'Strafer' Gott, previously commander of the division's support group, where the success of his columns against the Italians had been based on aggression plus the current principles of dispersion, mobility and flexibility. Gott's charm, calm under pressure and capacity for seeing a solution in the most difficult circumstances earned him respect and admiration from his British colleagues. The division itself had no shortage of experience over the previous twelve months but whether the appropriate lessons had been learned was another matter.

Few Italian units had been involved in the 'Battleaxe' fighting, so the popular conclusion drawn by the British from 'Compass', of complete lack of respect for Italian combat prowess, was unchanged. Propaganda photographs of lone Tommies escorting columns of demoralised Italians into captivity had been a reasonable reflection of the advantage that the better trained, better led, more mobile and motivated British infantry had over foot bound, half trained conscript Italian soldiers. But in playing to the chauvinistic view of their enemies to which many British were already conditioned, it ignored the determination with which the Italian artillery had fought, as had their tanks at Beda Fomm. It led to serious underestimation of their armoured and motorised units.

Training for Operation Crusader

By October 1941 British Intelligence had recognised the effectiveness of the German 50mm Pak 38 anti-tank gun as well as the 88mm gun in an antitank role, had noted the improved armour of the German main battle tank, the Mk III, and the effectiveness of German supporting artillery in keeping British tanks at a distance.[32] But it is difficult to identify any measures taken at regimental level to counter these threats and despite the defeat in 'Battleaxe' there was a widespread view that the German performance had not been particularly impressive.[33] German formations of up to 100 tanks had advanced slowly, supported by field artillery and anti-tank guns opening

---

31   Henry Maule, *Spearhead General: General Sir Frank Messervy* (London: Odhams Press, 1961).
32   TNA WO 169/1174: 31.10.41 Eighth Army Int Review No. 4. 'German Tank Tactics in Libya'.
33   IWM, 7/21/2/6 Tuker 12: The Germans were 'Not particularly good. If thrown off original plan they take 3 hrs to get going again for they call in their comds, get into a huddle and then give verbal orders.' LHCMA Creagh Papers: 'Generally speaking German tactics were rigid and rather stereotyped.' CAC, Corbett 3/16: 'Recent German conduct has been to advance with a mass of tanks, in successive waves on a narrow front and in considerable depth ... Such massed formations cannot be handy and expert in tactical manoeuvre. Their action tends to conform to pre-arranged plans, carried through, where possible, to the letter.'

fire at two or three thousand yards range where they were safe from the return fire of British armour. The solution proposed was to either ambush them from hull down positions or to 'advance at full speed from three sides, firing hard on the move' in order to close to effective 2-pdr gun range.[34] Firing on the move had been an article of faith with Hobart and the pre-war Tank Corps, and, given plenty of practice, achieved a hit rate of 20-33 percent.[35] Bearing in mind the 2-pdr gun's inferior sights and relative inaccuracy at medium or greater ranges even when stationary, it had some theoretical virtue if closing with enemy tanks was the only option. In practice it exposed British armour to German anti-tank guns and led to greater losses for the British than the Germans. Though 7th Armoured Division had seen how effective German artillery was in discouraging British tanks' advance, British artillery was not brought under the control of armoured unit commanders to similarly harass a German advance.[36] And the combined arms battle groups formed by German units were wrongly assumed to have a similar purpose to British Jock columns – harassing opposing reconnaissance units or supply columns – while in reality they were intended for taking on and destroying enemy units.[37]

In the autumn of 1941 4th Armoured Brigade under Brigadier Alec Gatehouse was re-equipped with the new Honey tanks and acquired a new role independent of 7th Armoured Division, training with its own dedicated infantry battalion and artillery regiment. This was along the lines of the armoured brigade group structure now adopted in England. 4th Armoured Brigade's losses during 'Battleaxe', when their meagre artillery support was moved on to another task, and later when ordered to 'rally forward' beyond the protection of infantry, provided food for thought for both Gatehouse, and for Brigadier Harding, formerly Brigadier General Staff to O'Connor and now BGS to Godwin-Austen at XIII Corps, the main infantry formation of Eighth Army. Both brigadiers appreciated the absolute necessity for armour to train with supporting arms prior to action and for infantry and armour to understand each other's limitations. At XIII Corps Harding was able to work with Brigadier Watkins of 1st Army Tank Brigade and organise at least some training between infantry and armour. Watkins thought the principles laid down in British training manuals were sound but commented that 'they are not sufficiently understood', possibly an acknowledgement that the official training manuals were neither much read nor made complete sense.[38] His gospel was that the assistance of tanks was 'essential to the

---

34 TNA WO 169/1185: Sp Grp War Diary 27.6.41.
35 Thomas L. Jentz, *Tank Combat in North Africa* (Arglen, Pennsylvania: Schiffer Military History, 1998), p. 59.
36 TNA WO 169.1185: Sp Grp War Diary, 27.6.41.
37 TNA WO 169.1185: Sp Grp War Diary, 11.7.41.
38 For example, training pamphlet MTP 23 is confused over the number of squadrons in a tank regiment and in all seriousness suggests that infantry in action can be alerted by flag signals from a tank to give the tank 'necessary assistance which will often consist of pushing the tank out of soft ground.'

other arms but [tanks] equally require the fullest possible assistance from all other arms'. Infantry must understand that they 'have to get hold of an objective and be prepared to hold it against immediate counterattack, especially tank counterattack… they must learn to follow-up a tank attack closely and at speed…they must understand thoroughly the weaknesses and limitations of tanks as well as their capabilities'.[39]

Infantry brigade & battalion commanders had most to learn:

> It has been a common thing for commanders to send our tanks, quite unsupported, to "clear up the situation" in fact using tanks as cavalry… The fault lies, of course, not with the commanders or with infantry or other arms, but in the fact that they are never given the chance to train with tanks; in the whole period I have commanded this brigade I have only once had an opportunity to carry out exercises on the ground with troops… note the relative boldness of German Infantry, as compared with our Infantry, in the presence of enemy tanks… they have a wholesome respect for tanks, but they fully understand them and their weaknesses … are well accustomed to training and working with them.[40] So far, in this country, control [of developing tank/infantry co-operation] has been in the hands of senior officers who, in most cases, are principally interested in the armoured division, and have no experience with army tanks; Army tank formations have been treated as the "Cinderella" of the RAC… what is required cannot be achieved by occasional consultations between Army Tank Bde commanders and action on a grade II staff level at GHQ ME.

His methods proved successful in the autumn offensive, Operation 'Crusader'. Both XIII Corps and the garrison in Tobruk successfully attacked the encircling Germans in co-operation with RTR Matildas, mounting night attacks at low cost in well-rehearsed tank/infantry operations.

The Indian Connection

It was clear to the Eighth Army that conditions in the Middle East were very different to those under which Home Forces trained, and that it was up to them to evolve their own tactics. A major source of both reinforcements and guidance for the Middle East was India for which the Middle East was the only prospective theatre of war until Japan entered the war in December 1941. From 1940, 4th and 5th Indian divisions were employed in Egypt and Eritrea, the 10th Indian Division in Persia, 3rd Indian Motor Brigade was stripped from a nascent Indian armoured division and sent to

39   TNA WO 201.527: These comments were made by Watkins in December 1941, but clearly refer to the training period in the autumn.
40   R.L Dinardo, *Germany's Panzer Arm in WWII* (Mechanicsburg, Pennsylvania: Stackpole Books, 2006) corroborates this view of German infantry/tank basic training.

Libya early in 1941, and training and thinking in India was dominated by events in North Africa. The Quetta Staff College already provided military education for commanders and with the raising and training of 1st Indian Armoured Division much thought was given to how troops should be employed in the novel circumstances of mechanised warfare. A leading British exponent of armoured warfare, Major General George Lindsay, had been posted to India in 1935 after he was judged to have failed in his command of the improvised armoured division in the previous year's Salisbury Plain exercises. With the outbreak of war his experience was now thought to be of value and his 1939 talk on 'Modern Formations' – echoing the official title of Charles Broad's 'Purple Primer', the RTC's handbook of the 1930s – gives an idea of Indian Army thinking at the time.[41] Dispersion, mobility and separation of the arms were his themes: dispersion should confuse the enemy, mobility would allow concentration on the decisive point and make supply and movement easier, while separation of tank and infantry units into armoured and unarmoured brigades was necessary because 'Experience shewed that armoured and unarmoured troops cannot be associated in one formation like a Brigade'. Tanks working closely and therefore slowly with infantry were deprived of their 'speed and latitude of manoeuvre' and would therefore be more exposed to antitank fire: his conclusion was that 'AFVs must always be a specialised arm and never mixed in another type of unit'. He envisaged infantry and heavy tanks used in the maximum possible mass to break through enemy defences: 'The Artillery & MMGs put the tanks home, the tanks put the infantry home and the infantry protect the tanks by mopping up the anti-tank weapons.' Cooperation rather than integration, in fact. The Mobile Division's fast tanks should be kept away from the breakthrough battle, to move through fresh and intact to paralyse enemy command, control and communications in the area immediately behind the battlefield. He favoured a strategical offensive combined with tactical defensive, using mobility to seize points which the enemy must counter-attack, while operating on a wide front to confuse the enemy, disengaging when necessary to concentrate fighting power at the decisive point to destroy their forces. Much of his argument was to be embodied in the tactical philosophy of the armoured divisions of Eighth Army until the late summer of 1942.

The man charged with raising the first armoured formation in India, a country that was to provide two million soldiers in the struggle against Fascism, was Major General Tom Corbett, Inspector of Cavalry in India. Corbett took his responsibilities seriously, was straightforward, loyal and hard-working. He was however not widely respected for his intellect, and in postwar correspondence his contemporaries sometimes refer to him as 'poor Tom'. He had read Liddell Hart and absorbed the view that armoured forces should use mobility and dispersion like the Mongols of old,[42] and he had read

41   CAC, Corbett Papers, 'Modern Formations'.
42   Though in Corbett's case he wrote of Scythians, perhaps confusing them with Parthians, since almost nothing is known of Scythians except for the occasional horde of gold artefacts.

enough Fuller to envisage fleets of tanks operating independently of the main army. His convoluted prose does suggest a mind lacking complete clarity. He thought 'the prevalent idea of similitude to cavalry, navy, etc, [was] erroneous.'[43] He was clearly a 'modernist' in military terms, a firm believer in mobility, speed, 'radius of action',[44] dispersion to confuse the enemy and then taking advantage of the enemy's mistakes, though without countenancing the possibility that mistakes might be committed by one's own side. He was interested in psychology,[45] believed that British soldiers were 'intense individualists, and hate being drilled, co-ordinated and mucked about … intense individualism is our greatest asset….at the bottom of all our enterprise, our self-control, our avoidance of political extremes – when it goes our Empire will also go.' Initiative depended on a robust individuality. 'We are most fortunate in dealing with a rank and file that is not complex ridden, and which is malleable, loyal, intensely practical, and Game.' His admiration for the British soldier was commonplace among his generation of commanders, as was his disdain for the Germans: he thought rigid German discipline suited trench warfare but 'that sort of discipline will not survive war of movement for long'. His first training directive in July 1940 was based on a perception of Germany superiority in numbers of heavily armed and armoured tanks and he saw a solution to the problem: 'disadvantage in firing power can be counterbalanced by advantage in circuit of action [range of vehicles] … the relative differences in armament can best be neutralised by light elements by exhausting the enemy's range of action, harassing his supply services and avoiding battle until his disabilities have been fully exploited'.[46]

In effect he was advocating jock columns before they had been invented, drawing on Liddell Hart's and Fuller's prescriptions for mobile warfare. Corbett like Lindsay was an advocate of dispersion: 'Concentration must be more in time than in space…Undue concentration in a restricted area by cramping manoeuvre restricts initiative, surprise and adjustment to the rapid progress of events'[47] and he dismissed 'the teaching that maintains detachment is contrary to the principle of concentration. The suitability for detachment of armoured formations is in many respects their primary characteristic… detachments must be made and with the utmost boldness… the commander who fails to appreciate this ignores the fundamental characteristic of armoured troops and will only achieve feeble and commonplace results.'

Against a numerically superior enemy, initiative 'can usually best be retained by concentrating the maximum striking power in succession against the enemy's threats with a view to defeating him in detail', a tactic which does imply that the enemy

43   CAC, Corbett Papers, 2/21, 1936.
44   'Circuit of action' is the rather awkward phrase used in place of 'range' by Broad in his 'Purple Primer' of 1931, IWM, 03(41).2/4.0, LBY65757, p. 20.
45   CAC, Corbett Papers, 2/33.
46   CAC, Corbett Papers, 3/9, 11/7/40, Training directive No 1 of 1st Armoured Div. in India.
47   CAC, Corbett Papers 3/14, 1st Armd. Div. Instruction No. 3 27/3/41.

has conveniently followed a similar doctrine of dispersal and allowed one's own side time to concentrate. It was unfortunate that training programmes in India as in pre-war England were hampered by the lack of equipment for exercises to examine the practicality of such doctrine – armoured cars and lorry borne infantry were not an adequate substitute for tanks. He was not keen on verbal orders which he thought needed confirmation 'to prevent misunderstanding, doubts and omissions' and wireless security needed 'the greatest care', the implication being that written orders were to be preferred.

Since 1st Indian Armoured Division was intended for service in the Western Desert, there was close liaison between Corbett and the Middle East – he visited the Western Desert in 1940, reports on 'Compass' were circulated to India, and elements of the division were sent to Egypt in 1941. A draft of a Military Training Pamphlet post-'Battleaxe' indicates the contemporary thinking on tactics in India and the Middle East in the autumn of 1941:

> The primary role, constant and predominating, of armoured formations is the defeat of hostile armoured formations ... Recent German conduct has been to advance with a mass of tanks, in successive waves on a narrow front and in considerable depth ... Such massed formations cannot be handy and expert in tactical manoeuvre. Their action tends to conform to pre-arranged plans, carried through, where possible, to the letter. If these rigid plans can be upset hostile improvisation on the spur of the moment will be difficult. [They could be upset by] superior training, mobility and manoeuvre, by the initiative and skill of commanders...The ability to fire accurately on the move will confer upon a force full manoeuvre in combat, power to maintain the momentum of attack and ... liberty to withdraw or to pursue.[48]

Corbett agreed with Lindsay that the chief virtue of armour was its mobility, and that mobility 'shackled' as during 'Battleaxe' deprived British armour of its ability to manoeuvre, the best weapon against German concentrations. He interpreted German concentration of armour as a psychological flaw: 'The German tendency to huddle is due to restricted wireless but is also a manifestation of his anxiety to ensure co-ordination and perhaps of his distrust of subordinate commanders ... a packed mass cannot manoeuvre or adjust their broadsides rapidly.'[49] Visiting the Middle East just before 'Crusader', he found 'tactical doctrine somewhat vague ... no comprehensive conclusions from recent experience had been worked out and recorded'[50] and thought that his Indian organisation, with greater 'homogeneity' in the armoured brigades, by which he meant a single tank type and few supporting troops, compared favourably

48   CAC, Corbett Papers, 3/16.
49   CAC, Corbett Papers, 3/19 Training Instruction No 11 Nov 1941.
50   CAC, Corbett Papers, 4/7.

to the Western Desert model. He envisaged tanks combining with armoured cars and close support mortar platoons (to put down smoke) using their mobility to embark on operations extending up to 400 miles in range and up to a week in duration. It was clear to him that 'It is impossible to get close cooperation between armoured forces of the Cruiser type and an infantry formation' though 'of course there can, and should be, cooperation of effort in the general sense.'

Brigadier Eric Dorman-Smith, nicknamed 'Chink' for his supposed resemblance to his regiment's Chinkara antelope mascot,[51] was the Director of Military Training in India from 1937. He had a reputation for unorthodoxy and intelligence. Rather like Liddell Hart and Fuller, he took ideas to their logical extremes, not always considering the circumstances in which his solutions were likely to be applied. Clever, ambitious, unconventional and a keen soldier with, unusually, a love for the army itself more than the regiment, he saw himself as a professional and an intellectual in an army dominated by amateurs and dullards, especially those from the socially fashionable regiments.

Dorman-Smith lacked friends among his contemporaries – only Freddie de Guingand, Montgomery's future Chief of Staff, admitted to a liking for him – and he aroused harsh criticism: sarcastic, arrogant, conceited, offhand are some of the comments he inspired. He was not a team player in any sense, he engendered no loyalty from subordinates and seems to have felt none to the military institutions with which he worked, whether it was his regiment, staff college, headquarters unit or the War Office. He claimed after the war that as a Catholic Irishman he felt something of an outsider in the British army,[52] which had a significant number of officers of Protestant Ascendancy background, including of course both Montgomery and Sir Alan Brooke. His career shows a pattern of early enthusiasm in a new posting, frustration if his views were ignored, antagonism from both superiors and subordinates and a departure to a new situation. His lectureship at Camberley Staff College for 16 months instead of the normal 3 years, and command of his regiment, the Northumberland Fusiliers, for only 12 months, were both unusually brief appointments. In an army that was based on concepts of duty and loyalty, it is notable that so many of his superiors were prepared to tolerate him for the sake of the insights that he could contribute. His career in India illustrates the nature of his relationship with the army and shows why he was often looked at, and listened to, with some scepticism. As Director of Military Training in India from 1938-40, he worked closely with Auchinleck, then Deputy Chief of the (Indian) General Staff, on the modernisation of the Indian Army, but antagonised Messervy by criticising the conduct of an exercise. Messervy retaliated with negative comments on Dorman-Smith's paper 'Extended Warfare', which

51   Dorman-Smith's regiment was the Northumberland Fusiliers. His son explained the nickname: 'The nickname relates only to the Chinkara antelope that the 1st Bn NF had in India prior to 1914. The Chinkara did not go to England when the Bn returned in 1913 hence the remark "We've got our Chink back" when D-S joined the Bn in February 1914.'
52   JRL GB133/1/3/2/5, letter to Lt Col John Lucy, 15 July 1961.

advocated a battle group rather than a divisional organisation.[53] Dorman-Smith later accused the Adjutant General of lying, was highly critical of the complacency of the Indian military establishment in the first year of war, and left India in pique for a less prestigious job as commandant of a new Staff College in Haifa.[54] Cassels, the Commander in Chief in India, was not sorry to see him go but nonetheless wrote to Wavell, his opposite number in the Middle East, that Dorman Smith 'has been a very great success out here as DMT and I have a very high opinion of his energy and outstanding ability'.[55] One wonders how far Cassels' favourable reference was designed to speed Chink on his way.

Dorman-Smith had been a useful brigade major to Wavell ten years earlier, and before long Wavell summoned him from Haifa to assist in the planning of an attack on the Italian advanced positions. This was to be led by Lieutenant General Richard O'Connor, who also knew Dorman-Smith and respected his intellect though well aware of his idiosyncrasies.[56] The rehearsal on 26th November for the initial attack did not convince O'Connor or Wavell that it would achieve either surprise or the decisive success that was needed. With only a single infantry division for the assault role, and a series of fortified camps to be taken, a setback at the beginning would jeopardise the entire operation. The upshot was a meeting of Wilson and O'Connor and their chief staff officers, Brigadiers Galloway and Harding, with Dorman-Smith representing Wavell. Between them they produced a plan titled ' A Method of attack on an entrenched camp in the Desert'.[57] It was a model of simplicity, matching O'Connor's limited resources to the task, relying on surprise, speed, timing and co-ordination of artillery, infantry and armour. Key points were artillery fire for deception and demoralisation rather than destruction, the assault to be under command of the tank battalion CO with infantry in bren gun carriers in close support of the tanks to protect them at the point of entry, and lorried infantry arriving within ten minutes to complete the mopping up process. Some aspects are similar to Lindsay's suggestions for tank/infantry assault in his 1939 'Modern Formations' paper, which Dorman-Smith would certainly have seen and it is reasonable to suppose were part of his contribution. He claimed credit for the deceptive aspect of the artillery bombardment which was a major factor in achieving surprise. It reflects the high standard of training of the prewar army that such a novel plan could be successfully implemented without further rehearsals.

53   Maule, *Spearhead General*, p. 204.
54   JRL GB133/2/1/35. In Dorman-Smith's obituary (The Times 21/5/69), Liddell Hart
       inaccurately claimed that 'As DMT in India, he ran up against opposition in his efforts
       for modernization and was "eased out" early in the war to the post of Commandant of the
       new Middle East Staff College'.
55   CAC, Barnett Papers, BRNT1 letter 17/9/40.
56   O'Connor thought Dorman-Smith 'extremely clever...rather supercilious and arrogant,
       and talked down to people and certainly made no pretence of hiding his feelings if he
       disliked or despised anyone.' Graecen, p. 102.
57   Liddell Hart Centre for Military Archives, O'Connor Papers.

Dorman-Smith then faced a series of disappointments. He was returned to Haifa from where he watched the plan succeed, heard that O'Connor had been overruled in a request for him as his BGS, and then discovered that John Harding was preferred for the position.[58] He was bored with his task of educating middle ranking officers in staff duties and left much of the work to his Chief Instructor, Freddie de Guingand. He eventually found a ringside seat at events when he was given a post at Middle East HQ as liaison officer between O'Connor and Wavell, and in that role accompanied O'Connor to the victory at Beda Fomm. His report on the battle was approved by O'Connor but not circulated, and a temporary appointment as BGS ME under Arthur Smith, Wavell's Chief of Staff (whom Dorman-Smith had gratuitously offended by mocking his religious beliefs many years earlier),[59] ended in June 1941. Chink's comment was that 'In a group which is out of accord with my views I'm an awkward and destructive component'.[60]

Following Rommel's initial advance and O'Connor's capture, Beresford-Peirse had taken command of XIII Corps for the 'Battleaxe' operation, the first major attack on the Afrika Korps. He had a liking for Dorman-Smith who he suggested should be 'a kind of brains trust for commanders'. He sent Harding to consult Dorman-Smith on the plans. Dorman-Smith suggested isolating the key German position at Halfaya with a strong British anti-tank screen and forcing Rommel to counterattack, keeping 7th Armoured Division in reserve on the flank for the appropriate moment when Rommel's counterattack failed.[61] It was certainly an improvement on the actual plan, and whether Harding, who did not care for Dorman-Smith,[62] adequately reported this advice to Beresford-Peirse is not known. The failure of Operation Battleaxe and the arrival of Auchinleck as Commander in Chief Middle East gave Dorman-Smith hopes for advancement but despite meetings with Auchinleck in July and October 1941 he remained still marooned, as he saw it, in Haifa. Auchinleck's choice of Neil Ritchie, junior to Dorman-Smith, as deputy chief of staff left him even more despondent. A letter from his wife in India alerted him that senior officers were 'being brainwashed by anti-Chink propaganda'. This rumour seemed to be confirmed when London vetoed Auchinleck's request that Dorman-Smith be appointed Director of Military Training in the Middle East. The final straw was the news in November that Ritchie had replaced Cunningham as Eighth Army commander during Operation Crusader. Dorman-Smith resigned his post as Staff College Commandant, writing that 'I must go on being passed over because I am too brilliantly disturbing'.[63]

58 Graecen, *Chink*, p. 165.
59 Graecen, *Chink*, p. 93.
60 Graecen, *Chink*, p. 180.
61 JRL GB133GOW1/2/10.
62 Adrian Stewart, *Six of Monty's Men* (Barnsley: Pen & Sword, 2011). E-book edition, loc384, Chapter 2.
63 Graecen, *Chink*, p. 187.

Brigadier Francis Tuker had been Dorman-Smith's Deputy Director of Miitary Training in India. He was regarded by Dorman-Smith as a brilliant soldier, 'a practical visionary in his own right'[64] and was later recognised to be an outstanding divisional commander. As an Indian Army officer he was the natural choice to succeed Dorman-Smith as DMT in India and he held the position for over a year until appointed to command 4th Indian Division in North Africa early in January 1942. He subscribed fully to Corbett's view of mobility and range as the key elements in armoured warfare and believed that 'We cannot afford blindly to imitate enemy methods temporarily successful. To beat the enemy we must out think him'.[65] He worked with Dorman-Smith on a concept he called 'Area Warfare', a reaction to the British experience of linear trench warfare of 1914-18. In his view, Great War 'linear' warfare had been countered by the British development of assault tanks to break the enemy's heavily defended line, creating breaches which lighter faster tanks could exploit. The campaigns in Poland in 1939 and France in 1940 confirmed to Tuker that linear defence was ineffective in modern operations. But lack of information on the actual German methods made accurate deductions by him and others impossible. He believed that if the Poles had concentrated on defending two or three areas rather than trying to hold a line, they could have held out for four or five months & inflicted 500,000 German casualties. He also believed that in 1940 a French strategy of defended areas interspersed by mobile forces would have been more successful against the Germans than the Maginot Line.[66] He did recognise, like Lindsay, Corbett and Dorman-Smith, that 'without some sort of doctrine of war, one cannot possibly make up one's mind clearly as to what form strategy will take' and thought that the standard British Army handbook, Field Service Regulations, 'fell to the ground because it never gave the Army a clear picture of what modern war was.' In October 1941 he regarded doctrine and advice from England as inappropriate for North African operations since British formations were geared to the eventual re-conquest of Europe, an operation that would involve armies in heavy fighting, 'shoulder to shoulder: their moves must be at first of only a few miles and always in contact: they will be forced to lay siege to and reduce great fortified work almost from the outset. With us, the picture is different. We move freely and unopposed over great areas.' It was therefore up to the army in India and North Africa to evolve their own doctrine and tactics: 'We are not only up with other people but well ahead in tactical doctrine and training ... The Staff School at Haifa [i.e. Dorman-Smith] tell every officer to try to get hold of every pamphlet and T.M. from India.'[67]

Tuker also noted that area defence had, under Dorman-Smith's leadership, been taught in India for the previous 18 months and after returning from a month-long

64   Graecen, *Chink*, p. 141.
65   IWM, Tuker Papers, 71/21/2/3.
66   IWM, Tuker 71/21/2/5 DMT's address of 23 September 1941.
67   IWM, Tuker 71/21/2/6, note C, para 61.

tour of the Middle East in the autumn of 1941 he was pleased to report that the fortress system of defence by areas was now being adopted, pointing this out on a map of the Western Desert and Syria: 'BTE's [British Troops in Egypt] system will hold provided it is provisioned fully and can continue to operate an offensive, mobile armoured field force.'[68] Corbett, subscribing to the same theory in November 1941, wrote 'In area warfare, the field fortress, on which our mobile striking forces pivot, form an indispensable part … There are many of them in the Middle East. All have proved their worth'.[69] However he manages to cite only one by name, Tobruk, as a success for its role in holding back Rommel. A paper, 'Organization and handling of Field Army', from Tuker as Director of Military Training at this time, illustrates his and Corbett's views on combined arms and armoured divisional organisation. Echoing Liddell Hart's prescription in 'The British Way in Warfare', it describes the light mobile element (reconnaissance and protective), heavy mobile element (armoured divisions) and fighting element (infantry divisions and 'I' tanks) of which an army should be composed:

> The primary role of the heavy mobile element is offensive action against the enemy's heavy mobile troops. The fighting elements are the moveable bases for the mobile elements … [they] must be ready to take immediate advantage of the defeat of the enemy's mobile troops…The importance of the primary role cannot be overstressed. The second role of the heavy mobile element is close cooperation with the fighting element in battle … exploiting the success gained by the 'I' tanks; or they may penetrate the enemy area from a flank or the rear. … The outcome of the armoured battle will depend principally upon manoeuvre.[70]

The paper envisages the armoured division's field artillery being decentralised to the brigades so that immediate support was available when required.[71] The Support Group should be abolished and its tasks performed by the 'fighting element'.[72] since 'inclusion of infantry as an integral part of an armoured division in place of an armoured brigade destroys homogeneity and reduces considerably the power of manoeuvre of the formation as a whole'. A single infantry motor battalion per division would suffice for mine clearance and similar tasks. Corbett disagreed with Tuker's suggestion that 'Armoured divs must be prepared to act offensively in close cooperation with other formations, against prepared defences.' His comment was an emphatic 'No – Have an I[infantry] tank bde instead. Don't fritter away lightly Armoured and scarce mobile troops.' These comments, written just before 'Crusader', may have been driven by the

68 IWM, Tuker 71/21/2/6 25/8/41 DMT's Tour of ME to 25/9/41.
69 CAC, Corbett Papers, 4/3.
70 CAC, Corbett Papers, Note from DMT 'Organization and handling of Field Army', 4 November 1941.
71 Corbett has given this an emphatic pencilled tick on this document.
72 Another pencilled tick from Corbett.

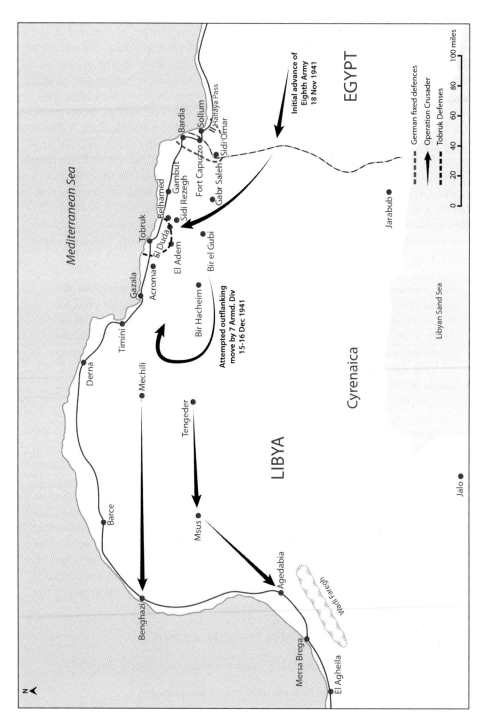

4. Operation Crusader

failure of armour against emplaced antitank weapons in 'Battleaxe'. Neither Tuker nor Corbett make any reference to infantry, artillery and armour training together. Their views are a return to the thinking of Hobart in 1940, of the Experimental Mechanised Force of the early 1930s, and of Liddell Hart's and Fuller's theories of mobile manoeuvre warfare.

The Winter Battles, 1941-42

In 'Battleaxe' a direct attack on German positions along the frontier had been tried and failed. Now Auchinleck looked at alternatives. He considered a long outflanking move south and west of Tobruk to cut off the Panzergruppe from its supply lines, but this was ruled out because of the vulnerability of such a dispersal of forces to a counterstroke. The eventual plan, 'Operation Crusader', was for 7th Armoured Division to take on and destroy German armour, in accordance with Corbett's vision of 'the primary role of the heavy mobile element', before turning to relieve Tobruk, while the infantry of XIII Corps masked the German frontier defences and covered British supply lines. A brigade of heavy tanks would support the infantry, but Freyberg in particular was concerned that this would not suffice if his New Zealanders were attacked by both panzer divisions. He insisted that an additional armoured brigade should be close enough to help his division should the need arise. 4th Armoured Brigade was therefore to be initially placed under the control of XIII Corps with the task of protecting the infantry divisions. The plan was approved by Auchinleck on 3rd October. But doubts began to emerge as the details sank in. On 21st October,

> 'General Norrie pleaded to be given a free hand in his task of destroying the enemy armour without being hindered with the additional task of protecting the left flank of XIII Corps. His aim was to move all his armoured brigades to a central position from which he could strike hard in any direction'.[73]

Norrie maintained that the presence of XXX Corps automatically covered Godwin-Austen's left flank and wished therefore to control the operations of 4th Armoured Brigade until the threat from the panzer divisions had been removed. But Godwin-Austen and Freyberg were insistent that their infantry divisions needed more armoured support than the infantry tank brigade assigned to them.

Norrie once again raised the question of 4th Armoured Brigade on 14th November at the final planning conference. Godwin-Austen stated that he could not give Norrie complete freedom to employ this brigade, and his concerns and those of Freyberg carried the day. Belief in the mobility of the armoured units and their ability to concentrate when required, in line with Fuller's pre-war concepts, outweighed any perceived risk of their defeat in detail.

73   TNA WO 201/358: Eighth Army Operations September 10th to November 17th 1941.

The 7th Armoured Division's new commander, Vernon 'Strafer' Gott, was 'an enigma', according to the late Field Marshal Carver[74]. His British subordinates were inspired by his charm, presence, calm under pressure and ability to find solutions in the most difficult circumstances. South African and New Zealand officers were less impressed. In 1940, leading the Support Group of 7th Armoured Division, he made up the Jock columns that were so effective against the Italians. In May 1941 he led a scratch force that held the Germans on the Libyan-Egyptian frontier and in June his Support Group provided flank protection for the 'Battleaxe' offensive. Divided into four columns it had negligible influence on the main battle, and its detached role deprived the tank regiments of artillery support. In the reorganisation following Wavell's departure, Gott took over the division. It is difficult to see just what the division's tactical philosophy, under Gott, was, though its structure followed the 'Organisation of 7 Armd Div' paper previously quoted. In the event the division's two tank brigades, 22nd and 7th Armoured Brigades, went into action that November with just one infantry company and one field battery each, sufficient for no more than local protection at night when replenishing. The bulk of the division's infantry and artillery was concentrated in the Support Group, whose role was once again to occupy country unsuitable for tanks, to act as a pivot on the flank of armoured brigades when required, or to form jock columns – in other words to work in conjunction with armour rather than being integrated with it on the German model. Anti-tank guns were regarded as infantry equipment within the Support Group, and so were once again unavailable to add fire power to the armoured regiments as did the German anti-tank guns.

The 22nd Armoured Brigade had landed in the Middle East on 25th October and had spent most of the time since implementing essential vehicle modifications and acclimatising to desert conditions. They had time for only a single exercise between arrival and the start of the offensive on 18th November.[75] Its three TA Yeomanry regiments cultivated a carefully nonchalant style: 'The yeomanry spirit held. Routine duties were performed without orders being necessary. When they were given, the old formula "I'd like you to…," "will you please…" "Be a good chap and go…", persisted.'[76] 2nd Royal Gloucestershire Hussars in particular prided themselves on 'the Yeoman outlook', enjoying the tendency of its informal approach to disconcert overly serious regular officers.[77] But little help was given them by more experienced units: the only advice one of their squadron leaders received, when he asked an officer of 7th Hussars for tips on fighting, was, 'you go in, you come out, you go in again, and you keep on

74   Field Marshal Lord Michael Carver, *Dilemmas of the Desert War*, p. 145.
75   Major Stuart Pitman, *2nd Royal Gloucestershire Hussars* (Uckfield: Naval & Military Press reprint of 1948 edition), p. 4. The exercise involved the seizing of an objective vital to the enemy and repelling the counterattack. Entirely appropriate, but far from what happened in the following three weeks.
76   Pitman, 2RGH, p. 5.
77   Pitman, 2RGH, pp. 71, 73.

doing it till they break or you are dead'.[78] On the second day of the Crusader offensive, at Bir Gubi close to 7th Armoured Division's path to Tobruk, 22nd Armoured Brigade was ordered to eliminate the Ariete Division when the Italians did not retreat as expected. Ignoring the advice of the experienced 11th Hussars to arrange artillery and infantry support, Brigadier Scott-Coburn ordered a charge at the Italian positions, overran some of them at considerable cost and then was forced back due to insufficient infantry to clear and hold the position. Captain Robin Dunn drove past the site some weeks later:

> 'When they viewed the enemy the gallant Yeomen had metaphorically drawn their swords, stood up in their stirrups and charged the enemy. The result was clear for us to see as we crossed the battlefield. A confused column of about 50 British tanks were sitting stationary and derelict in the sand with, at their head, a battery of damaged Italian guns with trenches and abandoned equipment lying around them. Some tanks were about a thousand yards from the guns and the column extended to within 50 yards of them. It was a sobering sight and described the battle better than any words.'[79]

The more experienced 7th Armoured Brigade under Brigadier George Davy was equipped with the oldest tanks in Eighth Army supplemented by a number of Crusaders. Davy's Nelsonian order of the day, 'This will be a tank commander's battle. No tank commander will go far wrong if he places his gun within killing range of an enemy',[80] read to all tank commanders before the offensive by their COs, proved insufficient as a tactical instruction. Twenty-four hours after crossing into Libya there was still no reaction from the Afrika Korps, so Cunningham changed the plan from inviting a decisive clash in the open desert to proceeding to the relief of Tobruk. 7th Armoured Brigade and the Support Group headed to Sidi Rezegh near Tobruk from where they aimed to join up with the defenders of Tobruk and drive off the Germans. However, the Support Group's weakness in infantry allowed the Germans to retain the nearby heights. The panzer divisions arrived to support the German infantry units, and there ensued an immensely confused four day battle, characterised by attack and counterattack, in which the British never brought to bear their overall superiority in tank numbers. 7th Armoured Brigade was effectively wiped out and its remaining elements withdrawn. A remarkable feature of the battle was the outstanding leadership of Brigadier Jock Campbell of the Support Group. Standing up in his staff car and identified by a dramatically large flag, he personally led tank reinforcements into the fray as they arrived. The subsequent award of a Victoria Cross was unique for someone of his rank, resounded through the army and earned him a letter of congratulation

---

78   Pitman, 2RGH, p. 5.
79   Dunn, *Sword and Wig*, p. 35.
80   Liddell Hart Centre for Military Archives GB0099, Davy manuscript memoirs and notes.

from Major General Ravenstein of 21st Panzer Division, his opponent in the battle, taken prisoner a couple of weeks later.

Brigadier Gatehouse's 4th Armoured Brigade, veterans as were 7th Armoured Brigade, was organised on brigade group lines with a full battalion of infantry and a regiment of guns integrated with the armour and had developed tactics of its own before the opening of Operation Crusader. Sergeant Wardrop of 5RTR was delighted at the success of the brigade's new combined arms methods. He revelled in 'a running scrap in which they [the Germans] lost six and as it got dark we closed in on them and duffed up another three. All night long we scotched them up...The big experiment of guns, tanks and infantry was proving a huge success, by this time we were operating like clockwork.'[81]

The guns travelled 2,000 yards behind the tanks with a Forward Observation Officer who could put rounds on target within about three minutes of the regimental commander's order. Meanwhile the armoured regiment would be pushing round to outflank the enemy.[82] Gatehouse seems to have led his brigade with skill, varying his tactics, as necessary. Wardrop again:

> '[W]e took on 21st Panzer Division that day and why not, it was 20 November - Cambrai Day! "Forward Five" and we got into line and advanced to the fray. We held them for about an hour and during that time the 3rd Tanks and 8th Hussars were pushing in from the left and right and shooting them up from the sides. They turned and ran for it, leaving nine behind.'[83]

Even the straightforward charge was an option: summoned to help 7th Armoured Brigade at Sidi Rezegh the next morning, 'there they were – a long line of [German] Mark IIIs and 50mm anti-tank guns, so we went to town on them ... it was decided to give them the old charge again. Quite frankly, I was not so strong for this charging business, although we continued to do it until about the next year at Knightsbridge, but off we went.'[84]

In a letter to Auchinleck two months later, Gott was to say that 4th Armoured Brigade was the most successful of the armour in 'Crusader', 'well trained in a very sound system of support and co-operation between all arms ... especially between the guns of the Bde Grp and the Armd regts.'[85] It seems that Gott and 7th Armoured Division had either rejected or were unaware of Gatehouse's methods prior to the battle, perhaps because Gatehouse's brigade had been assigned to a role covering the infantry of XIII Corps and was not directly under Gott's command.

81   George Forty, (ed.), *Jake Wardrop's Diary* (Stroud: Amberley Publishing, 2009), p. 40.
82   Forty, *Wardrop*, p. 26.
83   Forty, *Wardrop*, p. 38.
84   Forty, *Wardrop*, p. 39.
85   John Rylands Library, GB133AUC659, letter 27/1/42.

13. Captured Panzer Mk III. (The Tank Museum Bovington 0691-65)

14. Burning Crusader tank. Photo taken by a German tank crewman. (The Tank Museum Bovington 14-1838-C5)

Having mauled 22nd Armoured Brigade at Bir Gubi on the opening day of the battle, the Ariete Division needed to be destroyed or masked. The South African Division was given the task on the 19th November, but their commander Major General Brink was reluctant to attack, claiming that Ariete's tanks were manned in part by Germans,[86]and therefore more formidable than Norrie's orders implied. On the 20th his 5th Brigade was ordered to Sidi Rezegh to help 7th Armoured Brigade in restoring the link with the Tobruk garrison. Brink took five hours to begin the move and stopped a dozen miles short, unwilling to continue in the dark, leaving 7th Armoured Brigade isolated and to be nearly annihilated the followng day. Pienaar's 1st Brigade was equally dilatory in following up on the 22nd to mask Ariete, leaving a substantial gap between it and 5th Brigade, which the Afrika Korps was quick to exploit. Rommel gathered both his panzer divisions and on the 23rd with the Ariete he launched them at the 5th Brigade, destroying it and scattering the armoured units that fought with it, though at heavy cost in both tanks (losing 72 out of 162) and men.[87] To exploit the chaos he had caused, Rommel took his two armoured divisions and the Ariete on a 72 hour drive away from the battlefield to disrupt British communications, destroy their supply dumps and relieve the pressure on his own garrisons along the frontier. It was a move that, had it succeeded, would have been lauded as an exemplary demonstration of Liddell Hart's strategy of the indirect approach. The operation has gone down in history as 'the dash to the wire'. But he was stoutly beaten off on the frontier by 4th Indian Division who reduced German tanks by another 20, and he failed to locate the British supply centres. His absence gave Eighth Army time to recover its own damaged tanks, reorganise its units and bring up the New Zealand division to renew the attempt to relieve Tobruk. Cunningham, though not his subordinates, believed the battle lost and wanted to break it off. His BGS, Brigadier Galloway, on his own responsibility obstructed the issue of Cunningham's retreat order and alerted Auchinleck to Cunningham's loss of nerve. Auchinleck appreciated that the Germans were also feeling the strain of the week-long fight and replaced Cunningham on 26th November with his own Deputy Chief of Staff, Major General Neil Ritchie. His instructions were to keep the presssure up. 4th and 22nd armoured brigades, for once united, got the better of 15th Panzer the following day but withdrew from the battlefield to leaguer at dusk allowing the Germans to safely rejoin the Panzergruppe.[88] As the number of tanks on both sides diminished, British superiority in infantry, artillery and supplies began to tell in what became an attritional struggle. Even German officers were impressed by the British 'unfailing will for victory – a hardness and stubbornness which must be admired and which never flagged, even

---

86   Katz, *South Africans vs. Rommel,* p.115. Another South African report claimed that Ju87 Stukas with Italian markings attacked with such determination that they must be flown by German pilots.

87   General Sir William Jackson, *The North African Campaign 1940–43* (London: Batsford, 1975), p. 169.

88   Mellenthin, *Panzer Battles,* p. 94.

in situations which seemed to be hopeless'.[89] On 7th December Rommel ordered a withdrawal to the west of Tobruk.

The Eighth Army was too battered to follow up without some reorganisation. Norrie's XXX Corps might have been the best choice for the pursuit since Norrie was an armoured commander with an HQ equipped for mobile warfare – he was a believer in forward control, via a small mobile tactical headquarters.[90] But Ritchie transferred 7th Armoured Division to Godwin-Austen's XIII Corps and gave him the task. 'Pip' Roberts, one of Norrie's staff, later said that:

> Ritchie felt he could handle Godwin-Austen of XIII Corps more easily than Norrie: they both had infantry minds. There was a sort of club spirit among the armoured commanders from Norrie through to the divisional and brigade commanders which Ritchie found difficult to deal with.[91]

It shows the lack of harmony among Eighth Army's commanders that even if Ritchie did feel more at ease with Godwin-Austen than with Norrie, Godwin-Austen himself 'had never been able to establish an easy relationship with Ritchie'.[92] At all events, the pursuit was not a success. Godwin-Austen sent 4th Armoured Brigade on a seventy mile journey to outflank the entire Panzergruppe and attack them from the rear while 4th Indian Division assaulted them frontally. But problems with refuelling the armour and difficult terrain were to delay and frustrate 4th Armoured Brigade. They were forty miles distant when a sharp counterattack (described in Chapter 2) halted the pursuing 4th Indian Division and bought enough time for Rommel to pull his troops back.[93] 7th Armoured Division's support group had played no part in the outflanking attempt, being deployed in jock columns to protect supply lines from what was at this stage a non-existent threat. Ritchie wrote to Auchinleck that it was 'quite infuriating' that the outflanking movement had failed and implied that Godwin-Austen was to blame,[94] though Gott as divisional commander seems a likelier candidate for censure,[95] bearing in mind the excessive depth of 7th Armoured's move and the dispersal of its brigades. And then Ritchie's BGS, Brigadier Galloway, with the backing of the RAF put forward a proposal to cut off the Afrika Korps near

---

89   Reidel, Chief of Staff of 15 Pz Div quoted in Gudmunsson, *Inside the Afrika Korps*, p. 256.
90   TNA WO 216/85 Norrie's Report, 12 July 1942.
91   Major General G.P.B. Roberts, *From the Desert to the Baltic*, (London: Kimber & Co 1987) p. 59.
92   Carver, *Harding*, p. 89.
93   Unexpectedly difficult terrain is the generally accepted reason, but 5RTR War Diary (entry 16.12.41) Bovington records that it was considered 'unsafe' to move the refuelling column up to 4th Armoured Brigade. German armour was more prepared to risk running out of fuel than the British, Gudmundsson, p. 227.
94   Carver, *Harding*, p. 89.
95   JRL, Auchinleck Papers GB133AUC562 letter 17/12/41 Ritchie to Auchinleck.

Antelat in a repeat of O'Connor's strike the previous year, but this was rejected by Ritchie.[96] This drive would have forestalled the tank reinforcements which Rommel received through Benghazi in the last week of December and 'Crusader' could well have achieved a decisive victory.

The 22nd Armoured Brigade now took over the task of pushing the Afrika Korps back, but suffered two unpleasant reverses at the hands of the newly reinforced panzer divisions. On 26th Decenber after moving south on Eighth Army's intelligence report that the enemy had 'very few tanks left and that a "great opportunity" existed to cut off his withdrawal to Tripoli by bold action', they were attacked by about 80 newly landed tanks with the inevitable supporting infantry and anti-tank guns.[97] Losing 42 of their 108 tanks, half from breakdowns, they withdrew behind the formidable Wadi Faregh, but were then outflanked and forced back yet again, losing another 30. The brigade was taken out of the front line early in January and replaced by the newly arrived 1st Armoured Division.

The Msus Stakes

It became the custom in North Africa for the rapid advances and retreats during each change of fortune to be ironically nicknamed as if they were prestigious races at fashionable race meetings. The Benghazi Handicap, as Rommel's first advance in the spring of 1941 had been called, was now followed by the Msus Stakes of January 1942 and succeeded by the Gazala Gallop in the summer – even the Germans caught the habit, christening the Alam Halfa battle in September 1942 'The Six Days Race'.

Difficulty in supplying 1st Armoured Division, fresh to the desert and inexperienced, meant only its Support Group could be maintained at the front. Its 2nd Armoured Brigade began a training programme 50 miles east of Agedabia in 'a new doctrine of combined action of armoured units and Field and Anti-tank Arty in close co-operation'.[98] This was presumably based on Brigadier Harding's summary of his and Watkins' views in their December pamphlet on armoured and infantry co-operation which stipulated that 'tanks will never be committted to action without adequate arty and anti-tank support.'[99] One would question how useful 2nd Armoured Brigade's combined arms

---

96   CAC, Galloway Papers, CLWY 1/5 Letter to Charles Miller 22/7/63 'Neil [Ritchie] refused to let it go. I believe he consulted the Auk which, if so, was a very unfair thing to do ... I will never forget that bitter disappointment all my life... I am absolutely certain that much, if not all of 1942 could have been avoided.' Galloway, instrumental in foiling Cunningham's order to break off the battle three weeks earlier, had a furious row with Ritchie over the issue and was sent back to Cairo where he took up Ritchie's former job. His proposal and the RAF's enthusiasm for it are mentioned in Tedder, *With Prejudice*, p. 199, but Tedder is clear that Ritchie was also keen on it – it seems therefore that it may have been vetoed by Auchinleck.

97   TNA WO 169.1294: 22 Armd Bde 1941 war diary

98   TNA CAB 106.662: Messervy's Report, February 1942

99   TNA WO 201/527: Tactical Handling of armoured formations.

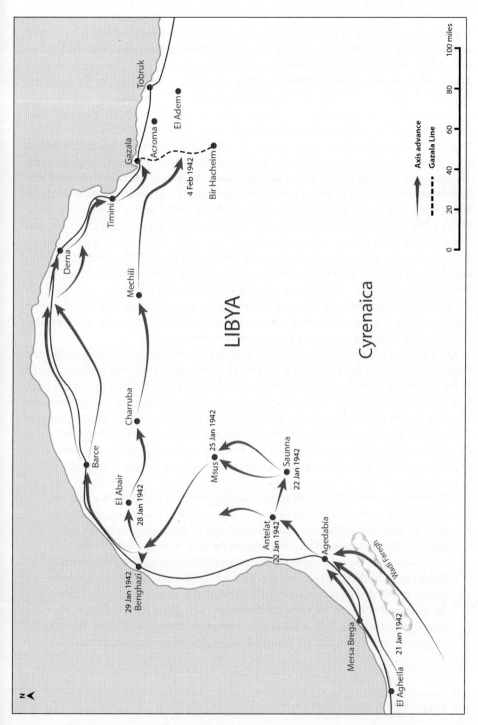

5. The 'Msus Stakes' – Rommel's advance to Gazala

training was when the Support Group was deployed further forward and not involved in the training. The division's commander, Major General Lumsden, who had led an armoured car regiment with distinction in France in 1940, was wounded on New Year's Day in an air attack and Messervy took over. Meanwhile, closer to the front, the Support Group were introduced to desert warfare by Jock Campbell.

Campbell was in ebullient mood, greeting the Support Group with 'Rommel's had the stropping of his life, keep him on the run!,'[100] and giving them a week's introduction to column techniques before returning to Cairo. The Support Group's jock columns then moved up to harass and inflict maximum losses on the enemy. Eighth Army HQ was sure that the enemy posed no immediate threat and Messervy planned that in February 4th Indian Division would pin the Afrika Korps in its position at Mersa Brega while 1st Armoured Division made a 200 mile outflanking move to cut them off. Air Marshal Tedder, Commander in Chief of the RAF in the Middle East, was less confident than his army counterparts, putting Eighth Army's only partial victory down, mostly, to 'an excess of bravery and a shortage of brains.' He wrote to London on 13 January that 'The Army have themselves remarked to me two or three times, "We are still amateurs" – strange for a professional Army but true. Now, unfortunately the 22nd Armoured Brigade who might have been expected to have lost their amateur status, are being relieved by a new Armoured Division who are new to real war, so I am afraid we shall have to expect some more bloody noses.'[101]

He was more perceptive than he knew. Rommel's intelligence chief had noted that Eighth Army would be inferior in numbers while its supply route was still obstructed at Bardia (the redoubtable Hauptmann Bach was once again holding out to the last), and Rommel launched an attack on 21 January to take advantage of the opportunity. The supply situation had prevented British armour closing up to the front to support 1st Support Group, and in difficult terrain the wheeled columns of the Support Group could not escape the tanks of the Afrika Korps and came close to destruction. Its artillery regiment, 11th Honourable Artillery Company, lost most of its guns:

> We tried to carry out an orderly retreat, moving from one positon to the next and delaying the enemy as much as we could by fire. But this was almost impossible, the gun platforms buckled in the soft sand, the tie bars broke, radiators boiled and half shafts fractured. One after another the guns were hit or their tyres were punctured ... As the men worked to keep the vehicles moving two groups each of about fifteen Stuka dive bombers appeared overhead and came screaming down releasing their bombs on our stricken battery. By this time, the tanks had closed up again and although we engaged them over open sights from the depression where we were stuck, yet another gun received a direct hit, leaving us with only two guns. Eventually we managed to get clear of the depression and after

100 Dunn, *Sword and Wig*, p. 37.
101 Tedder, *With Prejudice*, p. 218.

driving for a further ten miles formed close leaguer at about 6.30pm. It had been a disastrous baptism of fire for the HAC.[102]

The following day the DAK advanced rapidly along the coastal road, outdistancing both the 201st Guards Brigade and the remnants of the Support Group, and by the evening of the 23rd Messervy's plan of holding a line and counter attacking had failed – the enemy had reached and passed the line before 2nd Armoured Brigade could take up its position, the usual German combination of anti-tank guns and armour inflicting heavy losses on the armoured regiments. Eighth Army HQ still believed that German strength amounted to no more than two battalion groups totaling a couple of dozen tanks (though the HAC had reported 40 in its initial contact) and therefore ordered a defence line at Saunnu by 1st Armoured Division, backed by 4th Indian Division under Major General Tuker.[103] German troops moved so fast that they reached Saunnu before the British but, following orders to encircle the enemy and moving east to close the trap, unintentionally left a gap through which the Armoured Division escaped. By the evening of the 25th British troops had continued north past Msus, comprehensively outfought, outpaced and outmanoeuvred by the German armoured units, not least because of the absence of artillery support: 'our guns could not compete at this speed and most of our columns were running a bad second to the enemy tanks'.[104] Divisional HQ was chased 5 miles beyond Msus, and Messervy, irritated by unrealistic orders to take up a position from Charruba to el Abiah on the Benghazi-Mechili track, ordered a concentration at Charruba from where he could counter a threat either to Benghazi or Mechili. Godwin-Austen rightly ordered the evacuation of Tuker's 4th Indian Division from Benghazi, but Tuker was then dismayed to be told by Eighth Army, where Ritchie was now working under Auchinleck's supervision, to halt the evacuation and counterattack, and was then angered by suggestions that he was faint-hearted. Godwin-Austen as Corps commander was supposedly in charge but found he was being cut out of the chain of command by Ritchie, backed by Auchinleck. Meanwhile Rommel sold a remarkable dummy that appeared to threaten Mechili and sent 1st Armoured Division racing back north from Charruba, allowing Rommel to head west through the Jebel Akhbar to Benghazi.

The 1st Armoured Division lost 30 guns and 94 tanks, more from breakdowns and fuel shortage than through battle, being reduced to 18 tanks by the time a defence was stabilised at Gazala.[105] 4th Indian Division escaped annihilation. One brigade succeeded in retreating to Tobruk while the other was forced to fight its way south and then eastwards through Axis forces. Godwin-Austen resigned, his position impossible when it was clear to his staff and subordinates that he did not have the

102 Dunn, *Sword and Wig,* p. 38.
103 TNA WO 201.2696: Report on Withdrawal El Agheila- Gazala, January-February 1942.
104 TNA CAB 106.662: Messervy's Report, February 1942.
105 TNA CAB 106.662: Messervy's Report, February 1942.

confidence of his superior, inspiring a comment from Freyberg, 'when the butler and the footman fall out, it is usually the footman who leaves'. Tobruk clearly could not be abandoned but maintaining the previous siege from April to December 1941 had been extraordinarily costly in terms of shipping, aircraft and troops and it had been decided by the Army, Navy and RAF commanders in chief that it would never be undertaken again. Now, after the retreat to Gazala, 'it was decided that, contrary to previous intentions, every effort would be made to hold Tobruk.'[106] With 80 cruiser tanks left, of which only 20 were fit for more than one action, Ritchie was told to develope a defensive position in the general area Gazala-Tobruk-Bir Hacheim but to avoid becoming invested in Tobruk and, should the danger of this appear imminent, he was to withdraw to the Libyan/Egyptian frontier, 'and that this position must be held.' The question of how Tobruk would simultaneously be held, or whether it could be held in those conditions, was not addressed.

Crusader Post-Mortem

Eighth Army, Auchinleck and Whitehall now had considerable food for thought as to why British formations struggled against German troops and what should be done to improve their performance. Trust in the leadership had been undermined though not yet to the extent of affecting morale which, being based on the regiment rather than faith in the 'top brass', remained high. Robin Dunn, wounded in the debacle, summed up the feeling: 'We did not have much confidence in our leaders or our equipment; we admired Rommel and had respect for the Africa Corps as clean fighters. But we had immense pride in our own regiments and those of our brigade and in our ability to 'see off' the enemy in spite of everything. We were pretty bloody minded'.[107] Sergeant Wardrop felt much the same: 'We were never licked; we knew we had chased them once and could do it again'.[108]

In Eighth Army, it was Auchinleck, Norrie and Gott who led the post-battle analysis of 'Crusader' and the January defeat. Ritchie, at heart a staff officer rather than a commander, was not much more than a channel for Auchinleck's views. Auchinleck and Norrie both kept faith in the jock column which they saw as instrumental in keeping pressure on Rommel when the respective tank forces were worn down, and which in November 1941 had certainly disrupted the Afrika Korps' logistics to the point where as Auchinleck wrote on 5th December, its fight was not sustainable:

'his thrusts seem to have petered out under the attacks of our jock cols...The jock columns of which more and more are being organised are just what we want. They piquet his movements and give him no rest, and are, I hope, giving

106 TNA WO 201.379: Ritchie's Report on Ops, May-June 1942.
107 Dunn, *Sword and Wig*, p. 41.
108 Forty, *Wardrop*, p. 46.

15. An Axis supply convoy, the target of Eighth Army's jock columns. (Imperial War Museum MH 5565)

us command of that enormous no man's land … They seem to suit our peculiar genius for fighting, and are certainly going at the enemy with the greatest relish and vigour… I think the Hun finds them somewhat unorthodox.'[109]

Auchinleck was already an advocate of the brigade groups which in late 1940 had become the norm in England, and to adopt what could be seen as a more powerful and flexible jock column was entirely logical from his experience of 'Crusader'.[110] It did not however take into account that the jock columns were successful only in the absence of armoured opposition, and that infantry brigade groups unsupported by tanks would be as vulnerable as jock columns to enemy armour. He saw the problem as poor tactical leadership of the British armour, which he blamed for the loss of so many tanks by 22nd Armoured Brigade at the end of December, forcing the deployment of the newly arrived and inexperienced 1st Armoured Division. He wrote to Ritchie that 'confident leadership and tactics are needed to make up for inferiority of armour… British soldiers

---

109 JRL GB133AUC520, letter to Arthur Smith 5/12
110 Although by May 1942 British armoured divisions had been restructured to one armoured brigade and one motor infantry brigade with the artillery under a brigadier. This was a move away from the brigade group concept.

with inferior tools...if properly led will as in the past beat better equipped enemies'. But he himself had no solution. He wrote to his Chief of Staff Arthur Smith, 'We have, as you say, a hell of a lot to learn about handling armour on the battlefield … Please have the Indian handbooks on the handling of armoured formations carefully studied. I feel they are ahead of Home in some ways – more realistic. .. our tactical school (senior wing) needs stirring up and re-modelling.'[111] Moreover, he told the new CIGS Alan Brooke on 7 January that he was 'seriously disturbed at the apparent lack of tactical ability in our RAC commanders … the two leaders who have been outstanding in the recent fighting between the opposing armoured forces are Gott - an infantryman – and Campbell – a Gunner' [Auchinleck had not then heard of Gott's commendation of Gatehouse of the RTR].[112]

Gott's leadership in keeping his troops fighting was impressive but his handling of the armour is open to criticism, and though Campbell was inspirational at Sidi Rezegh and the award of his Victoria Cross rightly caught the army's imagination, the Support Group under his direction was throughout 'Crusader' used more to form jock columns than to support the armoured brigades. Nor did Auchinleck, Gott, Norrie or Campbell appreciate that a significant factor in 1st Armoured Division's January defeat

16. Major General Campbell, Lieutenant General Auchinleck and Brigadier Gatehouse, February 1942. Campbell, at the wheel of the Ford in which he had led 7th Armoured Division the previous November, was killed shortly after this photograph was taken. (Amberley Publishing)

111 JRL GB133AUC524, letter 6 December 1944.
112 JRL GB133AUC603, letter 1/1/42, 617 letter. 7 January 1942.

had been yet again the detachment of its Support Group into jock columns operating separately from the armour. Though Eighth Army did not lack determination and the will to win, it remained to be seen whether improved equipment and reorganisation of divisions into brigade groups would compensate them for the limited tactical ability that derived from lack of an adequate doctrine.

Back in Cairo in February following Godwin-Austen's departure, Auchinleck began to consider a reshuffle of his commanders and reviewed their performance. Gott's reputation was still high and he took over XIII Corps. The charismatic Campbell, his replacement at 7th Armoured Division, was killed in a car accident in February and was succeeded by Messervy. Both Auchinleck and Ritchie had doubts about the recently arrived Major General Lumsden, wounded in December and now recovered to find his 1st Armoured Division had been heavily defeated in January under the temporary command of Messervy. Lumsden distrusted Messervy from then on.[113] Auchinleck thought 'Lumsden talks a good deal and is a bit mercurial',[114] while Ritchie clearly had doubts but the details in his letter to Auchinleck are unfortunately illegible.[115] Ritchie considered dismissing Tuker after the January debacle but Tuker and 4th Indian Division were in any case to be withdrawn from Ritchie's command.[116] Casting Tuker as a scapegoat would have been extraordinary, for his performance had been exceptional. It is clear from Tuker's letters and Dorman-Smith's comments that Tuker and Ritchie were quite incapable of working together.

Ritchie was a talented staff officer who made his name as Brigadier General Staff to 2nd Corps in 1940 and hugely impressed Brooke, the Corps commander, in the very great difficulties of the retreat to Dunkirk. But his only command of troops was in peacetime as CO of the Black Watch. He was younger than the corps and divisional commanders of Eighth Army and had no experience of frontline command. Despite Ritchie's great air of decisiveness, he was really rather indecisive, irritating Godwin-Austen by repeatedly asking for his opinion only to ignore it.[117] Brooke himself suggested Ritchie should return to Cairo as Chief of Staff for Middle East HQ now that the situation had stabilised, but there was a distinct shortage of candidates with enough experience to replace him in command of Eighth Army. Brooke suggested either the generally respected Beresford-Peirse, or Sandy Galloway who had proved his mettle during Crusader, but Auchinleck turned both down.[118] He told Brooke that Ritchie 'has gripped situation, knows what to do and has the drive and ability to do

---

113 Messervy was otherwise widely praised by all, including Ritchie: JRL GB133AUC702 letter to Auchinleck 12/2/42; 'I am sure he is a first-class commander.'

114 JRL GB133AUC696, letter to Ritchie 10/2/42.

115 JRL GB133AUC738, letter to Auchinleck 5/3/42.

116 JRL GB133AUC699, 11/2/42 letter from Ritchie.

117 TNA WO 259/73: Auchinleck to Brooke, 20 February 1942.

118 Even Dorman Smith was not unkind about Beresford-Peirse: 'a very genuine person, Anglo-Irish, and a fine divisional commander if obsoletely orthodox.' CAC, Barnett papers, letter to Barnett, 12 July 1958.

it I feel', words that are somewhat at variance with the close supervision he continued to bestow.[119]

Auchinleck informed Ritchie that he was sending Dorman-Smith up to Eighth Army to enquire into 'our present system of command and issue of orders etc. I feel we are still too rigid and hidebound and that we must modernise ourselves in this respect....It must be made clear that he is not snooping!'[120] Historians have usually represented that it was Auchinleck's intention to sound out opinion on Ritchie, but there is no evidence in Auchinleck's surviving correspondence that this was the case and it was during Dorman-Smith's trip to Eighth Army that Auchinleck was writing to Brooke defending Ritchie. In fact Auchinleck had already formally advised Eighth Army and its corps headquarters two days before sending Dorman-Smith that 'the old system of issuing orders and of control in general is not suitable for the swift moving warfare on very wide fronts that is likely to otain all over this theatre'.[121] He told Liddell Hart after the war that it was the 'cumbrous and static system of command and control'[122] that needed reform, to prevent the breakdown in communication when a headquarters was overrun or obliged to move, that was the reason behind Dorman-Smith's visit, not that Ritchie himself was the object of interest. Unfortunately Dorman-Smith had no respect for Ritchie, speaking of 'un embarras de Ritchies', and it would have been entirely in character for him to listen to complaints about the Army Commander and to dig for them as well.[123] He left behind him the damaging impression that such was his mission, having found a vociferous source in Tuker. On his return he reported to Auchinleck in the course of a whole Sunday that the Eighth Army was 'more like a club than a disciplined entity',[124] a 'poisonous' amosphere, a lack of disipline among the senior commanders with 'a "syndicate" method of command and the slovenly practices of which I had compained ... some "old boy" informalities which might become dangerous' and the loose employment of 'jock columns swanning about ... I'd thought I'd convinced him. Then I was sent to South Africa and I did not return until May 1942 to find there had been absolutely no change anywhere.'[125] He believed that Auchinleck's reluctance to sack Ritchie stemmed from the belief that his replacement would be Montgomery, who had beeen an uncooperative subordinate to Auchinleck in England in 1940. His visit left the impression in Eighth Army that Auchinleck had limited confidence in his Army commander, and that Auchinleck himelf was under the influence of Dorman-Smith, who was not favourably regarded.

119 JRL GB133AUC725, 23/2/42 letter to Brooke .
120 JRL GB133AUC696, 10/2/42 letter to Ritchie.
121 TNA WO 201/538: Auchinleck to 8th Army, Rear HQ, XIII Corps & XXX Corps HQs.
122 David French, *Raising Churchill's Army* (Oxford: Oxford University Press, 2000), p. 239.
123 Extraordinarily, Dorman-Smith had also offered to fill the vacancy of Chief of Staff to Ritchie, ignoring the impossibility of working effectively with a man he could not respect. JRL GB133GOW1/11/2 letter to John Connell 2/12/58
124 Lavinia Graecen, *The Desert Generals Part 1,* BBC Northern Ireland 2006
125 JRL GB133GOW1/3/2/1, letter to de Guingand 1 June 1964.

Lieutenant General Sir Alan Brooke had become CIGS on December 1st to be confronted within days by the Japanese declaration of war and a series of military disasters in the Far East, and the tone in his Diaries becomes a touch peremptory when further informed through December and January of North African setbacks just as he believed a victory had been achieved. An artilleryman who had utilised guns en masse in the successful offensive of 1918, he was not convinced of the benefits of operating brigade groups which by their nature decentralised control of artillery, especially having seen in exercises in England the previous autumn that 'one of the outstanding defects was the inability of commanders to stage even a divisional attack, owing to the universal custom of operating by brigade groups', though he accepted brigade groups were suitable for small scale operations.[126] But confronted with Auchinleck's note that 'The Armoured Brigade Group as a permanent organization is a necessity and I am not prepared to put armoured troops into battle in any other form',[127] he could not oppose the change.

Brooke encountered further resistance when he suggested the removal of Shearer, Auchinleck's Intelligence chief, whose assessment of German capabilities and intentions had been consistently poor, and it was six weeks before Shearer was replaced by Freddie de Guingand. Brooke also had an unspoken concern over Auchinleck's reliance on Dorman-Smith, described in Brooke's diary as a man with 'a most fertile brain, continually producing new ideas, some of which (not many) were good and the rest useless'.[128]

But his major issue was expressed on 21 January: 'What is lamentable and must be remedied is the lack of knowledge in most senior officers of the handling of armoured forces'.[129] Brooke thought a Major General with responsibility for armoured vehicles should supervise Eighth Army's armoured units, as was the practice in Great Britain, but Auchinleck insisted that a less senior individual under a Director of Military Training was more appropriate, perhaps because antipathy between the Royal Tank Regiment and cavalry units made a senior officer from either branch unacceptable to the other.[130] As Brooke admitted, 'Hobart's tour in the Middle East left such an unpleasant taste behind that all the Armoured Corps are still looked upon with suspicion!' though he thought 'things have moved on since Hobo preached his doctrine' – close all arms co-operation had now been accepted at home for the last 18 months,[131] at least in principle. Brooke had not yet visited Egypt and there is no sign that he appreciated how much North African armoured warfare in practice

126 JRL GB133AUC688, 6/2/42 letter to Auchinleck
127 JRL GB133AUC581, 5/12/41 letter to Brooke
128 Danchev & Todman (eds.), *War Diaries*, p. 224. In fact Dorman-Smith was not on Auchinleck's staff in any official role at this time. It was presumably news of Dorman-Smith's mission to Eighth Army earlier in the month that alerted Brooke.
129 JRL GB133AUC649, 15/1/42 letter to Brooke.
130 TNA WO 201.2870, Martel's report.
131 JRL GB133AUC688, 6/2/42, Letter to Auchinleck.

differed from British orthodoxy. Galloway suggested to him in March that a course for higher commanders would be beneficial: 'The Germans seem to have good supply competent leaders probably owing [to] systematic pre-war training and adherence to simple well tried principles which our Army seems to have mostly forgotten'.[132] Auchinleck was in full agreement on establishing such a course and he set in motion a Senior Commanders School to be based in South Africa. Unfortunately, he chose Dorman-Smith to lead it, and when Brooke heard he was quick to order it be moved to Palestine and headed by someone other than Dorman-Smith.

From London to report on 'Crusader' came Major General le Quesne Martel, one of the pioneeering spirits of armoured warfare since 1918. Now the Commandant of the Royal Armoured Corps, he was responsible for the recruitment, basic training, military doctrine, and equipment of all tank units, and for the officers of the Royal Tank Regiment – cavalry regiments continued to select their own officers. Brooke did not care for him or his tendency to try to make a private army of the Armoured Corps,[133] and he would not have been surprised to hear from Auchinleck that Martel still believed the 'RAC has to be a super-body on a plane above that of the rest of the army, and that no one who does not belong to it can understand the mysteries of handling armoured formations in battle.'[134] Auchinleck had already warned against Martel's 'hasty conclusions', in particular that having counted the basic numbers of tanks and guns on each side in early November Martel reckoned them equal and therefore was claiming the British won without any numerical superiority – presumably Auchinleck feared pressure at a later date to attack again without a clear advantage in numbers. Although he believed tactical thinking in North Africa was more advanced than in England,[135] Martel's conclusions do not differ greatly from Auchinleck's own thoughts on combined arms operations: 'before the war...the "all armoured idea" for tanks to go in alone had not been entirely eradicated. It is now even more clear than it was before, that armoured and unarmoured forces must cooperate for this first and most important role of destroying the enemy armour.'[136]

The ideal method 'when available' was to secure ground which is vital to the enemy, 'usually behind enemy lines'. It should be held with artillery and motor infantry, followed up by an infantry brigade group to free tanks for their mobile work. The enemy would be forced to attack to restore the postion, and 'while both sides are manouevering for position the armoured forces may clash. The enemy has been at pains to avoid a tank v tank action on the move at close range with us, as we have usually come off best.'

132 JRL GB133AUC742, 7/3/42 to Brooke from Galloway.
133 JRL GB133AUC649, 21/1/42 Letter to Auchinleck.
134 JRL GB133AUC640, 15/1/42 to Brooke.
135 JRL GB133AUC617, 7/1/42 to Brooke.
136 TNA WO 201.2870: Martel report.

Martel's faith in gunnery on the move lingered on and he misinterpreted the withdrawal of German tanks behind an anti-tank gun screen as German lack of confidence rather than appreciation of the anti-tank gun as the most efficient tank killer. His belief that the Eighth Army had outfought the Afrika Korps 'tank vs tank' could only have come from interviews with frontline officers – it pays tribute to their morale and determination if not to their powers of perception. It is noteworthy that his visit to Eighth Army seems to have resulted in a conversion to the area warfare doctrine, for in his report he advocates defended localities on which armoured forces can be based.[137]

Norrie was also much in favour of armoured brigade groups, but insistent that, referencing 'Battleaxe', three not two armoured regiments be included in each brigade group [138] with three armoured brigade groups in an armoured division.[139] He also felt strongly that a Support Group of two infantry battalions, two artillery regiments, and an anti-tank regiment should be included in the armoured division to 'provide a powerful pivot on which the armd bde gp can manoeuvre without depriving them of their essential supporting arms', as well as to provide jock columns which 'have been quite outstanding during these operations'[140] for observation and harassing duties. This would have amounted to a division of nine armoured regiments totaling 450 tanks, five infantry battalions, five field artillery regiments, the equivalent of two antitank regiments and all the necessary supporting armoured cars, AA units, engineer, signals, supply and administrative troops – even in the open spaces of the desert, this would have been an unmanageable mass of men and vehicles.

Gott's views cannot be fully known, but it is unlikely he differed much from Norrie, who frequently consulted him – a note 'Strafer agrees' appears on Norrie's proposal for a strong Support Group. The best indication of Gott's views is the long account of 'Crusader' he sent to London for Hobart,[141] his commander in the early days of 7th Armoured Division, in which he confirmed his continuing belief in jock columns: 'This phase of the campaign [to 1st December 1941] shows clearly the great value of the four mobile columns each composed of field guns, atk guns and motor infantry which a support group can provide.' Hobart was not impressed with British performance as related by Gott and pencilled in some acute comments:

[O]ne has the feeling that we occupied ourselves in finding out what the enemy were doing, and then harassing him with unarmoured columns. That we never had definite plans, or even objectives, and that we were dispersed in a sort of searching 'approach' dispersed all the time, never concentrated to give a maxi

137 TNA WO 201.2870: Martel's Report, p .3.
138 TNA WO 201.527: 30/12/41 Tactical handling of armoured formations
139 TNA WO 201.364: Letter to Ritchie, 30 December 1941.
140 TNA WO 201.364: Letter to Ritchie, 30 December 1941.
141 Liddell Hart Centre for Military Archives, 15/11/11 Hobart papers '7 Armd Div 18 Nov – 27 Dec 1941. Account by Maj-Gen Gott'.

punch, and always conformed to the enemy moves ... Attention of GOC [Gott] seems to have been given too much to his Sp[Support] Grp[Group]. He was never in a position to direct or lead personally his Armoured battles.

Gott claimed his attacks on German supplies had been decisive: he wrote that:

The big lesson of this period [up to 14th December 1941] was the disastrous effect which the destruction of a dump area can have upon a force. One of the reasons which precipitated the enemy's withdrawal from the Bir el Gubi area was that without his dumps, which we had destroyed, he could no longer maintain his force there.

Due to the enemy's skill in tank, anti-tank & artillery co-operation,

[N]o attack by our more lightly armed tanks was possible except by making a very wide detour and coming in on his soft-skinned vehicles. Although such a move on our part generally forced him to withdraw it was not easy to bring about.

Gott emphasized that 'Germans will not commit to a tank vs tank battle as such' but employ a very deliberate, careful approach with combined arms, being quite prepared to replenish halfway through the day under fire', methods that Hobart noted 'appear very inflexible and stereotyped and to require complete passivity on our part.'[142] Gott described his policy – one can hardly call it a doctrine – as:

Stubborn defence to his ferocious attacks and relentless pursuit of his orderly withdrawals ... [which will] wear him down and wear him out as assuredly as could any rapid and spectacular decision'. He added a list of lessons learned:

Lesson No. 1 – capture vital ground. The Sidi Rezegh battle 'crippled his armoured forces.'
No. 2 – Germans susceptible to outflanking, never tried to counter attack a turning movement.
No. 3 – Establish, protect and be prepared to shift a centre line for supplies.
No. 4 – All arms co-operation vital – therefore Armd[Armoured] Bde[Brigade] Grp[Group] must replace Armd. Bde.
No. 5 – Jock cols mobility & striking power allow enemy no rest and give security to the armd bde. The Support Group should supply jock columns.
No. 6 – Lorried infantry well equipped with atk guns were essential for holding ground.

142 JRL GB133AUC444, 20/11/41 letter from a Christopher Fuller to Auchinleck indeed bears this out, describing how for an hour a German armoured unit refuelled within a mile of British armour without being significantly disturbed by any British action.

Hobart's comments were: 'Almost all this is counter-action. Thought seems to be concentrated on how to avoid being beaten. Little light on how to beat the Hun, surprise him by new methods, or get ahead of him.' In reality the Sidi Rezegh battle had crippled 7th Armoured Division to a greater extent than the German units, and Gott made no suggestion as to how the new armoured divisions would be handled, with their armoured brigade groups, support group and, apparently, now lorried infantry as well.

In January 1942 Auchinleck brought Corbett from India to command a Corps in Iraq against a possible German strike through either Turkey or the Caucasus. At that time Corbett saw the jock column as essential to the defence,[143] though by February[144] he was aiming at 'flexibility, manoeuvrability and the closest association of all arms including the Air in mobile operations' and following the model of Gatehouse's 4th Armoured Brigade in 'Crusader'. And when the very able but exhausted Arthur Smith left his position as Chief of Staff of Middle East HQ in March 1942, Corbett's relationship with Auchinleck[145] ensured that he was Smith's replacement against the suggestion from Brooke[146] that Henry Pownall, recently chief of staff to Wavell in the Far East, be appointed. Given Corbett's inexperience of Middle East strategic issues and of managing a large GHQ, his appointment could only be justified by Auchinleck's view that his involvement with armoured forces[147] and his expertise in area and fortress warfare complementing the brigade group box tactic made him the appropriate candidate. But his conversion to Auchinleck's brigade group principle was very recent, and how effective he was in reshaping Eighth Army's doctrine at divisional level is open to question. Indeed, after the defeat at Gazala, Corbett explained to Brooke that in the ten weeks before the Germans attacked in May it had not been possible 'in the time to enlighten leaders; to complete the inculcation of a tactical doctrine which was obviously needed to take the place of the column and desert technique which had become the gospel of the desert army.'[148] As a result Eighth Army became caught in an unfortunate confusion between several distinct doctrines, none of which were ideal.

143 CAC, Corbett Papers 3/19 4, Ind Corps Instruction No 1 29/1/42 Para 16: 'It is important to develop the technique of harassing tactics. These have been most successful in recent fighting. Jock Columns should be formed and trained and made familiar with the country north of Baghdad.'

144 CAC, Corbett Papers 4/9, Reorganisation formations and units – MEF 7 February 1942.

145 CAC, Barnett Papers BRNT2, 25 August 1958.

146 JRL GB133AUC724, 21/2/42 letter from Brooke: Brooke suggested Ritchie rather than Corbett should replace Smith, and Galloway or Beresford-Peirse should take over Eighth Army. Dorman-Smith wrote of Auchinleck's fear that Montgomery would be sent out from Great Britain if Ritchie was reassigned.

147 JRL GB133AUC725, 23/2/42 letter to Brooke.

148 CAC, Corbett Papers 4/16.

4

Gazala and Tobruk

British Armoured Tactics Post-Crusader

Operation Crusader had deteriorated into a battle of attrition, British infantry supported by heavy tanks wearing down the enemy and jock columns strangling enemy supply lines. The dashing exploits of the jock columns attracted more attention but it was the work of the infantry and their artillery and armour in grinding down the Axis forces that won the battle, and a post 'Crusader' report from Brigadier Watkins of 1st Army Tank Brigade tries to build on their success.[1] Watkins had been forced to rethink his tactics after facing 'the efficiency and strength of German a/tk defences,' but night attacks with tanks at Belhamed on the Tobruk perimeter and at Bardia on the coast 'were carried out with the greatest success and practically no loss' employing a very highly trained tank battalion and in one case infantry of 2nd New Zealand Division, who 'were very experienced, highly trained generally, and had specialised in night work.' Watkins emphasised that what was required could not be achieved by occasional consultations between Army Tank Brigade commanders and equivalent level staff at GHQ ME. Harding, BGS at XIII Corps, held talks with Watkins and issued recommendations for tank/infantry cooperation that moved on from the tactics of December 1940, when infantry in trucks had followed Matildas from as far as 5000 yards.[2] His starting point was that 'an army tank brigade should form part of a normal division' and he emphasised that tank battalions must train with the brigades they would co-operate with in battle. All ranks needed to know capabilities of tanks and one another personally. Tanks should never be committed to action without adequate artillery and anti-tank support. Attacks were to be carried out in depth, artillery moving by turn in two echelons, and if the formation was attacked

---

1   TNA WO 201/364: Crusader Operational Reports.
2   TNA WO 201/527: Conversation with Brigadier Watkins 27/12/41 and Notes on employment of Armour, 4 January 1942.

by tanks, the echelon on the move would advance or withdraw to the one in position. Mobile infantry must be in close support for each echelon and engineer detachments were to 'immediately' destroy damaged enemy tanks. Stuart tanks were to work with columns in a reconnaissance or protective role, or as bait. FOOs would travel in 'I' tanks to bring rapid artillery fire to bear. As a working directive for the army tank brigades it brought the infantry tanks into the main battle and was a blueprint for engaging German units defending the 'vital ground' that Martel, Norrie and Gott all, very reasonably but without identifying any means of achieving it, believed should be seized to wrest the initiative from the Afrika Korps. Harding summed up XIII Corps experiences in tank/infantry co-operation and emphasised the need for artillery to accompany armour in a pamphlet, 'Lessons from Cyrenaica'.[3]

The rationality of Watkins and Harding and their practical training methods were a distance removed from the reliance on determination and jock columns that was at the heart of Auchinleck's, Norrie's and Gott's conclusions, not least in that Watkins and Harding were at last laying the foundation of a doctrine for armour/infantry combination. But there is no indication at all from the events later that summer that there was any further dissemination of their views, nor any training based on them. It was not until the October battle at Alamein that some of Watkins' techniques were fully adopted: attacks by moonlight and the use of smoke by day to help neutralise German defences, infantry with integral anti-tank guns so that tanks need not be sent out in advance of infantry (as at 'Battleaxe') to keep enemy armour at a distance, and in defence a counterattack role for armour within the area occupied by their own infantry. Alamein also saw armour integrated into the infantry divisions, 9th Armoured Brigade becoming a component of the New Zealand Division, and a battalion of Valentine tanks committed to each of 9th Australian, 51st Highland and 2nd South African divisions, all in sufficient time to allow familiarisation and training.

Planning and Training, Spring 1942

The failure of British armoured units to win the tank v. tank actions which they had sought during the winter battles forced Auchinleck and Ritchie – and Auchinleck kept a close watch on Ritchie's plans after the January debacle – to search for a tactical deployment of their new brigade groups that would give them an edge on the battlefield. It was evident from 'Crusader' that infantry brigades with their 25-pdr guns in an anti-tank role had been quite effective in writing down German tank strength when the Afrika Korps could be persuaded to attack them. It was of course an unwelcome prospect for the infantry to be left out in the open as a sacrificial bait – when Brigadier Caunter suggested as much to an infantry opposite number, 'it was altogether too much for him'[4] – but there was no reason why with competent

---

3   CAC, Corbett papers 4/14.
4   Liddell Hart Centre for Military Archives, Caunter Papers,

planning and organisation, and the new 6-pdr anti-tank guns, it should not have a reasonable chance of success. Harding had already broached the idea in his 'Lessons from Cyrenaica' pamphlet, emphasising the capacity of infantry brigades to fight off any attack 'given correct procedures on the move' and to ward off armour 'for extensive periods' given two hours warning, and as the new Director of Military Training he was in a position to introduce the system. Auchinleck fell in line with the idea when he wrote to Ritchie early in March on the 'mobile base organisation for bde groups' which he saw 'as the foundation for any future offensive operation' and that forming themselves into boxes complete with mines, wire and water should be practised as a drill.[5] A tactical note of March 1942 is clear that even for armoured divisions British artillery were now to be considered the main enemy tank destroyer and on encountering an enemy formation, box tactics were the preferred option:

> 'the first care of the commander must be to form a "secure base" or "pivot of manoeuvre". From this pivot, secure against counter-attack, he will prepare, launch and support his own attack; and within this pivot he will receive and defeat the enemy attack.'[6]

An armoured brigade could form a pivot with its own infantry battalion and artillery regiment, or an armoured division could do the same with its motor brigade group. The idea was extended to the strategic level: in addition to bringing Corbett to Middle East HQ as Chief of Staff, Auchinleck in April brought Tuker under the direct command of ME HQ, his 4th Indian Division tasked with organising defences against the possible German threat through the Caucasus by establishing the system he had outlined to Dill the previous autumn,

> 'defended areas … on which our reserves – mobile armoured and motorised forces – can pivot and strike at the enemy as he tries to pass through the gaps… the system of so-called "boxes" in the western Desert is based on essentially the same idea.'[7]

And in May Dorman-Smith returned to Middle East HQ as Corbett's deputy, bringing the three former colleagues from India back into active roles in the same theatre.

In the desert a 50 mile long belt of mines was laid south from Gazala, thirty miles west of Tobruk, to Bir Hacheim. This kept Tobruk securely out of range of German artillery. The minefield was backed by the 1st South African and the 50th Northumbrian divisions in defensive boxes, with the Free French Brigade in another

5   JRL, GB133AUC746, Letter to Ritchie, 7 March 1942.
6   TNA WO201/527 'Notes on Employment of Armour.'
7   JRL GB133AUC361, Auchinleck letter to Dill, 30 September 1941.

box at Bir Hacheim itself. The length of the line meant that the two southernmost boxes, held by 150th Brigade of 50th Division and the Free French Brigade, were isolated and out of range of supporting fire from their neighbours. Further brigade boxes to the east, at Knightsbridge and El Adem, gave depth to the position and protected the supply dumps building up at Belhamed for the next offensive. Gott's XIII Corps commanded the infantry divisions in Tobruk and the northern boxes, while Norrie's XXX Corps would command the armoured divisions and the central and southern boxes. Though this might lead to some confusion if either corps commander found himself tasked with an operation that required assistance from the other arm, the thinking was that brigade groups, whether infantry or armour, were now self-sufficient as far as supporting arms were concerned and could therefore be transferred from one division or corps to another according to need. Movement and navigation in the desert would be simplified by setting out a couple of hundred used oil barrels, each numbered and marked on the map of the defended area. Confidence in the flexibility of motorised troops was carried too far when the motor brigades of each armoured division, trained and equipped for a mobile role with armour, were also assigned static garrison roles, 201st Guards Brigade of 1st Armoured Division to hold the 'Knightsbridge' box south of Tobruk, and 7th Motor Brigade of 7th Armoured Division a box further south still at Retma. The armoured brigades were thus left each with just their integral infantry battalion and artillery regiment as their only immediate all arms support, and no thought was given to how the boxes, established with much expenditure of labour and resources, would be held if the troops in them were suddenly called into action in a mobile role. As it happened, neither of these motor infantry brigades fulfilled either their mobile or their static roles. 7th Motor Brigade was to be called upon for yet another task, supplying the besieged French garrison at Bir Hacheim, and two of the three battalions of 201st Guards Brigade were withdrawn from the Knightsbridge box to form battalion boxes several miles distant, where they were swept away in the eventual defeat.

By May 1942, there was pressure from London on Eighth Army, the only active British land front against Germany, to resume the offensive as soon as possible. Malta was under devastating aerial attack and naval losses made supplying Malta from Gibraltar impossible. Convoys from Alexandria to Malta could only be covered by the RAF from the airfields of Cyrenaica west of Tobruk, now in German hands. If Malta succumbed or was neutralised, an uninterrupted flow of supplies to the Afrika Korps would tip the balance to Rommel and endanger the British position in the Middle East. Eighth Army was therefore under increasing pressure to take the offensive. Its initial idea, according to Dorman-Smith, was for a 'frontal and orthodox advance from the Gazala salient towards Derna with a landing from the sea.' In a planning session with de Guingand and others at Middle East HQ on March 20th, Dorman-Smith was not short of criticisms, and when asked what he would do,

without having given any previous thought to the issue took up a large tiddly wink counter and placed it on the map some 30 miles south-west of Mechili, saying I would put a strong anti-tank & armoured force there and invite Rommel to attack me. If he declined I would repeat the performance nearer to Msus. At some point Rommel would have to give battle or quit the Jebel.[8]

Freddie de Guingand, who rather liked Dorman-Smith on a personal level and was not intimidated by his sarcasm, made a 'satirical comment' on this idea but Dorman-Smith's notion matched the widely accepted concept of seizing ground vital to the enemy and forcing him to attack to regain it. Eighth Army's offensive plan eventually called for the establishment west of Bir Hacheim of a number of brigade strength fortified boxes at 20 or 30 miles intervals that Rommel would be obliged to attack, with an 'advanced base' at el Gania. This would enable raids to Benghazi and southwards, aiming to bring enemy armoured forces to battle and then to advance further after they were defeated. It would be a staged affair with a prolonged pause before any further move to El Agheila, a process that in all would take three months.[9] With armour tied to the defence of the brigade boxes the plan risked surrendering the initiative to the enemy the further the line was extended. De Guingand, Carver and others dubbed it 'the cowpat strategy' – a glance at the map explains why – and after wargaming likely scenarios were sceptical of its prospects.[10] Carver, who as a staff officer working closely with Norrie was in a position to know, later wrote that Norrie and Gott believed Ritchie was too inclined to accept suggestions and orders from Cairo which did not reflect conditions at the front, and this belief 'was decisively strengthened by Ritchie's support for the plan.'[11] He records in passing that George Hatton, Norrie's unpopular BGS and a strong supporter of the plan, had come from India to Egypt – and it is possible that Hatton had been imbued with the notion of 'box' strategy and 'area warfare' while in the subcontinent.[12] In his report to the Vice CIGS on the summer's fighting, Norrie was to say, 'I have always disliked every form of box, (including the "kennels"),[13] "Cowpat" or defended locality, and I have never understood their real value.'[14] This does beg the question why he allowed his divisional motor brigades to be tied up in them. And in the event, he was to organise an additional, and as it turned out vitally important, box at Alamein in July.

Even after the defeat at Gazala, Norrie thought that 'The Armoured Brigade group system has proved to be satisfactory.' His XXX Corps had further refined it into what he (though no one else is recorded as using the term) called "The Regimental Packet System" which he believed 'also worked well provided training had been carried

8   CAC, Barnett Papers, B RNT1, Notes on Galleys for 'The Desert Generals'.
9   Tedder, *With Prejudice*, p. 277.
10   JRL GB133AUC822, Operation Buckshot map.
11   Field Marshal Lord Carver, *Tobruk* (London: Pan Books, 1972), p. 263.
12   Carver, *Out of Step*, p.98. Carver contemptuously describes Hatton as having 'no operational experience and an unprepossessing personality'.
13   'The Kennels' were a defended locality on the Libyan-Egyptian frontier.
14   TNA WO 216/85 Norrie's Report Ops, 26 May-8 July 1942.

out beforehand, and everyone knew each other.' It is clear from regimental records, where it is usually referred to as 'the regimental box', that the 'Packet System' meant devolving the brigade group's field batteries and infantry companies to the command of the individual armoured regiments. From Norrie's own remarks, it does not sound as if the dismantling and reassembly of the brigade group's supporting arms under service conditions was straightforward:

> Sufficient time had, in some cases, unfortunately not been available to obtain the best results from this intimate type of fighting. This system must be flexible, as there will be many occasions on which it will be more satisfactory for the Regimental Commander RHA to command his own guns. With good training and communications, it is quite practical to change over from one method to the other – in fact this is one of the objects of this method of grouping.[15]

Messervy had come to certain conclusions during the January debacle, which he expressed in a letter to Godwin-Austen on 27 January:

> You ask the fighting capacity of the Div. The men are in good heart … really think the chaps are first class and longing to down the enemy somehow. The trouble is, and we must really recognise the fact, that we are fighting the enemy armour the whole time with inferior armament, which makes it very difficult. … There were 120 German tanks on one flank only and half of these were Mk IVs… The Boche stands off at 3000 yds or so where he is absolutely safe and shells our guns and a/tk guns; he will never attack when we are ready for him. When he has knocked out most of our guns, then only he hits in hard with his Mk IIIs and Mk IVs and these are both always accompanied by very efficient Atk guns which drop into action to assist the tanks if they get into trouble… Unfortunately the Honey cannot really be regarded as a fighting tank.

He was less convinced than some of the value of harassing supply lines, having found that tank attacks on motor transport were surprisingly ineffective except in terms of dispersing them:

> A whole Sqn of German tanks went straight through [a battery's transport] firing for all it was worth; not a vehicle was put off the road though there were a lot of holes in all of them … I am quite certain that with Mobile troops in Desert country it is impossible to fight delaying actions – one has got to fight to a finish or else clear right out of it, preferably at night, to the next place where you have

15   TNA WO 216/85: Norrie's Report, 12 July 1942.

decided to fight. Colns achieve NO real delay; they can only harass. Enough for now. What times we endure!'[16]

After the situation stabilised, Ritchie watched Messervy's armoured division training in regimental groups in mid-February and reported to Auchinleck: 'the system was worked out by Frank Messervy ... I am sure the system is sound'.[17] It is likely that it was on the lines that Messervy had been considering in a letter to 2nd Armoured Brigade's commander,

> '[A] tactical drill by which we can bring the enemy on to our 25pdrs at times and let them have a direct close-range shoot. That would give our tanks the best chance of putting in a really effective counter attack from one flank using their speed to get there. ... There are distinct possibilities in placing [our 25 pdrs] behind high ground, where incidentally there is better cover as a rule, having a tank screen as a bait on the ridge. If the enemy advances on to the ridge, the tanks would withdraw, without seriously engaging, under a smoke screen, and the guns would get their shoot in as the enemy tanks came through the smoke. That sort of option is what you might call defensive-offensive tactics which give the best chance of giving the enemy a knock- out blow'.[18]

By early March Messervy's principal formation, 4th Armoured Brigade, was practicing its proven combined arms tactics and developing techniques of engaging anti-tank guns with the high explosive shells from its newly acquired Grants. In the first half of May it reconnoitred two positions from which it could advantageously absorb the first shock if the anticipated German attack came round the southern end of the Gazala line.[19] Its brigade exercise that month involved their 6-pdr anti-tank guns working closely with tanks, a counter attack by one regiment being 'assisted by all available fire covered by RHA and 75mm HE'.[20] But they were still in a relaxed state on 26 May, when 'bathing parties and leave to Cairo was going on as usual and there was no indication apparent to us of the storm that was to break on the following day.'[21]

2nd Armoured Brigade, new to the desert at the end of 1941, was composed of 'three fine regular cavalry units' with 'a most admirable self-confidence but tended to think as a result that there was not much for them to learn,'[22] according to David Hunt,

16   TNA WO 2/2695: Messervy personal correspondence, Letter to Godwin-Austen, 27 January 1942.
17   JRL GB133AUC722, letter to Auchinleck, 15 February 1942.
18   TNA WO 2/2695: Messervy personal correspondence, January 1942. 'Defensive-offensive' was a concept much favoured by Liddell Hart.
19   Bovington Tank Museum Archives, War Diary 8 Hussars.
20   Bovington, War Diary 3RTR
21   Bovington, War Diary 8 Hussars
22   David Hunt, *A Don at War* (London: Kimber, 1966), p. 92.

an Intelligence officer at Eighth Army HQ. They had been badly battered in January when they and 1st Armoured Division's Support Group were deployed separately and as a result both formations had been defeated in turn.[23] In the spring the brigade did a certain amount of column work that involved action against the enemy and its exercise on 1 April practised 'different methods of attacking with an armoured Bde Gp.'[24] Their new Grant tanks arrived at the beginning of May. Grants' armour turned out to be largely resistant to all but 88 or 76.2mm fire[25], and later to the 'long' 75mm of the Mk IV Special. There are frequent reports of them surviving a dozen or more hits. But their high profile made them conspicuous targets and where Grants fought alongside Crusaders and Stuarts, Grants were often knocked out rapidly at ranges of up to 2000yds, presumably by the 88 and 76.2mm guns accompanying the panzer divisions. At that range the Grant's gun and sight was not accurate enough to reliably knock out even an enemy antitank gun. Further details of gun v. armour performance are given in the appendix, but in summary the 167 Grants with the regiments on 27th May were superior to all German tanks other than the couple of dozen Specials. As one German participant recalled, 'The American Grant tanks were a nasty surprise since their main armament outranged both the Panzer III and IV.'[26]

17. 6-pdr gun and crew. (IWM E018895)

23   Dunn, *Sword and Wig*, pp 37-40 .
24   Bovington, War Diary 10 Hussars.
25   TNA WO 231/93: Gazala Command Study, Appendix 13.
26   Behrendt, *Rommel's Intelligence*, p. 156.

18. Grant tanks moving up to the front, June 1942. (The Tank Museum Bovington 0096-H3)

The 6-pdr anti-tank batteries joined 2nd Armoured Brigade only two days before the battle. The 2-pdrs that they replaced had proved too fragile to be towed across the desert and had been carried 'portee' on trucks. They were passed on to infantry regiments, going into action days later with their new crews often only half trained.[27] The 6-pdr was much more robust and so better suited to being towed, was less conspicuous thanks to a lower profile and therefore more survivable. The gun's performance was quite similar to the German equivalent, the 50mm Pak38. But crewed by the Royal Artillery, 2nd Armoured Brigade deployed them with their fellow artillerymen as protection for the field guns rather than with the tanks as in 4th Armoured Brigade. In the event they were rarely fired until things were becoming very desperate and then German tanks were quick to distinguish 6-pdrs by their muzzle flash from the less lethal 25-pdrs and concentrated fire to knock them out efficiently.[28] Even at the time Robin Dunn thought 'It seemed to many of us that the 6-pdr would be far more

27   James Colvin, 'Eighth Army Operations May-July 1942', *Journal of the Society for Army Historical Research,* Summer 2019, Vol. 97, No. 389, p.172.
28   IWM, Dunn's Diary Notes, 1 June.

effective if used offensively',[29] working with the armour, consolidating the ground taken and protecting their flanks, as was the German practice. But overall 2nd Armoured Brigade's artillery and armour seems to have worked well together and gave the 115th Infantry Regiment of 15th Panzer Division a severe handling on the first day of the German attack.[30] As Dunn wrote in his memoir:

> The Armoured Brigade Group with its combination of General Grant tanks, 25-pdrs and 6-pdr guns proved itself a very formidable combination. Much of the success of 2nd Armoured Brigade was due to the fact that all the Regimental groups had lived and trained together for three months. All the officers knew one another intimately and could appreciate what the others were likely to do. Although we all wore different badges we were all intensely loyal to the Bays Group.

His reference to regimental groups, and repeated references to the Bays group in particular, seem to indicate that Norrie's Regimental Packet was the system that 2nd Armoured Brigade was following, Many years after the event he told this writer that they trained hard up to 27 May, adding 'Not that it did us much good.'

Despite being in the same division as 2nd Armoured Brigade, 22nd Armoured Brigade adopted a different tactical system. Instead of the Regimental Packet, it followed the pivot group concept, and according to a post war memoir of 2nd Royal Gloucester Hussars, achieved the worst possible outcome, splitting resources into penny packets and confusing the troops. From the beginning of the year the tank regiments had been given a new concept in training – the 'Box', consisting of a battery of guns, a company of infantry, and a troop of antitank guns to support each regiment:

> In theory an immovable strong point, with the armour kept ready to counterattack … In practice Boxes were in danger of facing the wrong way or locking tanks up inside their confines, thus preventing any manoeuvring, or of just being overrun…Training with the box was very muddling.'[31]

The war diaries of the other two regiments in the brigade confirm this unsatisfactory practice: 4th County of London Yeomanry describes their regimental box operating largely independently of the tank squadrons until it was overrun on 6 June, and though 3rd County of London war diary states that it was the Brigade Box that was overrun, it does make clear that it was operating out of contact with the armour. It is clear from later remarks that in the name of flexibility the Brigade Box was on call to be

29   IWM, Dunn's Diary Notes.
30   IWM, Dunn's Diary Notes. Dunn counted 400 prisoners, 16 guns and 34 lorries destroyed or captured.
31   Pitman, *2RGH*, pp.50-51

split up into Norrie's 'Regimental Packets' as required to support individual armoured regiments, but there is no indication that this worked satisfactorily. A TEWT – a Tactical Exercise Without Troops – on handling Grant squadrons was held on 2 April when 'the principle of employing three composite battle groups of all arms in advance of the Tank regiments and to form a pivot of manoeuvre appeared satisfactory'.[32] This was presumably part of the 'Packet' system training. There is no mention of any other training with infantry though the Brigade did find time to send its men on liaison trips with the RAF and the navy.

1st Army Tank Brigade, equipped with Valentines, was deployed in support of Gott's XIII Corps, but trained in a cruiser rather than infantry support role. It also used box tactics: as in 22nd Armoured Brigade, their Brigade Box operated separately from the armoured regiments and when the Box called on them for help the regiments found that too often it was a false alarm or that they arrived too late – 'All very confusing and very, very tiring,'[33] as one of their squadron commanders recorded. It would seem that though armoured doctrine as ordained by high command recognised the importance of all arms co-operation, lower down the chain of command the concept was badly misunderstood. The notion of a decisive tank v. tank clash in which the infantry and artillery were bystanders lingered on, while infantry regarded armour as a rescue service for them.

The multiplicity of tank types, in addition to misunderstood or partially adopted doctrine, made regimental training inconsistent. Regiments in 1st and 7th Armoured divisions had either one or two of their three squadrons equipped with Grants, the others being either Crusaders or Honeys. The 1st and 32nd Army Tank Brigades in XIII Corps were equipped with Matildas and Valentines respectively. All these tanks had different characteristics of speed, reliability, armour protection and in the case of the Grant, armament. Squadron training was further influenced by the experience of the tank crews and therefore was anything but consistent. Individual regiments developed their own tactics: in one, tanks fired volleys of five or ten rounds rapid of 2-pdr shells on the squadron leader's command in the hope that the unnerving effect of an impact or a near miss would deter the enemy advance even when the round could not penetrate.[34] The 10th Hussars of 2nd Armoured Brigade believed that the use of smoke would enable them to close with the enemy to a range where their 2-pdrs might be effective before dashing back into the smokescreen, naval fashion, for cover.[35] 9th Lancers, also of 2nd Armoured Brigade, made much use of smoke and was one of the very few units to emphasise the value of the close support Crusaders whose function was to provide smoke cover.[36] German tanks on the other hand were

32   TNA WO 169/4251: 22 Armd Bde War Diary, 2 April 1942.
33   Stuart Hamilton, *Armoured Odyssey* (London: Tom Donovan, 1995), p. 46.
34   Stuart Hamilton, *Armoured Odyssey*, p. 44.
35   P. Griffiths, *WWII Desert Tactics* (Oxford: Osprey, 2008) p. 60. The 10H War diary records a successful attack on anti-tank guns on 2 May using this tactic.
36   TNA WO 169/4481: War Diary 9th Lancers.

unwilling to silhouette themselves by advancing through smoke, so smoke was also used by the British as a defensive barrier.[37] 8 RTR found the protection provided by the Valentine's heavy rear armour plate and engine made it worth taking up positions facing away from the enemy with the turret reversed, permitting a rapid exit if the situation became difficult, or slowly reversing to within effective range of the enemy if more aggressive action was ordered.[38] There was no longer any mention of tanks firing on the move.

Eighth Army's Defensive Plan

While Eighth Army was under pressure to take the offensive to regain control of Cyrenaica, Ritchie also had to cater for a German attack. It would be wrong to assume that the Gazala line was intended as more than a trip wire. The unmanned sectors of the minefields stretching five and ten miles either side of 150th Brigade's positions were never going to do more than buy the day or two of time it would take the enemy to clear a path through them, but the direction of the main enemy assault would thereby be identified. Ritchie's BGS, Brigadier Whiteley, made clear in his evidence to the Enquiry after the fall of Tobruk that Ritchie's defensive plan actually rested on a box system similar to the 'area warfare' doctrine advocated by Tuker and Corbett:

> The Battle was intended to be fought not on the Gazala Line, but in the general area Gazala-Hacheim-el Adem-Tobruk. One could not see how the battle was going until possibly Tobruk or el Adem had fallen. It was all one big area. If the Battle were lost, the withdrawal would be right back to the frontier. It was all one position with considerable depth and Tobruk and el Adem were part of that depth. Later as more troops came up, Belhamed, Sidi Rezegh and El Duda formed another defensive zone adding to the depth. These two [Tobruk and El Adem] were always part of the main position.[39]

It would seem from Auchinleck and Ritchie's correspondence in May 1942 that Auchinleck did not fully understand this, for his repeated advice to Ritchie on the direction of Rommel's main effort implies that 8 Army's intention was to halt the Axis attack on the Gazala Line, and when that failed he was insistent that the new defensive position should shield Tobruk, not use it as a bastion. But Ritchie, according to Whiteley, was clearly looking to entangle the Afrika Korps in a network of fortified boxes which would support the armoured brigades' battle against the Afrika Korps while jock columns attacked Rommel's supply lines.

---

37   Dunn, *Sword and Wig*, p. 289.
38   Stuart Hamilton, *Armoured Odyssey*, p. 46.
39   TNA WO 106/2235: Operations 26/5-2/7/42 Report of Court of Enquiry, p.14

Whiteley also testified to Auchinleck's concern over a penetration of the centre of the Gazala line as the worst possible case. There was no intelligence that indicated an attack in the centre, and Rommel was short of the reliable infantry needed for an assault through minefields. Nonetheless, following Auchinleck's comments, 'Plans were revised so that the Knightsbridge locality could be developed as a pivot on which the armour could operate in the centre area.'[40]

The northern and central sections of the Gazala line and Tobruk itself were under Gott's XIII Corps, while the southern bastion of Bir Hacheim was under Norrie's XXX Corps. Norrie controlled both 1st and 7th Armoured divisions, which were to counterattack the Afrika Korps whether it broke through the centre or advanced south round the Gazala Line. Ritchie believed Rommel would choose the southern approach in combination with a diversion in the north but under pressure from Auchinleck he catered for an attack in the centre, aiming to buy time if the southern route was taken by positioning an additional two infantry brigade groups south and east of Bir Hacheim to slow a southern enemy advance. This made XXX Corps an unwieldy mass of three armoured and five infantry brigade groups with only two divisional headquarters to manage them. And the armour's defensive tasks of covering the infantry boxes might be at odds with its mobile role of defeating the Afrika Korps. Tuker was therefore sent up on 26 May to take command of four of the infantry brigade groups,[41] and install them into defensive boxes. This reduced 7th Armoured Division to a single armoured brigade since its 7th Motor Brigade was now assigned to a box under Tuker's command.[42] 1st Armoured Division's motor brigade group, 201st Guards Brigade, was already dug in at Knightsbridge, and equally unavailable for mobile operations, so the three armoured brigades now had for immediate support only the infantry battalion and field regiment integral to each of them. This was despite Auchinleck's repeated insistence on the importance of associating infantry and artillery in adequate numbers with armour and fighting the divisions 'as divisions and not scattered about in brigades'.[43]

Tuker was astonished to be given his new task of commanding 'the left flank of the Army' since he had made clear that he had no confidence in Eighth Army's plan or in

---

40   TNA WO 106/2235: Operations 26/5-2/7/42, Report of Court of Enquiry, p.14

41   TNA WO 106/2235: Operations 26/5-2/7/42, Report of court of enquiry. These were the Free French Brigade at Bir Hacheim, 3rd Indian Motor Brigade SE of Bir Hacheim, 7th Motor Brigade at Retma, 29th Indian Brigade at Bir Gubi, plus two armoured car regiments. 3rd Indian Motor Brigade was rushed up with half its complement of wireless sets and anti-tank guns and by no means fully trained. IWM, Tuker Papers, 71/21/2/9.

42   Carver, *Out of Step*, p. 67, states that 7 Armd Div was to retain control of 7 Motor Bde after the arrival of Tuker – this was not Tuker's understanding. In the event 7 Motor Brigade rather than working with 4 Armd Bde, formed columns to raid DAK supply lines and to resupply Bir Hacheim until its evacuation on 10-11 June. See Playfair, *Official History*, vol iii, pp. 235-7.

43   Tuker, *Approach to Battle*, p. 99.

its commander.[44] He had told Harding in February that extending the Gazala line to Bir Hacheim 'would lead to the ruin of the Eighth Army as it was a magnet to drag all Eighth Army's reserves to its relief. It had no water for one thing! Moreover it meant nothing. It protected nothing but desert.' He had aired the same views to Norrie in March and on the 15th of that month had told Corbett 'the same thing in more detail for 24 hours'. Now in May, on taking command of the four brigade groups, he intended to make 3rd Indian and 7th Motor Brigades fully mobile and, against orders, put them into action harrying Rommel's communications:

> If I was then removed from command of that flank I should have been satisfied. The next man could play the time server if he wished, I never have, would not and never will.[45]

In Norrie's XXX Corps cohesion between the two armoured divisions was not improved by poor relations between their commanders and significant differences in their tactical views. Messervy of 7th Armoured Division thought the armoured corps was 'wrongly permeated with the doctrine of getting into "battle positions" and getting the enemy to attack them there rather than thinking of closing with the enemy by mobile attack.'[46] Lumsden of 1st Armoured Division on the other hand saw little future in attacking enemy positions and was to be 'extremely vehement' when Messervy later proposed a counter attack. Lumsden was comfortable with the idea of boxes as pivots of manoeuvre to trap the enemy between armour and the infantry and believed that a static box's manpower would be useful for night patrolling against the enemy. Messervy believed that boxes were symptomatic of the defensive mindset that tried to cater for the enemy's every move, and that they split resources and saddled armoured commanders with immobile troops. Messervy and Lumsden's personal and professional differences were accentuated during the battle when in the name of flexibility Norrie switched brigades from one divisional headquarters to another – within a week of the battle commencing Lumsden's 2nd and 22nd Brigades were under Messervy, and Messervy's 4th Brigade under Lumsden. Not only were divisions not being fought as divisions, the brigades were not under the divisional commanders who had trained them and with whom they should have developed mutual understanding and confidence. Lumsden later confirmed his lack of confidence in Messervy and the troops trained by him when he declared to the Enquiry that he had been unimpressed by the standards of 4th Armoured Brigade.[47]

44   Tuker, *Approach to Battle*, p. 105.
45   IWM, 71/21/2/6, Tuker Papers.
46   TNA WO 106/2235: Operations 26/5-2/7/42 Report of Court of Enquiry, Messervy's testimony.
47   TNA WO 106/2235. The witness statements to the Court of Enquiry into the operations 26/542 to 2/7/42 are remarkably frank, perhaps because many felt they no longer had favourable expectations for their careers.

German Preparations for 'Operation Venezia'.

Early in May, Axis airpower had neutralised Malta and supplies were flowing relatively freely to the Panzerarmee. It was clear that a British offensive was likely in June and that it would be preferable to take the initiative with a pre-emptive attack, for which there were now sufficient reserves of fuel and ammunition. Under the codename 'Venezia', Rommel was directed to defeat the British forces, take Tobruk, and advance to the Egyptian frontier but on no account to move into Egypt itself. Instead, after the capture of Tobruk, resources would be concentrated behind an airborne assault on Malta led by a German parachute brigade together with an Italian parachute brigade that had been trained up by the Germans. The capture of Malta would finally solve the problem of protecting Rommel's supply line to North Africa.

The Panzerarmee was full of confidence in their leadership, equipment and tactics. The heavy defeat of 1st Armoured Division in January had been accomplished more through manoeuvre than fighting, with light casualties and with a flair that elevated Rommel to mythical status among his opponents as well as his own men. Since then, fresh equipment had been shipped to bring the Afrika Korps up to its full strength of around 100 medium tanks in each of the two panzer divisions, plus some reserves. New equipment included 19 of the improved Mk III tanks with a much more effective 50mm gun. A handful of the latest MK IV with a 'long' 75mm gun, easily a match for the Grants, reached the front in June.' These two improved models were known as 'Specials' to the British forces and will be referred to as such to avoid the complication of the German classification. Frontal armour of all German medium tanks was now entirely proof against British 2-pdr fire. A large number of 76.2mm anti-tank guns captured from the Russians, less conspicuous than the 88mms and with performance almost as good as the 'long' 75mm, now supplemented the 50mm guns. A few 88s were mounted on halftracks (known as Dianas) and some 76.2mms on tank chassis (known as Marders). They were more mobile and quicker into action than the towed anti-tank guns and effective against Grants at ranges up to 2000 yards, a distance where the Grants' return fire was hampered by their poor sights.[48] Accounts differ as to how many Marders were available, 100 or more in June by one account,[49] and no more than sixty in total during the campaign by another, so perhaps not more than one *abteilung* (27 at full strength) at any one time.

Italian motorised units were less of a soft target now that they included towed 88mm guns plus their own 90mm equivalents, and the Ariete division had a unit of 24 Semovente self-propelled 75mm guns which, with hollow charge ammunition, were capable of destroying any British tank.[50]

48   JRL GB133AUC962, Messervy's comments on Gazala battle, 29 July 1942.
49   TNA WO 231/93: Command Study in North Africa. 117 is the figure mentioned. It is not certain that number were present in May 1942.
50   Ian W. Walker, *Iron Hulls, Iron Hearts* (Marlborough: Crowood Press, 2006), p. 109.

19. Marder self-propelled anti-tank gun, in this case utilising a redundant Czech 38t chassis. (The Tank Museum Bovington 10962-002)

20. Panzer Mk IV Specials. (The Tank Museum Bovington 2901-C4)

21. Italian Semovente 75 mm self-propelled gun. (The Tank Museum Bovington 2945-C2)

The Afrika Korps had continued training on their well-tried principles and reached a formidable level of teamwork which enabled them to adapt when faced with unforeseen problems. They were quick to react to the firepower of the new Grant tanks and the 6-pdr anti-tank guns, knocking them out rapidly in the opening stages of the battle even though they suffered heavy losses in the initial encounter. One of their all arms battlegroups took prisoner Major General Messervy on the first day of the attack. After escaping he was able to describe their methods. His captors consisted of a column of 8 armoured cars, 6 tanks, 2 platoons of lorried infantry, 4 self-propelled guns, 4 towed 88mm guns and 24 towed 50mm anti-tank guns:

> Very nearly every first line vehicle was trailing either an a/tk gun or an ammunition trailer for the guns; even the staff cars had trailers. The battle drill was to "follow my leader", who flew a huge red swastika from his car. If any opposition was met, the a/tk sub units would all be led into action in the required direction by their leaders standing up in the trucks and holding a red disc above their shoulders. They would come very quickly into action in the open, their towing vehicles remaining within 20 yards of the gun, and open intensive fire. Meanwhile the rest of the column would move on without check, the a/tk guns disengaging and re-joining as soon as the danger had been averted.

They did not really bother with dispersal, unlike Eighth Army which treated it as an article of faith. They were apprehensive of artillery fire but were not concerned with the air threat: 'the officers would assume an indifferent air, putting one hand in the pocket and not looking up, while the men opened fire with every weapon available. Nobody took cover or even lay down.'[51] The RAF at this time was somewhat outnumbered and significantly outclassed by the German fighters, due to the demands of the Far East war and short deliveries of fighters from the United States. However, its performance was to improve significantly by the end of June, thanks not only to the extraordinary efforts of the aircrew but to a highly efficient ground organisation that kept landing strips open until the last moment during the retreat.

German tactics had evolved a little to accommodate their new weaponry but essentially in attack used the same deliberate advance of mixed battle groups that had been observed by the British the previous year. Mark IV tanks would open fire at about one mile range. Under protective fire from these tanks and the artillery, assault guns, anti-tank guns and infantry with full equipment would be brought up. The infantry opened machine gun fire on defending artillery and anti-tank guns at long range. As soon as fire concentration was superior to the British defensive fire, the tanks attacked in three waves, part of the infantry following 200 yards behind the last wave. Artillery, self-propelled guns and infantry were thrown in to support the assault, firing as long as possible as the armour closed, with some use of HE shells. Reconnaissance forces – Mk II tanks, armoured cars and 50mm anti-tank guns – meanwhile protected the flanks.[52]

German wireless intelligence continued to build on its successes. When static, British units followed wireless procedures and made every effort to avoid giving away information that might be useful to the enemy, but in action discipline was often abandoned. In the early stages of 'Crusader' wireless security had been so tight that it was more than twenty four hours before Rommel would believe an advance was under way, and he was only convinced by hearing the announcement on the BBC. Under the stress of battle during 'Crusader', in an amateurish attempt to deceive the enemy, Eighth Army had used slang and Christian names rather than codewords. Terms such as 'Frank's boys' for 4th Indian Division (commanded by Frank Messervy), 'Coffee' for C-in-C, or 'Uncle George's eldest son' for 5th South African Brigade (part of 1st South African Division commanded by George Brink) were not difficult for the Germans to unravel.[53] Some British units persisted in this habit until the end of 1942.

The Afrika Korps' Captain Seerbohm ran a Wireless Intercept Company that produced exceptional results during Eighth Army's January debacle. When the line stabilised at Gazala, British wireless security improved again. Screening work by armoured car units and excellent camouflage added to the difficulty that German

51   TNA WO 201/2871: Report by Norrie on ops, May-June 1942.
52   TNA HW1/676: Report on German Tactics, 26 June 1942.
53   Behrendt, p. 125.

intelligence had in assessing British numbers and location of units. But as the situation became more fluid and under the stress of combat through June and into July, Seerbohm's 'circus' of tents and equipment, often closer to the front line than was safe, was sometimes able to pick up British signals more clearly than the intended recipients. The liaison officer responsible for reporting the information to Rommel found that 'Rommel often had signals in his hand before the enemy commanders to whom they had been addressed'.[54] In modern parlance, Rommel was able to work inside his opponents' decision cycle.

The German intelligence service could pick up British signal traffic from as far as Palestine,[55] but their most useful asset was what they called 'The Good Source'. An Italian clerk in the US Embassy in Rome had copied the American Military Attaché's secret code and passed it to the Abwehr in Berlin. German intelligence could now read the messages that Colonel Fellers, the American military attaché in Cairo, was sending to Washington. Fellers was an important channel for the British, who fed him with top secret information in addition to what he gleaned for himself – Dorman-Smith was among his official contacts[56] – and from January 1942 his messages were being decoded and passed to Rommel. Throughout the summer battles details of the British armour state, its losses, replacements and actual strength, and reports on the morale and leadership of Eighth Army, encouraged Rommel to maintain pressure despite the casualties his troops were sustaining. This information and details of the alarm in Cairo is likely to have been behind the change in the Axis plan to pursue Eighth Army into Egypt instead of halting after the fall of Tobruk to capture Malta. The leak was discovered on 29 June. The American codes were immediately changed and The Good Source dried up.

Overall, British intelligence had not distinguished itself since the arrival of Rommel. A certain amount of bad luck played a part. In March 1941 Ultra had quite correctly informed Cairo that the newly arrived Rommel was under orders to act defensively. Given the demands for troops in Greece, it was therefore a reasonable risk to remove 7th Armoured Division from Cyrenaica since there was no way of knowing Rommel would disobey orders and attack. But Wavell's intelligence chief, Brigadier John Shearer, was more inclined to try to forecast Rommel's likely moves rather than analyse what information was available. He badly misjudged the tank strength of the Afrika Korps before the Battleaxe offensive, and badly underestimated the strength of the reinforced Afrika Korps in January 1942, despite eyewitness reports of new German tanks at the front. It was only after considerable pressure from Brooke that Shearer was replaced by de Guingand. Even then de Guingand was frustrated that the increasingly valuable information coming from Ultra was not being fully used – he found later that Montgomery was much more receptive to its value.

54 Behrendt, p. 170.
55 TNA WO201/2871: Report by Norrie on ops May-June 1942.
56 Information from D-S family.

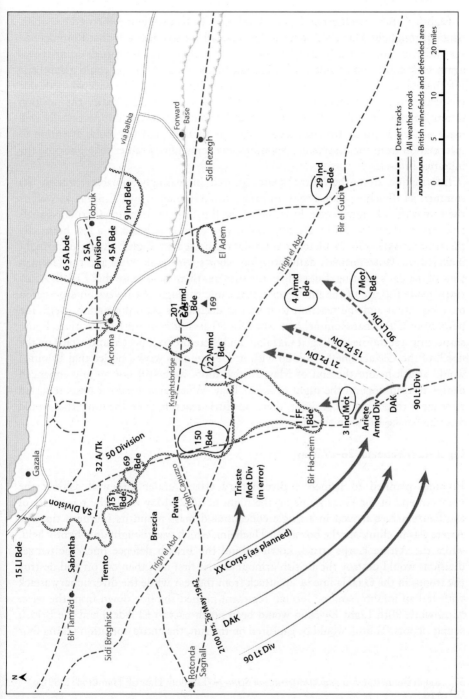

6. Gazala – Opening Day

Eighth Army's intelligence had a useful asset in its excellent armoured car units, which throughout May 1942 covered the Gazala Line so effectively that Rommel had very little idea of its depth or of Eighth Army's strength. British signals security was again reasonably good while units were not in action, so Rommel could glean little information on location or numbers of units. Eighth Army's Y Service was valuable in intercepting the Panzerarmee's communications and could identify the position of unit headquarters by radio location. But the information was not necessarily well used: one criticism of Ritchie's leadership was that he paid too much attention to information from the Y service, responding to enemy moves rather than grasping the initiative himself.

Information from the 'Ultra' source proved increasingly valuable through the summer, as Bletchley Park began to master the German army's Enigma as well as the Luftwaffe's Enigma code. From mid-June the delay in decoding German signals and transmitting the information to Cairo was steadily reduced to a few hours. By the time of Alamein in October information passed to Eighth Army each night included the Panzerarmee's daily situation reports with tank states and the German view of the day's fighting. But early in the summer there is no sense that Eighth Army really made full use of the intelligence that came through. As always, interpretation of information and the reaction to it was as decisive as the information itself. The news from Ultra that Rommel had asked for 80 assault craft misled Auchinleck into suspecting a seaborne landing at Gazala,[57] and therefore to expect a land attack on the north of the Gazala line to link up with it. Despite two weeks' notice that Rommel would attack before the end of May, British units were still not on any enhanced degree of readiness on the night of 26/27 May. When armoured car units reported movement throughout that night, there was little reaction from the units that would face the Afrika Korps in the morning.

Operation Venezia, 26-27 May.

Rommel planned to launch a diversionary attack under Cruewell against the northern end of the Gazala line on the night of 26/27 May while the remainder of the Panzerarmee moved in a single concentrated mass round its southern tip. The Ariete was to eliminate the box at Bir Hacheim, which was thought only lightly held, while the Afrika Korps struck north behind the British defence line. The panzer divisions would destroy the British armour on the first day, then cut off and destroy the troops in the Gazala line by an attack from the rear while the diversionary attack with Italian infantry and a German regiment pinned the line down from the west. Meanwhile 90th Light Division would head north-east to El Adem and the British supply depots. Tobruk would be captured on the run, the entire operation taking four

---

57   Ralph Bennett, *Ultra and Mediterranean Strategy* (London: Hamish Hamilton, 1989), p. 116.

days. Once British troops had been expelled from Libya, the Panzerarmee would halt on the Libyan/Egyptian frontier until Malta had been taken and Rommel's supply line finally secured.

German intelligence was poor, unaware of the depth or extent of British minefields or of the strength of the box at Bir Hacheim. A last minute change of orders to move further south round Bir Hacheim failed to reach the Trieste division which continued directly to the minefields and, fortuitously, was to create a supply route through them for the Afrika Korps in the following days. On the main axis the speed and violence of the German assault drove in the British reconnaissance screen during the night, then at around 8:00 a.m. the bulk of the Italian Motorised Corps crashed through Tuker's unfortunate 3rd Indian Motor Brigade before it could establish a box. It lost most of its guns and 500 men and was eliminated from the battle. 7th Motor Brigade resisted longer but was driven from its position at Retma. Tuker, his role superseded by events, returned to Cairo. The Free French halted the Ariete at Bir Hacheim, knocking out 32 tanks before the Italians followed the Afrika Korps north to help cut off the British divisions in the Gazala Line.

British armoured car units had reported Rommel's move throughout the night but neither 1st nor 7th Armoured Division reacted in a timely fashion. After the event, Carver at XXX Corps claimed that on hearing the wireless reports from British armoured cars he repeatedly warned 7th Armoured Division of the advance but was ignored by Messervy's GSO1, Harold Pyman. Norrie was reluctant to directly order Messervy to move.[58] Messervy on the other hand claimed that his own warnings, which Norrie denied receiving, were ignored and that he, Messervy, received 'from a staff officer'[59] instructions to make no move. The records that might clarify what happened no longer exist: 7th Armoured Division's wireless log was lost when the headquarters was overrun, Carver handed a surviving copy of XXX Corps' wireless log over to his successor, Patrick Hobart, the nephew of Major General Percy Hobart, who read it – and destroyed it, so the true story of who was most at fault will never be confirmed. Robin Dunn, commanding a troop of 25-pdrs in 2nd Armoured Brigade, commented to the writer that general opinion at the time was, '7th Armoured Division were asleep'.

4th Armoured Brigade received orders from Messervy to take up its carefully reconnoitred positions where it could have delayed the Afrika Korps and supported Tuker's brigades but was still on its start line at about 7.30 when it was struck by 15th Panzer.[60] Of its three regiments, 8th Hussars lost all but three and 3RTR all but five of the 26 Grants they each started with.. The two regiments were amalgamated for the reminder of the battle and the brigade was temporarily disabled as a fighting unit.[61]

58   Carver, *Dilemmas*, p. 77, and Carver, *Out of Step*, p. 134.
59   Maule, *Spearhead General*, p. 175.
60   TNA WO 169/4216: 4th Armoured Brigade war diary.
61   Playfair, vol. iii, p. 224.

The 15th Panzer Division also lost heavily but continued north while 4th Armoured Brigade retreated to the El Adem area, but thanks to Eighth Army's impressively efficient recovery and repair of damaged tanks came back into action a few days later. Messervy's divisional headquarters was also caught unawares, was overrun and Messervy captured.

Lumsden was mindful of Auchinleck's opinion that an attack in the north should be catered for, and that the most dangerous threat would be an attack through the centre of the Gazala line. At 1st Armoured Division he disputed Norrie's view that the German advance around Bir Hacheim represented the main thrust. From 3:00 a.m. onwards on the 27th, he argued against Norrie's request that his 22nd Armoured Brigade be moved to support 4th Armoured Brigade, which as it turned out was right in the path of the advancing Afrika Korps. When Norrie at last gave Lumsden a direct order at 7:00 a.m., 'Frizz' Fowler commanding the field artillery of 2nd Armoured Brigade was scandalized that Lumsden then ordered his staff to impose maximum delay in obeying.[62] The 22nd Armoured Brigade told XXX Corps that they could not move for another ninety minutes as they had not been given a warning order. 1st Armoured Division was finally ordered to "stand to" at 7:30 a.m. It was just at that time that the isolated 4th Armoured Brigade was struck. 22nd Armoured had not even begun its move when they in turn were surprised by 21st Panzer and forced north-east.

Lumsden's 2nd Armoured Brigade was positioned a mile east of Knightsbridge and engaged the enemy somewhat later, when they inflicted heavy casualties on 15th Panzer's infantry regiment. The brigade's guns and infantry had moved off with the tanks at 11a.m., believing the enemy column was to the south rather than to the west, so it was 2p.m. before they encountered 15th Panzer infantry and artillery. Robin Dunn and his battery were with the Bays regiment of 2nd Armoured Brigade. 'Off we went for the enemy guns. The cruisers would advance perhaps 400 yards at full speed, then halt & fire at the guns. We kept up a continuous barrage from the 25 pounders.'[63] The enemy column was overrun, and their gunners surrendered. 'Meanwhile we were being met by an accurate fire from a second position behind the first.' They destroyed 16 guns, 34 lorries and took 400 prisoners, though they did note that only two unwounded German officers surrendered, and that they were making every effort to escape. Dunn was elated by their success but believed the entire 115 Lorried Infantry Regiment could have been destroyed on that first day if 2nd Armoured Brigade had attacked even an hour earlier.

By the evening of the 27th, the German plan was in disarray. Losses to the fire of the Grants and 6-pdr guns had been heavy, the Ariete had been beaten off by the Free French at Bir Hacheim, Lumsden's 2nd and 22nd Armoured Brigades had remained intact and inflicted casualties as they fell back. The Panzerarmee finished

62   Dominick Graham, *Against Odds* (Basingstoke: MacMillan Press, 1999), p. 102.
63   IWM, 94/41/1: Private Papers of Sir Robin Dunn.

22. Honey tank on artillery observation post duty. (Imperial War Museum E16465)

the day without reaching the coast at Gazala and discovering the unexpectedly strong British forces behind the minefields between Gazala and Bir Hacheim. Their supply route round Bir Hacheim was now closed by British columns, 15th Panzer was out of fuel and separated by some miles from 21st Panzer Division who were half way between Gazala and Bir Hacheim. To Auchinleck and Ritchie it appeared on the 28 May as if the Eighth Army had Rommel trapped in exactly the area they had hoped. Auchinleck conceded that Ritchie's forecast of the direction of Rommel's attack had been correct and congratulated him by telegram,[64] suggesting that he move to the offensive now that the enemy armour was 'where you always wanted it. Well done you!' He continued his micro-management throughout the day, attaching a five page plan for a counter-offensive but also sending messages warning of possible further German attacks in the northern sector, including amphibious landings, 'in accordance with PINCER principle',[65] as he put it.

The subsequent defeat of Eighth Army at Gazala, in its impact rivalling Gallipoli and the fall of Singapore as among the most calamitous suffered by British land forces in the twentieth century, had its roots in the setbacks of the previous twelve months

64   JRL GB133AUC881, Message to Ritchie, 28 May 1942.
65   Carver, *Dilemmas*, pp. 81-2.

and the inability of British commanders to evolve a practicable doctrine and therefore a common philosophy through which they could work. Defeats had reduced confidence in leadership above regimental level, and when a crisis posed tactical problems for which there were neither precedents nor a coherent doctrine, dissension spread among senior officers. It is not difficult to apportion blame for the failings in generalship, but it is more to the point to look at some of the significant themes of the battle from the British perspective. The themes are lack of confidence in the leadership as evidenced by the response of units to orders, the failure of such doctrine as existed, and the dissension between commanders. These flaws were largely the product of the institutional and cultural aspects of the British army discussed earlier.

Rommel's Crisis: 28 May to 1 June

28 May saw the Panzerarmee trapped between the British 150th Brigade Box and the bulk of the British armour. 15th Panzer Division was immobilised by lack of fuel and 21st Panzer Division made little progress northward to the coast, but the Ariete Division held off British armour as Rommel gathered in such of his supply columns as he could find and sought a new supply route through the British minefields, one that would be less hazardous than the journey round Bir Hacheim. 22nd Armoured Brigade watched the immobilised 15th Panzer whilst 2nd Armoured Brigade moved up to attack Ariete. But the move started late and was held up at dusk.[66]

On the 29th Ritchie was still optimistic and 'thought there was a chance of shelling the enemy to pieces while his own tanks & motor brigades attacked supply lines, believing the tactics of "Crusader" should work a second time,'[67] while Auchinleck was thinking in terms of a Liddell Hart style indirect manoeuvre by advancing to Rotonda and Mechili, respectively thirty and seventy miles from British lines. Neither was looking for a decisive tank v. tank action. 2nd Armoured Brigade attacked early along Trigh Capuzzo to close the gap in the minefield and prevent the dispersed German formations withdrawing back through it and concentrating once more. One regiment made progress through the German gun line, but German tanks counter-attacked, forcing tanks and guns back, knocking out the 6-pdrs, and the brigade was pushed back to Knightsbridge. By the end of the day Rommel had succeeded in concentrating his divisions behind Ariete's gun line and could turn to destroying the British 150th Infantry Brigade which was still obstructing his direct supply route.

British losses had been particularly heavy among the Grants and 6-pdr guns, but as Rommel turned his forces to concentrate on 150th Brigade, he appeared to be withdrawing, giving Ritchie and Auchinleck the impression that the Panzer Armee was weakening and that further pressure would exhaust his supplies. Thus on 30 May, though 4th Armoured Brigade diverted southwards, 2nd and 22nd Armoured

66   Dunn, *Sword and Wig*, p. 273.
67   Playfair, vol iii, p. 228.

Brigades were instructed to drive in the Ariete division that was Rommel's first line of defence against a counterattack. Dunn describes in his diary the reluctance of British armour to engage enemy tanks directly. His troop of 25-pdr field guns was detached from his regimental group to support an outflanking attack by 22nd Armoured Brigade's regiments from the north. The enemy consisted of about 25 Italian M13s, much inferior to any British tank. The attack was held up, then called off because of the perceived threat from four 88mm guns, precisely the kind of target which Dunn's troop was trained to engage. 'It all seemed rather tame I thought.'

23. 88 mm gun. Its bulk made this feared anti-tank weapon vulnerable once Eighth Army directed high explosive fire against it. (Imperial War Museum E077164)

The afternoon heat haze developed into a mirage that prevented observation and the attack was not remounted till 6pm with support from two more regiments of artillery. 'The CLY [County of London Yeomanry] went along the Trigh Capuzzo with all the dash that made them famous in November. I raced along on their right flank'. Over a ridge they saw eleven German Mk III tanks 1000 yards away. The Crusaders' 2-pdrs were ineffective at that range so Dunn found the CO of the tank regiment, with whom he had never previously worked, and 'told him I could support him with smoke if he wanted to close. I pointed out that he must still have two to one superiority in numbers. He was rattled.' He wanted further reconnaissance, there might be more tanks, certainly there would be antitank guns, and 'in any case he had reported the situation to the brigadier.' The action was to be broken off. Dunn 'was disgusted by the day's work.' The 3rd County of London Yeomanry had been detached from their own formation to make up for losses in 2nd Armoured Brigade and their war diary gives the impression that they lacked conviction.[68] Being separated from the colleagues with whom they had trained and coming under command of strangers cannot have helped their morale. Dunn later encountered 2nd Armoured Brigade's artillery commander, 'Frizz' Fowler, 'very angry and blinking and snorting with rage … Said the armour was "bloody sticky", that one determined squadron could deal with the anti-tank guns and then there was nothing to stop us. He finally disappeared in a cloud of dust.'[69] Both men had reason for their frustration: Ariete's armour and guns were the only serious opposition, for the panzer divisions were between five and ten miles to the north preparing their attack on 150th Brigade.[70]

Lieutenant Dominic Graham's battery was attached to the 2nd Armoured Brigade, whose tank units he described as 'windy, cautious and ineffective. It had not adopted the concept of combined arms action that we had practised in 1st Armoured Brigade'. He was forced to watch in frustration as the armour observed 50 odd panzers and supporting troops for most of two days without firing a shot at them. He was reprimanded and then laughed at for firing 50 rounds per gun from his battery (400 25-pdr shells in all) at them in sheer frustration. 'We shall never know what damage they did, but they forced the enemy to withdraw.'[71]

Lieutenant Colonel Roberts of 3RTR similarly was 'of the opinion that if only 22 Armd Bde would go forward they could shove the whole lot out.'[72] But Lumsden had formed the view that daylight attacks by tanks resulted in casualties for little gain – 2nd Armoured Brigade had itself been temporarily reduced to 30 tanks – and he saw a night attack on German anti-tank defences by infantry followed by an advance by armour as more likely to succeed. Lumsden saw the German 88s as decisive in beating

68   Bovington 3 CLY War Diary: '3rd CLY was put under command of 2nd Armd Brigade … The enemy was reported to be withdrawing West through the mine marsh, and orders were to maintain contact. In the morning, an attack was put in by the 2nd Armd Brigade with 3rd CLY on the right under cover of smoke, against enemy tanks on the ridge 377412. 3rd CLY was ordered to withdraw. A further attack was made in the late afternoon under smoke provided by the 25pdrs under command of 2nd Armd Brigade. 3rd CLY went wide round the right flank but this attack was also abortive owing to the fact that targets were obscured by the smoke and orders were received to rally'.

69   IWM, Dunn Papers.

70   Playfair, vol iii, map 26, p. 224.

71   Graham, *Against Odds*, pp. 103, 129.

72   TNA WO106.2235: Operations 26/5-2/7/42, Report of court of enquiry, Messervy's testimony.

off British attacks, though he appreciated the dire situation of the Panzerarmee: 'That day, the 30th, we definitely had him. We had him boiled, he was caught in there.'[73] Lumsden's aim now was to trap the enemy between the armour and the 150th Brigade box, but he was concerned about the security of the Knightsbridge position, though it is difficult to see where any threat to Knightsbridge came from at that time: 'It was on Knightsbridge I was pivoting my whole manoeuvre...the Knightsbridge position helped me and if that went my pivot went also so I couldn't use it for night patrolling against the enemy's guns and tanks which were at that time strong.' That night he did order up a column from the Knightsbridge garrison to attack German positions, but it was of no great strength and was repulsed with heavy losses in men and guns.

The plan for the 31st as detailed to Dunn was for a night attack by an Indian brigade followed by a dawn attack by 2nd Armoured Brigade to drive the enemy back over the minefield, columns to hold him there, 4th Armoured Brigade to work up from the south with one regiment each side of the minefield, and an Army Tank Brigade to strike down from the north with a South African column. 22nd Armoured Brigade,

24. German anti-tank gun in action, June 1942. It was more easily concealed and mobile than the 88mm. (Imperial War Museum MH005862)

73   TNA WO106.2235: Operations 26/5-2/7/42, Report of court of enquiry, Lumsden's testimony.

25. Ritchie failing to 'grip' his subordinates. Left to right, Brigadier Erskine, Lt Gen Norrie, Ritchie, Lt Gen Gott, Captain Singer, 31st May 1942. (Imperial War Museum E12630)

brought up to full strength, was to pursue and destroy. In all, five brigades from three divisions and two corps were to combine at a day's notice. It is not surprising that such a complex operation failed to materialise. 10th Indian Brigade of 5th Indian Division was ordered to carry out the initial assault on the night of the 31st but a raging sandstorm prevented reconnaissance and Messervy (escaped from captivity) cancelled the entire operation. On 1 June, the plan was modified to 50th Division forming a pivot from which forces could operate against the enemy position while 10th Indian Brigade formed a box from which to harass the enemy east of the minefield.[74] All this time 150th Brigade had continued to block Rommel's supply convoys, but shortly after noon on 1 June was finally overrun despite the fiercest possible defence. Its commander Brigadier Haydon was killed in the last stages of resistance. Rommel had now freed up his supply line, the British advantage had been lost and their plan had to be recast.

74   TNA CAB 44.97: Gazala Enquiry, Norrie's testimony, p. 81.

The problems for Eighth Army in this phase had started at the top. Since 'Crusader' Auchinleck's micromanagement of Ritchie denoted a lack of confidence in him which, being observed, did nothing to enhance his authority. Not only was Ritchie seen to be something of a mouthpiece for Auchinleck, who was in Cairo and out of touch, but even worse Auchinleck himself was thought by Gott and Norrie 'to be under the sinister influence of Dorman-Smith'.[75] Auchinleck's misjudgement of the direction of Rommel's opening assault and his attempt to cover against every eventuality led to faulty dispositions of the armoured brigades (though this should not have turned out as damaging as it did) and the unreality of his proposals for counter-attack – his suggestion on 29 May that 'all available light forces should strike hard at Mechili and even Benghazi', was delivered in person by Dorman-Smith and has his leitmotif all over it – cannot have helped. Auchinleck's known views on the direction of Rommel's attack may have contributed to Norrie's reluctance to order Messervy to alert his formations on the 27th, though Norrie's own 'management style' was also a factor: Carver describes Norrie as 'a charmer, a most persuasive and likeable man ... but there is no doubt – and I realised it at the time – that he was indecisive, and not firm enough with his subordinates.'[76] Both Messervy and his staff were dilatory in their reaction to XXX Corps warnings:[77] Roberts commanding 3RTR had been alerted at 0430 hours on the 27 May, but received no orders from 4th Armoured Brigade until after 0800 hours, by which time the Afrika Korps was almost on them. At 1st Armoured Division Lumsden's mercurial nature may have discouraged Norrie from alerting him with a possible false alarm, for, even when he did, Norrie's instruction that Lumsden should despatch his 22nd Armoured Brigade to join Messervy's division resulted in an 'acrimonious exchange'.[78] Dissension at the very top was reflected further down the command chain. Harold Pyman recalled later that, 'It was the only occasion during World War II that I heard British Divisional and Brigade Commanders tearing each other asunder over the wireless in the heat of battle' and he thought Norrie failed to either control or sack the offenders because he 'was far too nice a country gentleman to be sufficiently ruthless'.[79] The consensual command method that began with Auchinleck's oversight of Ritchie during 'Crusader' had evolved into a ponderous, safety first, procedural triumvirate of Ritchie, Norrie and Gott, with too much reliance on information from wireless intercept, resulting in plans to counter enemy moves rather than selecting an objective and pursuing it.[80] Norrie, and probably Gott also, saw Ritchie's early optimism as based on faulty appreciation and overconfidence,

---

75   Carver, *Dilemmas*, p. 11.
76   Carver, *Dilemmas*, p. 145.
77   Messervy's biographer claims it was 7th Armoured Division that alerted XXX Corps. The GSO1 responsible at 7 Armd Div, Lt Col Pyman, evades the issue in his memoirs. He destroyed the Divisional War Diaries when threatened with capture.
78   Carver, *Dilemmas*, p. 78.
79   General Sir Harold Pyman, *Call to Arms* (London: Leo Cooper, 1971), pp. 41-42
80   TNA WO216/85: Norrie's Report, 12 July 1942.

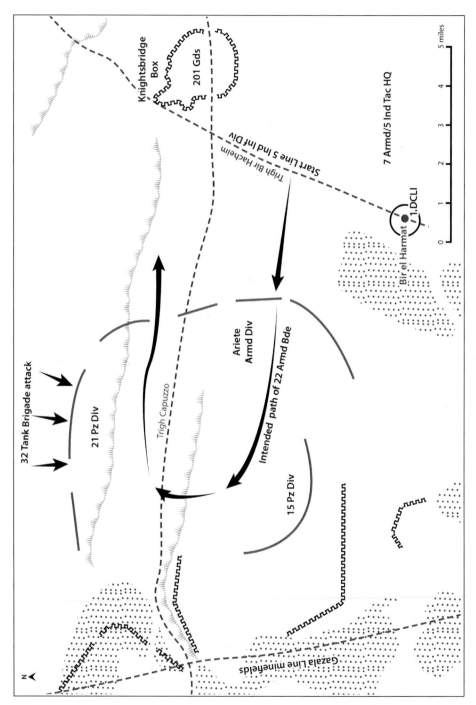

Knightsbridge Box

201 Gds

Trigh Bir Hacheim

Start Line 5 Ind Inf Div

7 Armd/5 Ind Tac HQ

Bir el Harmat

1 DCLI

Ariete Armd Div

Intended path of 22 Armd Bde

15 Pz Div

32 Tank Brigade attack

21 Pz Div

Trigh Capuzzo

Gazala Line minefields

N

0   1   2   3   4   5 miles

7. Gazala – 'Aberdeen'

'views which were not shared by myself or the Divisional commanders'. And by the time Ritchie, Norrie and Gott had received reports of the situation each morning, decided what action to take and passed their instructions to the front line units at the far end of the chain of command, it was too late for the orders to be put into full effect.

The introduction of armoured brigade groups with integral artillery and infantry had not encouraged deployment of divisions as divisions. There is no mention of motor brigades training with their armoured brigades. They were deployed separately and in neither armoured division were they reunited during this opening phase of the battle. 201st Guards Brigade remained locked in the Knightsbridge box while 7th Motor Brigade, recovered from its initial battering, was tasked with forming columns to harass German supplies and with convoying supplies to the Free French garrison at Bir Hacheim. Artillery and infantry support from these motor brigades would have strengthened the armoured brigades' attempts to drive in the Ariete's defence line and could have provided infantry for a timely night attack to relieve 150th Brigade as soon as its predicament became clear.

Considering the short period of time available to train on their new 6-pdrs and Grants, the gunners and armoured regiments did well with them in action, but heavy losses of these weapons were an ominous sign of the exceptional ability of the Afrika Korps to identify and neutralise an unexpected threat.

Operation Aberdeen, 2-6 June

British commanders were aware that, having missed an opportunity to crush Rommel, they must now attempt to regain the initiative. Ultra had revealed on the 31st that Rommel intended to remain stationary in the area that became known as the Cauldron and to lure British armour to destruction on the Panzerarmee's anti-tank screen. He would then counter-attack the remaining fragments.[81] A plan for an offensive by XIII Corps through the Italian-held sector to Temrad, 20 miles due west of the northern end of the Gazala line, had been mooted since 31 May. But with 150th Brigade gone, 50th Division no longer had the troops available and Pienaar, commander of 1st South African Division, refused to participate. Gott, 'optimistic as usual',[82] called in Briggs, the commander of 5th Indian Division, and asked him to 'consider' carrying it out. Briggs 'never thought harder in my life' before suggesting instead an outflanking move to the south round Bir Hacheim to attack Rommel's lines of communication. Briggs went off to start planning and to gather in his widely separated brigades:[83]

---

81   Bennett, *Ultra and Mediterranean Strategy*, p. 124.
82   Anthony Brett-James, *Ball of Fire: The Fifth Indian Division in the Second World War*, Chapter 14, <http://www.ourstory.info/library/4-ww2/Ball/fire07.html#ch14>
83   The 9th Brigade was manning part of the Tobruk defences, the 10th had been allocated to Army Reserve (it was the only formation in Army Reserve), and the 29th was garrisoning a box at El Adem. They were all separated by at least eight miles from each other.

Unfortunately, the armour intervened. It had been arranged that they should protect my right flank. Now they said they needed a day to refit. In my absence the whole plan was changed to a frontal attack against Rommel in his prepared position. And we were not to be a complete division after all.[84]

It was possibly just as well that the outflanking plan was cancelled, for it would have divided British armour, would have laid open British communications and supply depots to attack, and would have been itself vulnerable to a German counterstroke, but Messervy's proposal for a direct attack on Rommel's position in the Cauldron, the name given to the area now occupied by the Afrika Korps and protruding like a carbuncle from the minefield zone previously occupied by 150th Brigade, was precisely what Rommel was expecting. Gott was reluctant to take on any operation which was reminiscent of the frontal attacks of the First World War and neither he nor Norrie wished to command the assault. Lumsden became 'extremely vehement' at the idea that his 22nd Armoured Brigade be used for the operation,[85] and control of the brigade was passed to Messervy. In contravention of Field Service Regulations and training manuals that forbade divided command,[86] Ritchie gave responsibility for the operation jointly to Messervy and Briggs, who sited their headquarters together and arranged that they would alternate command depending on whether armour or the infantry were taking the dominant role at the various stages. It was 3 June before the plan was confirmed, and 4 June before the 9th and 10th Indian brigades of 5th Indian Division could be collected in from their positions, briefed, make their reconnaissances and assemble at their start lines for an attack before dawn on the 5th. The division had been well blooded against the Italians at Keren in Eritrea the previous year and was later to prove of stellar value in Burma but was fresh to the desert from garrison duties in Cyprus and had never trained or co-operated with armour. The plan is described by Messervy's biographer as 'to drive a wedge into the Cauldron with infantry brigade boxes'[87] drawn from 5th Indian Division. 10th Brigade was to break through the eastern face of the German salient, 9th Brigade was to follow up and establish a defensive box in the positions previously occupied by 150th Brigade. The infantry were described as 'self-protecting' against enemy armour, their protection being two pdr guns issued a week earlier. The 22nd Armoured Brigade, now under Messervy's command, were expressly told they had no responsibility for supporting the infantry but were to perform a 'milling'[88] attack moving west through the infantry

---

84   Brett-James, *Ball of Fire*, Chapter 14.
85   TNA WO 106/2235: Operations 26/5-2/7/42 Report of court of enquiry, Messervy's testimony.
86   TNA WO 231/281: Army Tank/Inf. co-op 1941Army Training Instruction No. 2 1941.
87   Maule, *Spearhead General*, p. 186.
88   It has not been possible to find any military definition of 'milling'. However the dictionary definition, 'moving around in a confused mass', adequately describes 22nd Armoured Brigade's manoeuvre.

and then turning north and east to sweep through the rear of the German forces holding the northern face of the Cauldron, which the Valentines of 32nd Army Tank Brigade were to simultaneously attack frontally.

Nothing went according to plan. A letter from a company commander in the 2nd West Yorkshire Regiment of 9th Brigade tells the story:

> We had to meet in the dark another Arty Regt whom we had never seen before and who had never seen us, and also a Sqn of tanks whom we had never met before. All this was supposed to take place in the dark and the attack to start at first light...The arty regt which was supposed to have met us on the starting line turned up two hours late...The Armd Bde reported the ground clear of enemy tanks, 20 mins later we were being attacked by enemy tanks! The Sqn of tanks which was supposed to have remained with us the whole day departed without even contacting our CO... Our two forward coys were overrun by enemy tanks and were almost completely written off. Eventually about 20 to 30 ORs came back from each company, but only one out of the 8 officers and he was badly wounded...In the afternoon our Brigadier came forward alone on foot at great personal risk to find the Bn... incidentally a first class man, most outspoken afterwards about the whole affair, and subsequently got the sack under the most unfair circumstances...Both Bde and Div [HQs] skidaddled on the evening of the 5th June as fast as they could go within a few minutes of telling us that there was nothing to worry about.[89]

The absence of an overall commander for the operation contributed to the chaos. Brigadier Carr of 22nd Armoured Brigade was emphatic that he reported numbers of enemy tanks in the course of his sweep. He later told a Court of Enquiry that 'It can only be assumed that the message from 22 Bde went to 7 Armd Div and was not relayed to 9 and 10 Inf Bdes.'[90] Lieutenant Colonel Langran of the 2nd West Yorks had a different point of view, reporting that two tanks of 22nd Armoured Brigade approached the West Yorks forward company, 'but withdrew without taking any action on being fired at by two enemy Armd cars.'[91]

Despite taking three days to mount the attack, faulty reconnaissance had misjudged the enemy positions so that the artillery bombardment and infantry attack fell mostly on empty desert. 22nd Armoured Brigade having been brought up to full strength still saw their role as exploitation rather than assault and Major Pitman of 2nd Royal Gloucestershire Hussars (2RGH) was unhappy with their task:

89   James Colvin, 'Eighth Army Operations May-July 1942', Journal of the Society for Army Historical Research, Summer 2019, Vol. 97, No. 389, pp.173-5.
90   TNA WO106/2235: Operations 26/5-2/7/42, Report of Court of Enquiry, p. 2.
91   TNA WO 106/2235; Operations 26/5-2/7/42 Report of Court of Enquiry p. 224.

[A] frontal attack by armour on a defended position, and an attack of this kind by cavalry tanks, though even then considered part of their role, is one of the surest methods of suicide that exists, and the plan, with memories of similar attacks in the past in our minds, did not tend to raise our spirits.[92]

The 22nd Armoured Brigade was halted by the concentrated fire of the Ariete's artillery, efficiently deployed in depth,[93] though the brigade's losses of 60 tanks out of 156 were to be more from breakdowns than from enemy fire.[94] Meanwhile 32nd Army Tank Brigade's attack in the north, supported by only a handful of infantry and in the event unco-ordinated with 22nd Armoured Brigade, brought about the destruction of all but a dozen of their 70 Matildas and Valentines.

Brigadier Fletcher of 9th Indian Infantry Brigade was scathing[95] about the planning and execution:

The operation known as ABERDEEN...appears to have ended with the destruction of 10 Ind Inf Bde and of four artillery regts, while 9 Ind Inf Bde has lost half a battalion and most of the fighting equipment of another. More serious perhaps than the material losses is the feeling which both the 2nd West Yorkshire Regiment and the 2nd Highland Light Infantry have that they were let down by the 22nd Armoured Brigade, to whom men of both these regiments refer in terms of uncompromising contempt. I think that therefore it would be useful to examine the operation, and to see what mistakes were made and what misunderstandings existed... If we examine this plan from the point of view of 9 Ind Inf Bde, we find that battalions were expected to advance in the dark over ground they did not know to an assembly area, the centre of which was marked by a barrel; to do a further advance to a point "EAST of B[arrel] 100" where they were to be joined by a battery of a regt they did not know (it had arrived two days previously from Iraq), and by a squadron of 4RTR which had already been in action in the dark.

Later that day the brigade was attacked by enemy armour:

Our left flank had evidently not been guarded. The protection of our left flank was such an obvious necessity that it never occurred to me to ask what that protection was. I assumed that my brigade would NOT be asked to advance five to eight miles into the enemy's position without adequate steps having been

92   Pitman, *2RGH*, p. 67.
93   Playfair, vol iii, p. 233.
94   Captain B.H. Liddell Hart, *The Tanks: The History of the Royal Tank Regiment*, Vol. II (London: Cassell, 1959), p. 173.
95   TNA WO 169/5077: 2nd West Yorkshire War Diary. A copy of the report was inserted into the diary.

taken to protect our southern flank ... There appears to have been a complete misunderstanding between 22 Armd Bde and 9 Ind Inf Bde as to the capabilities and tasks of the two brigades. 22 Armd Bde appears to have thought that a battalion could establish itself in a box in the desert in a matter of half an hour; while 9 Ind Inf bde thought that the 22 Armd Bde, with its 100 tanks, had been given the task of destroying the enemy tanks in this area in which it was to establish itself. In point of fact the 22 Armd Bde appears to have made no attempt to go to the assistance of 2 W Yorks when they were attacked by 40 tanks and 17 armd cars; and when the position held by 2 HLI was attacked by 40 tanks, the 22 Armd Bde began a slow withdrawal. Later it reported itself faced by 90 tanks. The opportunity of destroying the two small concentrations of enemy tanks had passed ... I consider that infantry who have to operate with tanks should be trained with them. There would not then be this wide divergence of opinion as to the tasks and capabilities of the two arms of a force engaged in any one operation. In the desert infantry require 48 hours in which to establish a box which can stand by itself against an enemy tank attack. In addition they must be allowed to lay mines ... The lack of mutual understanding and of common doctrine extended beyond the failure of tanks and infantry to understand each other. The two coys. of R[oyal] N[orthumberland] Fusiliers arrived in the concentration area at dusk on the evening before the battle. They had been stationed in Cairo without arms and unable to train; suddenly they were issued with arms and ordered to entrain for the front. This was not fair on the men.

Fletcher was not quite right that there had been no flank guard. The Duke of Cornwall's Light Infantry, arriving the previous day after a month-long journey from Iraq, was given a battery of guns from 7th Armoured Division and thrust into the role of guarding the southern flank of the attack. It was not fully trained and was short of carriers and antitank weapons. When command of the operation switched from 5th Indian Division to 7th Armoured, the DCLI's supporting battery followed instructions from their own division and departed, leaving the DCLI defenceless against German armour. Fewer than 100 of them survived.[96]

Unsurprisingly after his comments, Fletcher's career was terminated in July. One feels that the tone of his report was driven at least in part by anger at the destruction of his own battalion of the Highland Light Infantry in which he had spent his career and which he had recently commanded in action. His report is quoted at length because it illustrates the extent and the depth of Eighth Army's failings. These included a faulty doctrine of infantry boxes, a misunderstood practice of combined arms, tank units operating independently of their support group, confusion as to the respective roles and capacities of infantry and armour, lack of joint training, and a curious managerial style of leadership, where units and formations could be switched from one command

96   TNA WO 106/2235: Operations 26/5-2/7/42, Report of Court of Enquiry.

to another and small, random bands of men could be picked up and thrown into battle without preparation or planning. It was no longer even clear what the role of the armoured brigades was other than to manoeuvre without incurring too much risk from enemy fire. Pitman's belief that it was not really the task of 'cavalry tanks' to engage with serious opposition, despite his brigade being at least in part equipped with the well armoured Grants, precisely identifies the problem resulting from the lack of an armoured warfare doctrine.

In the war diaries of the three regiments in 22nd Armoured Brigade, 2RGH's tank losses on the 5th are not mentioned but in personnel they lost one killed, five wounded and one missing – 'remarkably light' as Pitman says.[97] 3CLY lost in all 16 killed, wounded and missing. If the proportion of personnel casualties to tank losses during Aberdeen were similar to what the brigade was to suffer later in September, this would indicate a loss in battle of no more than a dozen out of the 100 tanks in the two regiments. 4CLY war diary does not mention casualties at all, merely a great deal of moving back and forth, meeting 15 enemy tanks which was 'biting off more than we could chew' (their own strength was around 50 tanks) and concluding 'So ended a day of 24 3/4 hours, a really bad day'. There are no entries in any of 22nd Armoured Brigade's regimental diaries that contradict Fletcher's version of events. The official report for the cabinet office indicates that most of the brigade's losses were due to mechanical failure.[98] And it would seem that a significant proportion of the enemy tanks that had deterred them were Italian, from the Ariete rather than the Afrika Korps.[99]

Alternating command between between two headquarters for a single operation was expressly forbidden in Military Training Pamphlets. Carver believed that in this case twin headquarters were acceptable since 5th Indian and 7th Armoured division HQs were positioned close together. But it seems likely that divided command was the cause of the incompetent staff work that failed to locate accurately Ariete's main line of defence or to adequately guard 9th Brigade's left flank. Lack of a single command was also probably the reason for the failure to warn 9th Brigade of enemy armour at large in the Cauldron: 22nd Armoured Brigade informed 7th Armoured Division of the threat and normally the message would have reached Corps HQ and been passed to 5th Indian Division's units. Without a corps headquarters linking the divisions, the information was not passed on. Eighth Army HQ played no role in 'Aberdeen' save to send 2nd Armoured Brigade as reinforcement to 7th Armoured Division, where according to the Official History they 'received from it a number of orders which cancelled each other out.'[100] In fact Messervy later testified that because 2nd Armoured Brigade was unfamiliar with 7th Armoured Division's codes, when

97   Pitman, *2RGH*, p. 70.
98   TNA CAB 44/97: Operation Aberdeen.
99   Walker, *Iron Hulls*, pp. 123-4
100 Playfair, vol iii, p. 235.

they received the movement order 'they read West for East … this error was not discovered until it was too late to rectify.'[101] This was the predictable result of brigades being switched from one division to another.

Auchinleck's official despatch was to describe Operation Aberdeen as 'probably the turning point of the whole battle'. Rommel recorded that, after Aberdeen, he 'no longer expected any major relieving attack on our forces round Bir Hacheim and hoped to get on with our assault undisturbed'.[102]

Destruction of the Boxes, 6-17 June

It remained to be seen whether box tactics, having failed as an offensive tool, would be viable in defence. The Free French Brigade at Bir Hacheim had halted supplies to the Panzer Armee but now that Rommel had secured an alternative route through the area previously held by 150th Brigade, the Free French garrison, 3,600 strong, was becoming an expensive liability, requiring the full time efforts of 7th Motor Brigade and much of 29th Indian Brigade plus a substantial supply column to maintain,[103] and charged with political significance should it fall. Although Rommel had originally scheduled its capture for 27 May the defenders had beaten off Ariete's attack and subsequent assaults. After 'Aberdeen' Ritchie was inclined to evacuate but Auchinleck, always reluctant to give an inch, disagreed even though Bir Hacheim was no longer a hindrance to German supplies. Ritchie agreed to continue to hold Bir Hacheim despite the cost involved, and in an attempt to regain the initiative he ordered Gott to make a thrust westward through the northern section of the Gazala Line against the Italians, in the hope that German troops would be diverted to help their allies.

The only troops available were the two South African divisions, and Gott, 'after discussion with General Pienaar',[104] decided on a raid of brigade group strength. Even with this minimal request, Pienaar co-operated less than half-heartedly. He sent out a number of small detachments to find soft spots on 8 June. These suffered 280 casualties while failing to divert the Afrika Korps from concentrating on Bir Hacheim. The 15th Panzer Division now joined the Trieste and 90 Light divisions in the attack on the French, in what Rommel said was the hardest fighting he encountered in North Africa. No explanation has ever been offered as to why the British armour made no attempt to attack the Afrika Korps while it was largely occupied in this struggle, even though it must have been clear that the Free French brigade could not sustain its defence indefinitely without outside help. In 4th Armoured Brigade, Jake Wardrop and his colleagues in 5RTR could not understand it either:

101 TNA WO 106/2235: Messervy's testimony, p. 211.
102 Liddell Hart, *Rommel Papers*, p. 217.
103 TNA WO 106/2235: Operations 26/5-2/7/42 Report of Court of Enquiry, p. 17.
104 Playfair, vol iii, p. 238.

For about a week we pushed here and there all up and down the minefield, but it seemed to me that if they had got a lot of kit together and had one big push in one place, we could have done something definite. As it was, the units were just battering themselves to pieces in a lot of little scraps which were getting us nowhere.[105]

And Lieutenant Colonel Liardet, commanding 6RTR in the same brigade, also found himself involved in 'silly little attacks [which] went in, we lost a tank or two each time, this frittering of our armour contributed largely to our final downfall.'[106]

General Koenig, the Free French commander of Bir Hacheim, had no intention of having his brigade sacrificed, had made up his mind to evacuate and after 8 June refused to accept further supplies.[107] Reality eventually dawned on the British command, and the evacuation of Bir Hacheim was ordered for the night of 10/11 June. Anticipating a renewed German thrust to the coast to cut off the formations in the Gazala Line, Ritchie had used the four days' grace to establish battalion strongpoints to block such a move, using 2nd Scots Guards and the Worcesters from the Knightsbridge garrison, but Rommel was confident in his troops' ability to deliver a decisive blow and first turned east towards the weakened Knightsbridge box where the bulk of the British armour lay. Eighth Army still had an advantage in numbers of tanks.[108] But by now units had been so often interchanged, amalgamated and reformed that regimental cohesion was being lost, crews were sometimes strangers to each other and the tanks themselves were battered and failing. At this moment 15th Panzer Division became isolated in a move towards El Adem. Norrie saw that if Messervy combined 4th and 2nd Armoured Brigades, he could destroy 15th Panzer Division before the Afrika Korps could reunite. Messervy was more concerned that his supply line to Tobruk was now seriously at risk from the Afrika Korps and wanted to secure an alternative supply route from El Adem by combining his 4th Armoured Brigade with elements of 22nd Armoured Brigade and striking north. He set off to explain his plan to Norrie but ran into German units en route and was forced to hide in a disused well for several hours. The subsequent inaction and confusion, and the DAK's interception of Messervy's wireless message refusing to attack,[109] gave Rommel time to organise his next move: a strike by both his panzer divisions on 2nd and 4th armoured brigades on 12 June around the Knightsbridge box from both front and rear. By the end of the 13th not only had the British lost 150 tanks but they had been pushed off the battlefield, could not recover those tanks that might be repairable and were forced back towards the Egyptian frontier, leaving Knightsbridge exposed. The solitary Guards battalion left

105 Forty, *Wardrop*, p. 49.
106 Liddell Hart Centre for Military Archives, Liardet Papers, letter, 18 February 1943.
107 TNA WO201.379: Ritchie's Report on Ops, May–June 1942.
108 A total of 298 including 77 Grants versus 124 gun armed German and 60 Italian tanks. Playfair, vol iii, p. 239.
109 Mellenthin, *Panzer Battles*, p. 135.

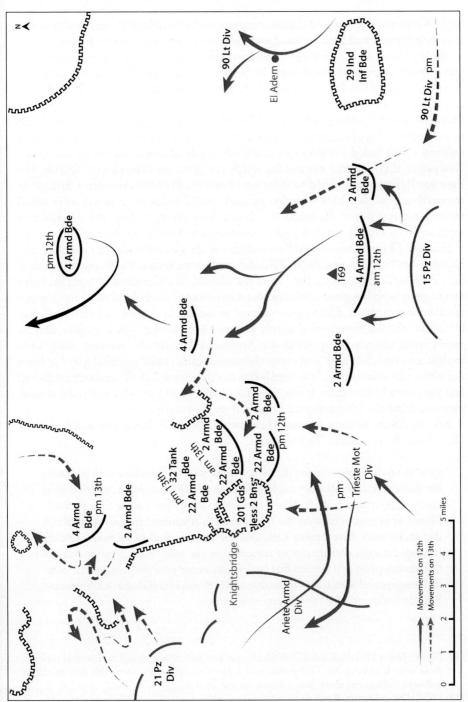

N

90 Lt Div

El Adem

29 Ind
Inf Bde

90 Lt Div pm

2 Armd
Bde

pm 12th
4 Armd Bde

4 Armd Bde
am 12th

15 Pz Div

169

4 Armd Bde

2 Armd Bde

2 Armd
Bde

pm 13th 32 Tank

am 13th 2 Armd
Bde

22 Armd
Bde

22 Armd Bde

2 Armd
Bde

pm 12th

201 Gds
less 2 Bns

Trieste Mot
Div

pm

4 Armd
Bde
pm 13th

2 Armd Bde

Knightsbridge

21 Pz
Div

Ariete Armd
Div

Movements on 12th
Movements on 13th

0   1   2   3   4   5 miles

8. Gazala – 'Knightsbridge'

in the Knightsbridge box, 3rd Coldstream, was unable to hold the German attack now that their armour had been defeated and the garrison made its way to Tobruk.

Robin Dunn's diary of this period was written up from the logs he kept at the time and gives an account of this decisive battle. By 11 June when Bir Hacheim fell, 2nd Armoured Brigade had been reduced to the Bays regimental group, with 50 tanks and Dunn's supporting artillery regiment. Together with 4th and 22nd armoured brigade they were a dozen miles south of a line between Knightsbridge and El Adem. Their mood was 'very lighthearted and cheerful' despite being sniped accurately by German artillery, insult added to injury by a captured 25-pdr adding to the enemy firepower. News came that Rommel was moving north-east from Bir Hacheim on Tobruk. The Bays battlegroup was ordered to move under command of 4th Armoured Brigade to the north-east as the DAK moved in parallel about 2 miles away. It was an identical move to the first day of the battle. 'We had defeated that, so there was no reason to suppose that we could not do it again. We went to bed full of confidence.'

Early on 12 June Dunn could hear shellfire to the east indicating an attack on the El Adem box. At 9:00 a.m. 30 Mk IIIs advanced on the Bays at Pt 169 but were halted on a crest 1000 yards off by the fire of the Grants. The Germans brought up three 88mm guns 'with the greatest boldness and unlimbered just behind the crest'. Dunn's 25pdrs drove them off. Enemy gun columns on the left flank were also driven off. But by midday the fire from several enemy batteries was causing tank casualties, and 50 enemy tanks advanced at speed on 4th Armoured Brigade who reversed slowly back to their gun line. Soon the gun crews themselves came under machine gun fire from the tanks. German success, 'was largely due to a number of Mk IV tanks, fitted for the first time with 88 mm guns. It was these formidable machines which played the main part in driving the 4th Armoured Brigade from the escarpment.'[110]

But the enemy advance exposed their own flank to the Bays, who still had eight Grants and thirty cruisers. To Dunn and,

> all of us on the spot it seemed that this was the perfect opportunity. Who knows but that a very different story might have been told of this battle if, at this critical juncture, 30 cruiser tanks had flung themselves at top speed at the enemy's flank. Pinned as he was in front by the fire of the 4th Armoured Brigade and 1RHA this shock must have broken him. But the decision had to be made quickly. It needed a high commander of initiative on the spot. Such a rarity was not forthcoming. Just as it seemed that victory was in our grasp we received the order to disengage and withdraw 4 miles due north. It was said that the 4th Armoured Brigade could not afford to lose any more tanks.[111]

---

110 IWM, Dunn Diaries, Book 4. The 88mm gun was not mounted on a tank at this time, so these must have been Mk IV Specials with long 75mm guns, not previously seen in action in North Africa, and more than a match for the Grants.
111 IWM, Dunn Diaries, Book 4.

The Bays group withdrew on Knightsbridge Box but 4th Armoured Brigade never received this order and 'we last saw them going at speed for Tobruk.' 22nd Armoured Brigade on the east of the box were attacked from the south. The Bays still further to the east were attacked on their own eastern flank before dusk, their resupply failed to arrive, and they became surrounded on three sides. As one of Dunn's colleagues said to him that evening, 'tomorrow will be the most bloody day you or I have ever spent.'

The 6RTR was one of the units of 4th Armoured Brigade involved in the same action. On 11 June they had lost several Honeys, but worse was to come. Their commanding officer, Lieutenant Colonel Liardet, wrote to his wife:

> 12 June was one of the worst in my memory. At dawn had remnants of 1RTR on the right flank with ten tanks and nothing on my left... later the Bays of 2nd Armd Bde came up on my left and gave me very welcome relief. About 1600 hours both flanking regiments were forced to withdraw and I was left very much in the air. I was unable to come back as ordered because I had a RHA Bty in action in the open about 600 yards behind the Rgt. I had to do a lot of running about to organise the withdrawal and as there was a lot of MG fire I was literally p --- ing in my breeches!! In the end poor old RHQ had to cover the withdrawal of the remains of 'C' sqn. We all got out less my written off Grants, five in number, and one 25pdr, and managed to rally all right. It was all most terrifying and my Fear Naught (Ha! Ha!) was hit no less than 14 times but never pierced.[112]

As dawn broke on 13 June, 22nd Armoured Brigade was still facing south with its right flank on the Knightsbridge box, while the Bays were now facing east with their backs to the box. Dunn could see the enemy column breaking leaguer a mile away. He halted their lorried component with artillery fire, but observation was difficult with the rising sun behind the enemy. Thirty tanks and some 88mm guns that were very well handled and made excellent use of the ground continued their advance. With 22nd Armoured Brigade on his right flank he moved back a mile extending the defensive line north from the Knightsbridge Box but by now the battlefield was becoming so compressed that enemy guns could bring him under fire from the rear. Dunn changed targets from the enemy transport to their tanks and halted their advance. The Bays were now reinforced by an infantry tank battalion with Matildas.

> The Matilda tanks were full of confidence and good cheer. They had come from Gazala where all was quiet. They said we only had to finish off this bit of armour here and all would be well. They were clean & well shaved & clear eyed & we, tired and unshaven after the hard fighting of the last day and a half, felt rather resentful of them.[113]

112 LHCMA, Liardet Papers, letter, 18 February 1943.
113 Dunn, *Sword and Wig*, p. 288.

The Germans began to pick off the infantry tanks at a distance safely out of range of their 2-pdrs, but Dunn again halted the German advance, by laying smoke through which the Germans would not advance. The Knightsbridge position was now surrounded on three sides and the Bays were down to two Grants and 11 cruisers. Three 6-pdr anti-tank guns under a subaltern unknown to Dunn appeared and he sent them out to the flank to further extend the line where, unsupported by armour or infantry, they were overrun by German tanks.

By mid-afternoon it was clear to Eighth Army that Rommel was switching his attack to cut off the troops in the Gazala line. In response Ritchie was forced to send the remnants of 2nd and 22nd Armoured Brigades north to hold off the Afrika Korps while 1st South African Division withdrew from their positions in the Gazala Line, moved through Tobruk and continued back to Alamein. The two remaining brigades of 50th Division was further inland and in a difficult position. The road back to Tobruk could not be held open long enough to evacuate them as well as the South Africans, so Gott organised an attack to the west through the Italian troops that held the front and then south around the entire battlefield until they met the coast road well into Egypt, a journey of about 200 miles. It was a move similar to 4th Indian Division's escape from Benghazi in January. They got through with few losses, overcoming resistance which had proved too much for Pienaar's men in their attack of 8 June, and 'the morale of those who got through was very high as they reckoned they had kicked the Italians all over the desert and pulled the leg of the Germans.'[114]

Without armoured support the Knightsbridge garrison, by now reduced to a single battalion, had to be evacuated to Tobruk, which according to Major Sainthill, second in command of the Coldstream Guards, was accomplished 'without much difficulty.'[115] During the process, Dunn's Honey tank encountered 20 German Mk IIIs and was knocked out. One of his crew was killed and he and the others wounded. Evacuated to Cairo and armed with the logs of his activities, Dunn wrote up his diary, assessing weakening morale of armoured units as the prime cause of the loss of the battle of Knightsbridge and thus of Gazala and Tobruk. He cited the earlier defeats of Eighth Army as due to inferior equipment – at Halfaya in Operation Battleaxe, at Sidi Rezegh and el Gubi during Operation Crusader (all before his arrival in the theatre), and at Agedabia and at Benghazi in January 1942. 'So they [the armoured units] had lost their dash', remaining inactive while the Germans manoeuvred around them. Dunn also noted the 'amazing adaptability' of the Germans in rapidly coming to terms with Grants and 6-pdr anti-tank guns, and the disparity in the leadership of the two armies.

On 14 July Auchinleck still hoped to hold a line from Acroma to El Adem which would safeguard Tobruk though it was clear to Ritchie that this was not feasible without an adequate armoured force. Corbett was sent to Ritchie at Eighth Army

114 TNA WO236/1: Erskine to Agar-Hamilton, 5 September 1950.
115 TNA WO 106/2235: Operations 26/5-2/7/42, Report of Court of Enquiry, p.156

HQ to emphasise 'the message from the C-in-C that the place [Tobruk] must not be allowed to be isolated', which by Dorman-Smith's account resulted in an impressive row between the two, Ritchie shouting 'I'm damned if I will [follow instructions]'.[116] Dorman-Smith said that if he had gone instead of Corbett he would have put Ritchie under arrest. Under pressure from London Auchinleck was insisting on holding Tobruk whilst knowing that it could not be saved from isolation, and once isolated could not withstand another prolonged siege. The issue was fudged to the extent that Tobruk was to act as the 'box' at one end of a new defence line, El Adem being at the other. This did not solve the problem of the lack of an armoured force between the two to hold off the DAK.[117] With only around 30 repaired tanks a day[118] coming forward, several days grace would be needed to rebuild 4th Armoured Brigade, so in order to form a mobile anti-tank defence Ritchie issued instructions on 16 June that infantry divisions were to provide columns of field gun, anti-tank and AA batteries each with an infantry company for local protection. The superfluous infantry and support units were to be moved back to the frontier for static defence. At this point events finally spiralled out of the control of the British commanders. Ritchie, having finally got Auchinleck's agreement to the temporary isolation of Tobruk, delegated to Norrie the decision whether El Adem, which had beaten off several assaults but was again under heavy attack, should still be held. Norrie passed the responsibility on to Messervy who ordered evacuation,[119] leaving the last bastion, Tobruk, isolated. On the same day 15th and 21st Panzer Divisions knocked out 30 of 4th Armoured Brigade's 90 tanks, in part because 4th Armoured Brigade's artillery had been detached to make up columns to support a newly arrived infantry brigade.[120] 4th Armoured Brigade withdrew twenty miles east to the Libyan/Egyptian frontier. On the 19th Auchinleck informed London that Tobruk, with 90 days supplies, could be held even if isolated from the frontier defence line and that even if isolated, the enemy would be 'unlikely to attempt to advance deep into Egypt unless our forces be decisively routed in the field or he has received considerable reinforcements.' With Eighth Army now back on the frontier of Libya and Egypt, and Tobruk isolated but holding up the Panzerarmee, Ritchie's intention was to rebuild a relieving force, a four or five week task at best. But free from interference by Eighth Army's armour, the Afrika Korps could concentrate on Tobruk and launched its assault at dawn on the 20 June. Tobruk's defences had deteriorated since the previous year, its minefields had been lifted to build the Gazala line, its anti-tank ditches had filled with sand and it was garrisoned by a ragbag of British and Indian battalions under the novice 2nd South African Division with a completely inexperienced commander. It capitulated early on the 21st.

116 Greacen, *Chink*, p. 200.
117 TNA WO106/2235: Operations 26/5-2/7/42 Report of Court of Enquiry, p. 18.
118 I.S.O. Playfair, vol iii, p. 254.
119 Carver, *Out of Step*, p. 116.
120 I.S.O. Playfair, vol iii, p. 257.

Perhaps the starkest of Eighth Army's failings in this phase is the lack of 'grip' by senior ranks. Neither Gott nor Norrie were able to get their divisional commanders to accept their orders or to act in accordance with their wishes, not only because of the friction of war but because the informal collegiate style that lessened the abrasiveness of a hierarchical command chain also allowed orders to be treated with an excessive degree of flexibility. This trait was to become even more pronounced in the following weeks. And Auchinleck's perceptible lack of confidence in Ritchie meant it was unlikely that orders from Ritchie to his corps commanders, or from them to their divisions, would be received with complete wholeheartedness.

On 22 June Auchinleck and Dorman-Smith flew up to Eighth Army HQ to confer with Ritchie. In a development of Ritchie's policy of 16 June each infantry division was now to reorganise into a 'brigade battle group' based on artillery with only enough infantry for close protection. Ritchie's plan was to gain time and stretch Rommel's supply lines by withdrawing 120 miles to Mersa Matruh, and to fight it out there, in accordance with Auchinleck's instructions.[121] Dorman-Smith noted Ritchie's 'usual slap-happy optimism … all was for the best, this was where we came before Crusader, soon there would be another Crusader',[122] presumably based on the hope of reproducing the previous year's success of jock columns strangling Rommel's supply lines. But Mersa Matruh was an awkward position to defend, of no significance other than as a water point and it was not possible to feel much confidence in Eighth Army's command: Ritchie inspired little in his subordinates. His BGS, Brigadier Whiteley, was clearly exhausted,[123] Messervy had been sacked leaving what remained of the armour in Lumsden's hands, Norrie and his XXX Corps headquarters had been sent back to Alamein to organise its defences, and a demoralised Gott still led XIII Corps. The recently arrived Freyberg, leading the only troops that were both fresh and experienced, refused to reorganise his New Zealand Division on Ritchie's lines and insisted on redrawing Ritchie's plan lest his men be trapped in Mersa Matruh. On 25 June, Auchinleck and Dorman-Smith flew up again, this time to dismiss Ritchie, take over Eighth Army and cancel the plan to stand and fight at Mersa Matruh.

---

121 TNA WO 106/2235: Operations 26/5-2/7/42 Report of court of enquiry. Whiteley, Ritchie's Chief of Staff, was clear that Ritchie was under orders to fight there.
122 JRL GB133GOW1/2/3, Appendix 1, p. 8.
123 Tedder, *With Prejudice*, p. 303. Tedder thought they were both 'completely whacked', Ritchie having a preoccupation with numbers of tanks of various types that 'seemed to have become an obsession.'

5

First Alamein and Change of Command

Dorman-Smith and Auchinleck

Dorman-Smith's letters and notes giving his account of the May-July 1942 period are often coloured with self-justification and personal animosities. But he left an outline written in the third person that is clearly intended to stand as a sober record of his role.[1] For a view of the state of British army doctrine practised in the desert rather than as prescribed in Great Britain his analysis repays examination. The army reforms of 1938 had introduced a 'triangular' infantry divisional structure of three brigades each of three battalions or regiments, plus supporting arms. This allowed flexibility, as the division could hold one or two brigades in reserve, depending on the situation, and a brigade commander would have the same flexibility with his three regiments. But in Dorman-Smith's view the organisation was still not flexible enough: 'This rigid divisional organisation had its equally rigid "tactical" doctrine, devised for the intensive warfare of western Europe, not for the extensive conditions of roomier theatres, where dispersal for example was necessary against air attack'.

He does not describe the 'equally rigid "tactical" doctrine', but one presumes he is referring to conventional direct attack, supported by divisional artillery, on an enemy position, and fixed defence in depth, supported by artillery and backed by armour, which he criticised during his time at Staff College. Armoured divisions similarly had a triangular structure, with two armoured brigades, each of three regiments, plus a third brigade in the form of a Support Group. Using the Support Group as jock columns separately from the armoured brigades destroyed the advantages of the triangular organisation of the armoured division and deprived the armoured regiments of the backing of the Support Group's artillery.

Dorman-Smith's remedy for the difficulties that Eighth Army experienced in June 1942 was to centralise the artillery, and to concentrate the Grant tanks, which alone

---

1   JRL GB133GOW1/12/16, Dorman-O'Gowan's narrative, n.d.

were capable of taking on the German armoured units, under artillery protection. Infantry in his view had a minimal role in the new paradigm of desert warfare and if there was insufficient transport to allow infantry to join the armour/artillery brigade battle groups, surplus infantry was to be sent back to Alamein. Divisions and corps were to move to each other's assistance 'and not remain supinely watching their specified front while decision was being reached elsewhere.' There were to be no more isolated divisional or brigade boxes in all round defence. Instead, infantry brigades (by which he presumably meant the new 'brigade battle groups') were to be not more than 10,000 yards apart, less if possible, with their own artillery. The front was to be kept fluid, moving at Rommel to regain the initiative when possible. Where possible, attacks were to be concentrated on Italian formations: 'Swat Wops' as he put it.

No matter how much the idea of fluid defence conformed to the mobility and flexibility extolled by Fuller, Liddell Hart and their disciples, it is difficult to see how the infantry brigade battle groups could be capable of offensive action. Fluidity was therefore not likely to mean more than retreat under pressure. Nor was it clear how the battle groups were to operate if artillery was centralised at divisional level and above. At Mersa Matruh Freyberg flatly refused to reorganise his division in this way and kept both his brigades intact. Without his action and the similar action of the commander of 9th Australian Division a little later, Eighth Army would have had no offensive capability at all in the following weeks, given the lack of confidence within the armoured units. Rommel in any case allowed no time for any reorganisation.

On assuming command of Eighth Army on the 25th Auchinleck informed Brooke 'Shall use DORMAN SMITH as my Chief of Staff leaving Corbett to represent me at GHQ' in Cairo.'[2] Dorman-Smith was informed by Corbett that 'the Chief was taking field command from Ritchie' and was taking Dorman-Smith 'as his companion. Nothing was said as to how DS would function, that could be left to events.'[3] Whiteley retained his official position as Brigadier General Staff of Eighth Army though his functions as principal staff officer to Eighth Army were largely superseded by Dorman-Smith. After a few days, the impracticality of the situation became apparent to all for, as Whiteley remarked, 'Chink being the sort of chap he is... started issuing all kinds of fantastic things to the Eighth Army'.[4] Dorman-Smith wrote after the war that 'It was the Auk who, without very clear thought, directed me to conduct operations alongside him... The result must indeed have seemed "fantastic" to Whiteley.'[5] From 28 June Auchinleck turned to Dorman-Smith for everything to do with operations but retained Whiteley as Eighth Army's titular chief of staff until late July which in Dorman-Smith's view 'was unfortunate and was later on the cause

---

2   JRL GB133/AUC957, 25/6 to Brooke.
3   JRL GOW/133 1/12/16, Narrative, p. 12.
4   JRL GOW/133 2/1/2, Letter to 'Michael' 1 December 1966. Whiteley, recorded in General Sir Ian Jacob's unpublished diary and quoted by Dorman-Smith..
5   JRL GOW/133 2/1/2, Letter to 'Michael', 1 December 1966.

of much mischief'.[6] It did however provide continuity of co-operation with the RAF with which Whiteley had organised a workable system, an important factor in the outcome. Dorman-Smith was Auchinleck's constant companion and tactical adviser, and so integral – he was even privy to the information from Ultra – to the events of the following weeks that he and Auchinleck can be considered as one mind as far as the tactical handling of Eighth Army is concerned.

During their flight to Mersa Matruh Dorman-Smith had lost no time in putting forward his ideas as to how Eighth Army should be reorganised and directed in the field, producing more than half seriously the latest edition of Liddell Hart's 'Strategy of the Indirect Approach' as a putative guide to Auchinleck's decision making.[7] Auchinleck, not renowned for a sense of humour and in no mood for flippancy, said he did not think he would have much spare time for reading. On arrival at Eighth Army HQ, the change of command and policy led to confusion and losses, through ambiguity over Dorman-Smith's responsibilities, poor wireless communications, and misunderstandings over a provisional retreat order. Ritchie had intended to hold the coastal flank at Mersa Matruh with the newly arrived X Corps, consisting of 10th Indian and 50th Northumberland divisions. The inland desert flank would be held by Gott's XIII Corps, comprising 1st Armoured and the New Zealand Division. The two corps would form two strong wings which could attack any enemy penetration through the weak centre of the position. But Auchinleck cancelled his previous order to fight it out there and summoned the Corps commanders to be briefed by Dorman-Smith on the change of plan.

Auchinleck did not take the opportunity to impose his authority in person, and this was matched by Gott's failure to attend, sending his BGS Brigadier Erskine instead. Erskine thought it 'a remarkable thing' that Auchinleck did not himself brief Eighth Army on the change of plan, instead giving the new orders through Dorman-Smith

---

6   JRL GOW/133 2/1/2, Letter to 'Michael', 1 December 1966.
7   Liddell Hart had sent Dorman-Smith the latest edition of this book which describes German tactics and strategy as 'avoiding head on assaults, and always seeking to find "soft spots" through which they could infiltrate along the line of least resistance.' See Captain B.H. Liddell Hart, *The Strategy of Indirect Approach* (London: Faber & Faber, 1941), p. 247. Although this is a correct enough description of German storm-troop tactics of 1918 from which interwar German military doctrine was developed, by the 1940s German practice involved bringing overwhelming force against the chosen point of attack rather than initially seeking the line of least resistance. Characteristically, Liddell Hart was suggesting that the Germans had adopted something similar to his own doctrine of the 'expanding torrent' rather than looking at the actuality. Liddell Hart was very widely read – his 1942 edition of 'Indirect Approach' (subtitled 'How to Win Wars') sold out at once. It would be surprising if Liddell Hart's work had not influenced the British army's attempts to find soft spots and manoeuvre its way to victory rather than find a practicable method of direct assault, just as Fuller had influenced the pre-war organisation and tactics of British armoured units.

only to 'water them down' the next day.[8] He made no comment on on his own chief's absence. Rather than fighting a decisive action at Mersa Matruh, the battle was now to take place over the 100 mile stretch of desert between Mersa Matruh and Alamein, with instructions that on no account were immobile troops to be committed to holding localities which could be easily isolated, all troops were to be kept fluid and mobile and to strike at the enemy from all sides. However, the armour was not to be committed unless a very favourable opportunity presented itself.

Lumsden's 1st Armoured Division at this time had 159 tanks of which 60 were Grants, significantly outnumbering and outgunning the DAK's total of around 60 tanks in all, but given the instructions it received it could not be blamed for being wholly ineffective. Lumsden was to testify that 'there were orders and counter orders on the evening of the 26th, sometimes under XIII Corps and sometimes under X Corps...I had five orders in one day from Army as to how the Bde was to be organised.'[9] On the 27th he 'was told not to attack unless a very favourable opportunity presented itself...[then] I got a message from Corps [i.e. Gott] to say it was all over: NZ Div didn't exist'.[10] Brigadier Erskine disputed this account, stating that 'It is not possible that Gott should have made such a remark to Lumsden', since Gott was fully aware of the New Zealand division's perfectly viable condition, was with them when they were attacked by 21st Panzer and remained with them throughout the day.[11]

As expected Rommel had launched his attack through the weak centre of the British position on the 26th and was by the next afternoon moving to encircle the New Zealand Division. Eighth Army and Gott's XIII Corps had each drawn up their own plans for withdrawal. With poor wireless communications confusing the picture for the corps and divisional commanders, XIII Corps issued its withdrawal order just as X Corps was preparing a counterattack into the DAK's advanced troops. Gott's intention for 27 June had been to hold his positions for as long as possible but he issued his plans for withdrawal in accordance with the new policy of a mobile defence. Neither he nor Holmes of the newly arrived X Corps had any idea of the weakness of the Panzerarmee. On that day 90th Light Division amounted to 1,600 men, 21st Panzer had 23 tanks and 600 very exhausted infantry, and each was isolated and beyond the reach of 15th Panzer's fewer than 40 tanks and 1000 infantry.[12] But 21st Panzer's boldness, encircling the New Zealand Division at Minqar Qaim despite efforts from the 3rd CLY and the Bays to hold them back, gave Gott cause to believe that his XIII Corps was at risk of being isolated and pinned down, contrary to Eighth Army's new policy. Late that afternoon both 1st Armoured and New Zealand Divisions received garbled messages from XIII Corps HQ that the New Zealand Division had already

---

8   TNA WO 236/1: Erskine to Agar-Hamilton, 5 September 1950.
9   TNA WO 106/2235: Operations 26/5-2/7/42 Report of Court of Enquiry, pp. 111-13.
10   TNA WO 106/2235: Operations 26/5-2/7/42, Report of Court of Enquiry.
11   TNA WO 236/1: Letter from Erskine to Cabinet Office, 1949.
12   Mellenthin, *Panzer Battles*, pp. 153, 155.

left Minqar Qaim and that 1st Armoured was at liberty to withdraw. Just at that moment Freyberg was wounded by shellfire and his successor Inglis, aware that Gott did not regard the New Zealand position as vital ground, set in motion his division's withdrawal to Alamein, the destination given in one of the plans. Gott himself issued his XIII Corps' own codeword for withdrawal a couple of hours later, but under a plan different yet again to that followed by the New Zealanders, having Fuka as the destination, some 100 miles short of Alamein. This was not what Whiteley at Eighth Army HQ had expected: he told the Court of Enquiry that Eighth Army's 'whole plan was that XIII Corps should attack North to help them [X Corps] out [of Mersa Matruh]…They were to hold the high ground until after X Corps had started … [but] XIII Corps just disappeared and left X Corps up the pole.'[13]

The New Zealanders fought their way through the Afrika Korps in a dramatic and bloody night battle, described by Rommel as 'a wild melee', in which his own headquarters became involved:

> The firing between my forces and the New Zealanders grew to an extraordinary pitch of violence and my headquarters was soon ringed by burning vehicles, making it the target for continuous enemy fire. I soon had enough of this and ordered the headquarters and the staff to withdraw to the south-east. One can scarcely conceive the confusion which reigned that night.[14]

Eighth Army HQ was not aware that the New Zealanders were going to withdraw and had ordered an attack by X Corps to relieve the pressure on them. The attack went ahead that night without much success. X Corps discovered in the morning of the 28th that they were now isolated and cut off in Matruh. They were ordered to 'slip out' after dark that day 'with whole force on broad front', being assured that Gott's XIII Corps would cover them, but their message informing Gott of the timing of the breakout only reached Gott half an hour after the breakout began. Even so, though 10th Indian Division suffered quite heavy losses, the bulk of X Corps including the two surviving brigades of 50th Division barged their way through the encircling Afrika Korps and arrived back at Alamein, disorganised and bewildered rather than demoralised.

The misunderstandings at Mersa Matruh are a measure of the confusion and exhaustion of all the senior officers and their staffs by this stage: Carver later calculated that over six weeks he averaged two and a half hours sleep per night.[15] Most of the New Zealanders and a good proportion of the other troops did fight their way back to Alamein through the encircling Afrika Korps, but in a state of disorganisation, and more than somewhat sceptical of their own commanders. 2nd West Yorks' survivors'

13   TNA WO 106/2235: Operations 26/5-2/7/42 Report of Court of Enquiry.
14   Liddell Hart (ed.), *Rommel Papers*, p. 238.
15   Carver, *Out of Step*, p. 119.

view of their superiors probably reflected the opinion of much of Eighth Army. After having their transport and artillery removed to make the New Zealand Division fully mobile in Ritchie's reorganisation, and spending a couple of weeks bathing in the sea for want of any orders, the West Yorks had been sent up to defend five aerodromes on the escarpment 15 miles east of Mersa Matruh, 'quite absurd as we had nothing but our rifles, and we couldn't even have stopped a single armoured car … In my opinion, it was entirely due to the RAF, (and the ordinary or common-or-garden Private Soldier), that the Generals were not entirely routed.'[16]

Dorman-Smith, who by his account had acquired the role of 'CGS Army Group', issued an Appreciation on 28 June in which he declared the intention 'to keep Eighth Army in being as a mobile field force and resist by every possible means any further attempt by the enemy to advance further eastwards.'[17] If neither Fuka nor Alamein could be held Eighth Army would fight on the western edge of the Delta, and would divide to defend both Cairo and Alexandria. A copy was sent to Corbett, who under the heading 'The Chief has decided to save the Army' issued detailed provisional orders for this plan and sent them to Gott. Dorman-Smith later acknowledged that 'The effect on Gott's mind, and on the acting commander of NZ Div, to whom Gott on June 29th unwisely repeated it, was to prove unfortunate.'[18]

Friedrich von Mellenthin, Rommel's Intelligence chief, wrote after the war that 'for the student of generalship there are few battles so instructive' as Mersa Matruh.[19] In the sense that it displayed how one force could achieve a complete moral superiority over another, this is certainly true, for the Panzerarmee took on a force many times its own size in infantry and guns, and was outnumbered nearly three to one in armour. Yet the Panzerarmee inflicted losses in personnel (mainly prisoners) amounting to at least its own size and drove the Eighth Army back 100 miles in disorder. Whether Ritchie, left to himself, would have succeeded in holding and defeating the Afrika Korps is not a question that is often considered. His columns which were supposed to at least delay Rommel's advance were swept away in minutes, but the three German divisions were widely separated, very weak in numbers and short of ammunition. The New Zealanders were fresh, as reliable as ever, some elements at least of 1st Armoured Division were prepared to counterattack, and with two more divisions in Mersa Matruh itself there was certainly enough firepower to overwhelm any of the German formations, or to beat off any assault that the Panzerarmee was capable of mounting. The decisive factor was moral rather than material: British commanders had little faith in Ritchie, and the change of command produced even more uncertainty. Given forty eight hours to stabilise the army, it might have been possible to fight successfully to a conclusion. Rommel was not inclined to be so generous.

---

16   Colvin, 'Eighth Army Operations', p. 176.
17   JRL GOW/133 1/12/16, p. 19.
18   JRL GOW/133 1/12/16, p. 19.
19   Mellenthin, *Panzer Battles*, p. 154.

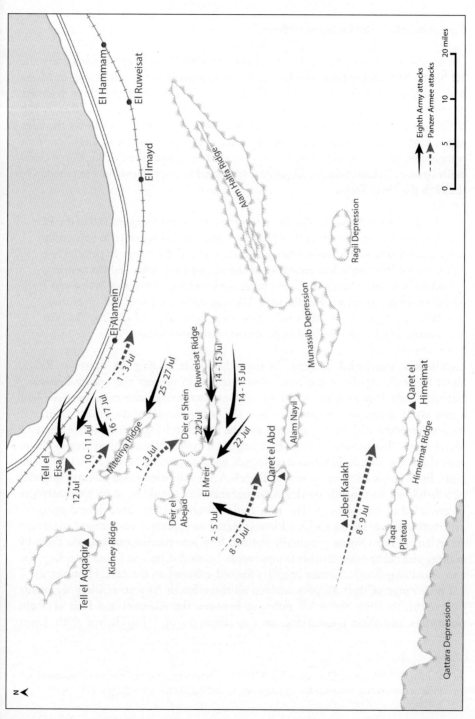

N

Eighth Army attacks
Panzer Armee attacks

0   5   10   20 miles

El Hammam
El Ruweisat
El Imayd
El Alamein

Alam Halfa Ridge

Ragil Depression

Munassib Depression

Tell el Eisa
12 Jul
1 - 3 Jul
16 - 17 Jul
10 - 11 Jul
Miteiriya Ridge
25 - 27 Jul
Deir el Shein
Ruweisat Ridge
14 - 15 Jul
14 - 15 Jul
22 Jul
1 - 3 Jul
22 Jul
El Mreir
Deir el Abejad
2 - 5 Jul
8 - 9 Jul
Qaret el Abd
Alam Nayil

Kidney Ridge
Tell el Aqqaqir

Jebel Kalakh
8 - 9 Jul
Qaret el Himeimat
Himeimat Ridge
Taqa Plateau

Qattara Depression

9. First Alamein

First Alamein – The Defensive Phase

On the fall of Tobruk, Norrie had been sent with his XXX Corps headquarters and 1st South African Division to Alamein to organise defences as a backstop to Mersa Matruh. Work had already started on the Alamein Line, consisting of three defensive positions spaced twenty miles apart, one at Alamein on the coast, another at bab el Qattara in the centre and the third at Naqb abu Dweis in the south on the edge of the Qattara Depression. Only the position at Alamein itself was anywhere near completion, the others being rudimentary to non-existent. The Afrika Korps could easily bypass all three unless a substantial armoured force operated between them. On the 28th the West Yorks,

> moved into the Abou Dweiss box, or Fortress "B", at the Southern end of the El Alamein line on the edge of the Quattara depression. We expected to find a fully prepared defensive position, with pill boxes, wire and AT mines. In point of fact there was nothing but an empty water cistern and a few holes and slit trenches, which were full of excreta. Over a year's work had been put into this line and I don't think anyone has had the sack. We may yet win the war! We spent three days here digging and, when the stores came up, wiring and mining. The men worked wonderfully, day and night, on very short water rations.[20]

Lacking any worthwhile armour, Norrie judged that holding the Ruweisat Ridge, about five miles south of the coast, was essential to prevent the enemy bypassing Alamein itself. Ruweisat was a 200 feet high east-west ridge, five miles long and half a mile wide, which gave observation over the northern half of the position. Since it was impossible to dig into the solid rock of the Ruweisat Ridge itself, Norrie created a fourth box at the westernmost tip of the ridge in a shallow depression at Deir el Shein, manned by the 18th Indian Infantry Brigade with supporting Matildas and anti-tank guns. By doing so he went counter to Eighth Army's directives that infantry brigades be refashioned into mobile battlegroups and that they should be in no circumstances be encircled or immobilised. The 18th Indian Brigade spent three days digging in. 1st South African Division's Dan Pienaar feared encirclement and refused to occupy the Alamein box. Norrie eventually shamed him into putting one brigade there by making clear that other British troops would be used if he was found wanting. The two remaining South African brigades formed columns to the east. However the 7 1/2 mile range of their 25-pdrs enabled all three South African artillery regiments to comfortably cover the 4 1/2 mile gap between the Alamein and Deir el Shein perimeters and their massed fire on the afternoon of 1 July halted 90th Light

20   Colvin, 'Eighth Army Operations', p. 176. 'Very short water rations' meant a maximum of four pints a day per man for all purposes, including personal washing and vehicles' radiators.

Division, now numbering no more than a reinforced battalion. With XXX Corps static and concentrated, the Corps artillery commander was also able to bring to bear his two medium regiments,[21] and the use of divisional artillery centrally controlled as a 'seventy-two gun battery' made its debut.[22] The German attempt to move through the Alamein line was halted by the intensity of the fire and nothing – not even the presence of Rommel himself – could induce the men of 90th Light Division to resume their forward movement.

Meantime, the 18th Indian Infantry Brigade at Deir el Shein, short of mines and wire, had dug in as best they could, then received instructions from Eighth Army on 1 July to revert to a mobile role.[23] The 80 lorries that they required for this change of plan did not materialise, so the brigade remained in place, All that day it held off an attack by both panzer divisions, the DAK losing 18 of its 55 tanks before overrunning the defenders in the evening. Calls to 1st Armoured Division for assistance went unanswered until late in the afternoon, too late to prevent the defence giving way.[24] Reasons given for inaction included lack of petrol, poor going, and a report from the division's armoured cars that all seemed to be quiet at Deir el Shein.[25] Dorman-Smith, 'who hated the whole concept of boxes' reacted to the news that the box had fallen with the thought: 'the last of the Bl ---- boxes'.[26] But in fact defensive boxes were an appropriate tactic when appropriately sited and supported, and it was only the lack, or failure, of supporting armour that made them untenable. There is no doubt 18th Indian Brigade achieved more in its static role, knocking out a third of the Afrika Korps' tanks, than it could have done as lorried infantry.

The 90th Light Division resumed its attack on the 2nd but was held by the South African brigades and a column of 10th Indian Division, while the two panzer divisions' renewed efforts to break through south of Ruweisat Ridge met what Eighth Army intended as a decisive counter offensive by the British armour. 22nd Armoured Brigade was ordered to move 16 miles west, then swing north to meet, engage and destroy the main body of enemy armour. These instructions did not impress one recipient, an artillery troop commander supporting 3rd CLY:

> The plan was utter nonsense, I at once told Bill [his battery commander]: those Mk IIIs that I had been reporting all morning were not there just for fun, and to expect us to break through them and all the acres of guns and MT and drive 16 miles behind the enemy's lines was crass stupidity.[27]

21   Carver, *Out of Step*, p. 124.
22   Bruce I. Gudmundsson, *The Seventy-Two-Gun Battery* (New York: MHQ Inc., 1991) and *The Journal of Military History*, Spring 1991, Vol. 3., No. 3, p. 36.
23   TNA WO 106/2235: Tobruk Enquiry, Norrie's testimony p. 296.
24   Seton-Watson, *Dunkirk-Alamein-Bologna*, p. 123
25   Playfair, *Official History*, vol iii, p. 341.
26   JRL GOW133 1/2/17, p. 24.
27   Seton-Watson, *Dunkirk – Alamein – Bologna*, p. 125.

They went forward two miles, ran into the advance of the Afrika Korps and the resulting standoff reduced German tank numbers to 26 by the end of the day against 22nd Armoured Brigade's 38 Grants and over 60 cruisers.[28]

For 3 July XIII Corps in the south was ordered to take the offensive with the New Zealand Division's two brigades and 5th Indian Division's single weak brigade. They were to drive west, then north to the coast to cut off and destroy Panzerarmee Afrika. Dorman-Smith blamed the failure of this move on the 'dour scepticism [that] pervaded the higher echelon of the New Zealand Division, inhibiting action', believing Corbett's provisional retreat order had discouraged both Gott and the New Zealand Division from taking risks.[29] Orders for infantry divisions to take on the Afrika Korps without assistance from British armour no doubt contributed to the New Zealanders' scepticism. No progress was made, but the Ariete Division lost much of its combat power when after boldly advancing by night its artillery column found itself at dawn isolated under the guns of the New Zealand 4th Brigade and was captured.

On 4 and 5 July Eighth Army continued to urge Gott and XIII Corps towards the enemy rear but decided on more limited objectives in view of limited strength and limited will among the troops and commanders to conform to what appeared to them to be unrealistic plans. A column from 7th Motor Brigade did reach Fuka on the coast 50 miles west of Alamein only to withdraw after shelling an airfield for half an hour, but column actions did not create major difficulties for the Germans. Though Dorman-Smith thought they made Rommel 'clearly anxious about his southern flank',[30] there is no evidence that such was the case. Nor was 1st Armoured Division, the only formation with any real offensive capacity, minded to force a breakthrough: Dorman-Smith watched 'in fascinated horror' as its commander, Lumsden, met with Norrie and 'immediately and brusquely' demanded that his division be relieved. 'Norrie tried but failed to calm him; Lumsden was over-excited and emphatically undisciplined.'[31] Norrie was replaced as XXX Corps commander by Ramsden, the commander of 50th Division, on the following day; accounts differ as to whether he resigned or was sacked.[32]

The Panzerarmee made one more attempt to break the Alamein position on the night of 8 July by attacking the New Zealand Division in its somewhat exposed position in the south, only to find that both the New Zealanders and 5th Indian Division had been already been withdrawn and the attack fell on their empty slit trenches at Bab al Qattara. The DAK was nonetheless in position to at least threaten another outflanking move round Eighth Army which on past form could be expected to retreat and disintegrate under the strains of mobile warfare.

---

28   I.S.O. Playfair, vol iii, p. 343.
29   JLR GOW133, 1/12/17 p. 26.
30   JLR GOW133 1/12/17, p. 30.
31   JLR GOW133 1/12/17, p. 29.
32   Major General Dorman-O'Gowan, "1st. Alamein: The Battle that saved Cairo" in *Purnell's History of the Second World War,* No. 36, p.989, and Carver, *Out of Step,* p. 128.

But they were forestalled when, on the night of the 9/10 July the 9th Australian Division, newly arrived from Syria and supported by the 44th Royal Tank Regiment, launched an attack at the northern end of the Alamein line. Together they had been ordered to take the low ridge of tel el Eisa about three miles west of the Alamein box so as to give some depth to the defences at Alamein. At the same time a South African brigade attacked from the Alamein box to the southwest.[33] The Italian Sabratha Division crumpled under an intense bombardment and the Australian advance was only halted by a scratch force of newly arrived German troops led by Friedrich von Mellenthin, the DAK's intelligence chief, reinforced as quickly as Rommel could bring up his armour from the south. The Australians did succeed in capturing tel el Eisa the following day, and even raided southwards, but Rommel had reacted swiftly to the danger to his communications along the coast road and sealed off the penetration. Eighth Army had not planned to exploit a breakthrough at this point and had no mobile forces ready to do so. Apart from the territory gained, the most significant outcome of the battle was the destruction of 621st Wireless Intercept Company and the death of Captain Seebohm, when the Australians overran its position. When Seebohm's liaison officer told Rommel that he had lost contact with his superior, Rommel asked where the company had been positioned. 'I showed him on the map. "Then it is *futsch* – lost!" he said, absolutely furious.'[34] Rommel continued his efforts to retake tel el Eisa on the 12 and 13 July with the greatest aerial support he could muster as well as 21st Panzer Division and all the army heavy artillery and launched yet another attack on the 14th. Recapturing Tel el Eisa and cutting off the Australians now holding the position would have been a major victory and could have opened the road to Alexandria. Von Mellenthin witnessed the engagement:

> Late that evening 21 Panzer attacked with the setting sun at their backs, and under cover of heavy bombardment. But again the attacking infantry moved too late so that the paralysing effects of the bombing were lost. Nevertheless we reached the coastal railway and might have done more had it not been for a galling fire from the Alamein Box. Fighting continued long after dark and the Australian infantry showed that they were the same redoubtable opponents we had met in the siege of Tobruk.[35]

It was now clear that British defences would need more than threats to force a withdrawal and that the effectiveness of their newly concentrated artillery fire would make any direct attack on their positions extremely costly. Rommel could only order a pause in the action while he built up armoured reserves for a mobile offensive. The Australians continued their local attacks on 16 and 17 July, and again on the 22nd,

33 I.S.O. Playfair, vol iii, p. 345.
34 Behrendt, *Rommel's Intelligence*, p. 170.
35 Mellenthin, *Panzer Battles*, p.167

when they expanded their their hold at Tel el Eisa and advanced about a mile south of Tel el Makkh, greatly increasing the security of the Alamein box and again alarming Rommel enough for him to commit his meagre resources of German infantry in counterattacks.

On 28 June, the Germans had launched their summer offensive in southern Russia and made rapid progress towards the Caucasus. As well as threatening Russian oil supplies, this brought into focus the long feared pincer movement through Persia that might reach Britain's own oilfields in the Middle East and link up with Rommel in Egypt. Auchinleck felt obliged to ask London to clarify whether the defence of Egypt should take priority over establishing a force in Syria and Persia strong enough to hold off an attack there. On 12 July Churchill replied that only by defeating, destroying or driving back Rommel's force could sufficient forces be released for a Syrian front. In Dorman-Smith's view, since there was no safe distance to which Rommel could be driven back, Auchinleck was obliged to accept this as an instruction for an immediate effort to destroy the Panzer Armee despite the battle-worn state of Eighth Army. However the strategic situation was not as urgent as Dorman-Smith painted it, for analysis in London concluded that, due to the distances, the terrain and the severity of the Russian and Caucasian winter, German forces could not reach the Levant before spring 1943.[36] Even Dorman-Smith conceded that as early as September reinforcements would arrive in Egypt from which the northern front could be reinforced.[37] A defensive stance was therefore quite feasible and the series of battles which Eighth Army undertook for the remainder of July seems to be as much a product of Auchinleck's determination and aggression and Dorman-Smith's fertile military mind as a strategically validated decision. Indeed, Eighth Army's operation orders numbers 89 and 90 of 4 and 5 July, well before Churchill's intervention, are already expressed in terms of 'pursue and destroy', and 'attack and destroy', consistent with the combativeness shown by Auchinleck during 'Crusader', and in his interventions in January and during the Gazala battle. It is however clear in retrospect that Eighth Army needed rest and reorganisation, time to allow units to reform and re-equip, men to return to their original regiments, new drafts to be absorbed, and for some at least a period out of the front line. To expect formations as battered as the divisions and brigades at Alamein to manage a series of operations as complex and reliant on co-ordination and timing as those planned by Eighth Army in July without rehearsal, training or a common doctrine, was hardly short of irresponsible. The demands made on the troops and the poor planning and staff work in every one of these actions are more reminiscent of first world war bungling than of the modernist military thinking on which Dorman-Smith prided himself. Equally, it was characteristic of Auchinleck's solitary nature and of Dorman-Smith's inability to engage that neither made visits to units to assess conditions, talk to commanders or try

36   I.S.O. Playfair, vol iii, p. 364.
37   I.S.O. Playfair, vol iii, p. 364.

to lift morale. There is not a single photograph or report of either so doing, and while the somewhat patchy morale of the army was clear to all, Auchinleck's requests to London for a restoration of the death penalty for desertion was hardly the appropriate remedy.

First Alamein – The Counter-offensives.

Eighth Army launched three major operations in July intended to to break through German positions with British mobile troops and drive back or destroy the Axis army. Each of these followed a pattern of a successful break-in by infantry followed by failure of the armoured forces to consolidate the gains made, and then German counter-attacks inflicting heavy losses. One New Zealand participant wrote of the 'incompetence' of Eighth Army:[38] it could more generously be seen as the 'friction' of war, at an extreme level, following disorganisation of units, changes in command and sheer exhaustion after seven weeks constant action. But the failures were consistent in nature with the reverses of the preceding month, Eighth Army lacking the doctrine that would have enabled units and formations to work together, confident that colleagues would perform their allotted roles. And once again the regimental, social and national distinctions of Eighth Army handicapped co-operation and mutual understanding.

The first of Eighth Army's counterattacks proper, Operation Bacon, aimed to take the dominant feature in the centre of the Alamein position, Ruweisat Ridge. While 5th Indian Division fought from east to west along the ridge, the New Zealand Division was to be launched against the western end from the south on the night of 14/15 July, with the assurance that after they took the ridge British armour would join them by first light to support them against the inevitable German counter attack. The New Zealanders were confident enough – they were veterans of Greece and Crete, Sidi Rezegh and Mersa Matruh – but Brigadier Kippenberger of 5th NZ Brigade doubted whether 1st Armoured Division would fulfil its orders to advance by night in support. New Zealand experience of tank/infantry co-operation had been with units of the Royal Tank Regiment with whom they had trained, not with the mostly cavalry regiments of 1st Armoured Division, whose reputation among the infantry by now was not the highest. Eighth Army's orders to 1st Armoured Division were 'To protect the Southern and Western flank of the NZ Div attack from first light 15th July'.[39] But the orders that 2nd Armoured Brigade received from 1st Armoured Division HQ stated merely that on receipt of a codeword they should 'be prepared to move' to exploit success or meet an enemy counter attack, in other words to await

---

38   Peter Bates, *The Dance of War: The Story of the Battle for Egypt* (London: Leo Cooper, 1992), p. 169.

39   TNA WO 169/4006: 1 Armd Div Op. Order 15.

instructions.[40] The New Zealanders, having worked successfully with British armour at night in the past, expected the tanks to be supporting them on the objective by dawn. The need for British armour to be on hand was the more critical since 4th New Zealand Brigade's position at first light was always going to be beyond the range of their division's field artillery. However 1st Armoured Division had not practised movement in the dark and did not see such a move as feasible. As during 'Aberdeen' there was no overall commander of the operation who could have taken into account the 'frictions' and have resolved the misunderstanding, for the New Zealand Division was under XIII Corps, while 1st Armoured and 5th Indian Brigade were under XXX Corps. Furthermore, a couple of mischances disrupted both the planning and the execution of the operation. Gatehouse of 2nd Armoured Brigade was wounded and replaced by Ray Briggs who arrived too late for the briefing to meet with the New Zealand commanders and discuss their requirements, and then 22nd Armoured Brigade, assigned to support 4th New Zealand Brigade's open flank from first light, was delayed into action after 'being called on to deal with a threat to the south west' the evening before. Their liaison officer accompanying the New Zealanders lost wireless contact 'due to the jamming of our wireless by the enemy' and was unable to summon the brigade up to support the New Zealanders, though he also heard and read later 'that Brigadier Fisher commanding 22nd Armoured Brigade got his map references wrong and did not appear in the right place.'[41] In the event although the New Zealand attack was outstandingly successful, overrunning the Axis defences and taking thousands of Italians prisoner, it was transformed into a heavy defeat as British armour failed to appear in time to halt the DAK's early counter attack. Brigadier Kippenberger of 5th New Zealand Brigade went in person in a failing Bren gun carrier to urge 2nd Armoured Brigade on. He eventually found their HQ, the staff all looking through their field glasses at the smoke rising from the ridge:

> The Brigadier received me coolly. I did my best not to appear agitated, said I was the commander of 5 New Zealand Infantry Brigade, that we were on Ruweisat Ridge and were being attacked in the rear by tanks ... Would he move up and help? He said he would send a reconnaissance tank. I said there was no time. Would he move his whole brigade? While he was patiently explaining some difficulty, General Lumsden drove up. I gave him exactly the same information. Without answering he walked round to the back of his car, unfastened a shovel and with it killed a scorpion with several blows... The General asked where we were and the Brigadier pointed out the place on the map. 'But I told you to be there at first light,' General Lumsden then said, placing his finger on Point 63.

40   TNA WO 169/4210: 2 Armd Bde War Diary
41   Major the Earl Haig, *My Father's Son* (London: Leo Cooper, 1999) p. 106.

Kippenberger was lost for words at Lumsden's insouciance. The New Zealand troops were less restrained. One officer wrote home:

> Our boys were supposed to have armoured support, as the Jerry always counter attack with tanks. Well our boys went through them like butter with the bayonet and gained the objective easily and started looking around for our tanks, not a tank of ours was to be seen, but they soon saw plenty of German tanks, they moved around and cut off a lot of our boys and shot them to pieces. As it turned out the Tommy tanks were sitting about two miles back waiting for orders!!! The crews were out frying sausages while our lads were being torn to pieces … it was a disgraceful affair, it's terrible to see the best troops in the world slaughtered like sheep because of those Pommie bastards.[42]

The 4th New Zealand Brigade's limited number of anti-tank guns were knocked out, its haul of prisoners was lost and such heavy casualties suffered that it never reformed as a brigade. Dorman-Smith's post war comment, 'It is still a matter of surprise that the commander of the New Zealand Division does not appear to have protested at the difficulty of his task',[43] indicates a loftiness similar to that of Lumsden and Briggs.

On 22 July another full blooded attempt, Operation Splendour, to write down the Panzerarmee followed a similar pattern. On this occasion Gott would direct the entire operation. Once again, an Indian Brigade would attack westwards to seize the last mile of Ruweisat Ridge while a fresh brigade of the New Zealand Division advanced by night from the south to the el Meir depression a couple of miles beyond the western tip of the ridge. Once again, the New Zealanders met their objective only to be overrun at first light by the DAK as 2nd Armoured Brigade, delayed by mines, was unable to support them in time. A follow-up attack by the three newly arrived and wholly inexperienced Territorial Army regiments of 23rd Armoured Brigade had been planned to exploit the breakthrough, in the belief that the defenders would be disorganised and vulnerable. It was launched despite the setback to the New Zealanders and ended in disaster with the loss of 93 out of 104 tanks. Unsupported by artillery or infantry, they ran first on to a minefield and then into the full strength of the Panzerarmee's anti-tank defence. The only positive of the occasion was to impress the nearby New Zealanders with the courage and determination of at least some of the British armour.

Ultra and other sources made it clear that the Panzerarmee was still stretched almost to breaking point despite a flow of reinforcements and the gradually increasing density of their positions behind minefields. Eighth Army planned its third attempt to break through as an attack by the Australians between the Ruweisat and Miteirya Ridges

---

42 Quoted in Jonathan Fennell, *Combat and Morale in the North African Campaign*, (Cambridge: Cambridge University Press, 2011), p. 80.
43 Dorman-O'Gowan, *Purnell's History*, p. 990.

26. Briggs and Lumsden. (Imperial War Museum E016464)

for the 24/25 July only to find that Morshead of 9th Australian Division objected on the grounds that his troops were nearing exhaustion from their repeated (and largely successful) local attacks in the coastal sector around Alamein. Morshead no longer had confidence in his Corps commander, Ramsden, nor in British armour's ability to support his men, and he invoked the right to refer to his government before accepting orders that might seriously endanger his troops. Ramsden suggested Auchinleck invite Morshead for tea, over which the matter was discussed and a compromise reached. The South Africans would first clear a gap in the minefields, the Australians would make the break into enemy positions and a British infantry brigade would advance through, clearing further minefields. The gap would be exploited by 2nd Armoured Brigade and 4th Light Armoured Brigade. Organising the deployment of five brigades from five different divisions none of which had previously worked or trained with each other required a 48 hour postponement of the operation. Dorman-Smith wanted the operation cancelled altogether, believing the delay allowed the Afrika Korps to regain its balance after the attack of the 22nd though there was no evidence that the Panzerarmee had been much troubled then, indeed von Mellenthin had regarded it as 'a disaster for the British' and 'very favourable to us and encouraged the hope that we could hang on at Alamein.'[44] However, Auchinleck favoured carrying it through.

Morshead's attack when eventually launched under the codename Operation Manhood failed in very similar circumstances to the earlier efforts: poor co-ordination between formations, difficulty in clearing and negotiating minefields, inability of armour to support the infantry in a timely fashion, and the rapid and efficient German counterattacks which overran two British and one Australian infantry battalions. Like Operations Bacon and Splendour before it, Manhood never even came close to the objective of destroying the Panzerarmee or driving it back to a safe distance from Alexandria. As part of an attritional struggle it could only have been counted a success if it had worn down Rommel's infantry and forced him to commit his armour in unsuccessful local counterattacks rather than husbanding it for a counter offensive. But this final battle of First Alamein did not succeed in wearing down Rommel's troops: within a month the Panzerarmee had reinforced and rebuilt its strength to reach its most significant advantage in numbers and equipment of the campaign.

The Panzerarmee recorded its opinion of the Eighth Army's performance in the summer, and it was not complimentary.[45] Its view of the high command was that British 'slowness and clumsiness, the lack of initiative and tactical versatility observed to date had not changed. There was no alteration in tactical planning if the battle developed in a way which had not been expected beforehand.'

It noted the lack of close co-operation between infantry and armoured formations other than a few cases of infantry formations supported by a few infantry tanks. Tank units held for exploitation followed up very slowly and were not nearly quick enough in exploiting the success gained by the lorried infantry. British armoured technique had improved to the extent that armour was used in brigade strength as opposed to squadron or regimental strength as in the previous year, but armoured commanders had 'not yet mastered the art of handling larger formations with speed and manoeuvrability'. In defence they aimed to extend their defensive line to outflank the attacking German force, resulting in a long thin line, itself very vulnerable to an outflanking move. Attacks were supported by heavy artillery fire, including HE fire from the Grants, but in attack no co-operation with anti-tank guns was observed. Concerning infantry, in defence 'the fighting was extremely tough and embittered. Hardly ever was it possible to put the enemy to flight. Either he withdrew according to plan or defended himself until he was annihilated or captured.'

British infantry tended to attack by night with the bayonet, turning to defence to await counterattack. The German view was that it was a very clumsy method, unsupported by artillery and vulnerable to counter attacks. The one British strength was their artillery, which had great versatility, good and plentiful observers, and useful range.

44   Mellenthin, *Panzer Battles*, p.169
45   TNA CAB 146/15: Appendix 9, p.202 DAK's Report on Fighting, May-July 1942.

Some in Eighth Army appreciated that their tactical methods needed examination. Early in July, Whiteley, who was still officially Eighth Army's chief of staff though much of his role had been taken over by Dorman-Smith, committed his thoughts to paper in a summary of how he believed the army's tactics should be modified in the light of the summer's experience.[46] He appreciated that speed of decision was vital, that time could be saved by quick and logical appreciations so as to avoid changes after orders had been issued, and by 'broadcasting the commander's intention and general plan, having due regard to secrecy' and 'cutting out lengthy discussions, gossip and unnecessary questions.' *Aufragstaktik* by another name, in fact. Frequent and regular information back to the senior commander in form of a running commentary would improve speed of decision and flexibility better than lengthy and out of date reports. Motor brigades must co-operate with armoured brigades and remain mobile, artillery was to form the basis of both defence and attack, while armour attacked enemy flank & rear rather than their front. In defence, since individual infantry battalions were not strong enough to provide all round defence against an attack in force by tanks while holding sufficient ground to house artillery in the quantity required, they must therefore be sited in groups, compact enough to cover ground with small arms, anti-tank and mortar fire. But like Dorman-Smith, Whiteley makes no attempt to analyse the reasons for the Panzerarmee's success, nor to look at its tactical methods, and, perhaps like Dorman-Smith with a nod to Liddell Hart's doctrine of mobility, seeks to match the Afrika Korps in manoeuvre warfare.

Change of Command

In the aftermath of 1st Alamein, a little more than a fortnight after the closure of the 'Manhood' offensive, Churchill and Brooke visited Eighth Army and Middle East HQ. Within four days they had replaced Auchinleck, Corbett, Dorman-Smith and Ramsden with Harold Alexander as Commander in Chief Middle East, Bernard Montgomery as Eighth Army Commander, de Guingand his Chief of Staff, Brian Horrocks commander of XIII Corps and Oliver Leese commander of XXX Corps. In an unexpected but remarkably smooth flurry of promotions, dismissals and imports of new blood, the management at Middle East and Army HQ and at division and corps level largely changed, except in the Commonwealth formations. One of the moves that illuminates the tensions in Eighth Army's command under the previous regime is that of Major General Richard McCreery.

Brooke had been keen since the beginning of the year to send out to North Africa a Royal Armoured Corps Commander to improve the tactical leadership of the armoured forces. This was not to Auchinleck's liking. In the wake of Martel's visit in January Auchinleck perhaps feared the advent of an Armoured Group system

46   TNA WO 201/452: Notes on the main lessons from recent operations in the Western Desert, 13 July 1942.

and wrote to Brooke to oppose Martel's conviction that 'the handling of armoured formations is so technical and delicate a business that the ordinary commander cannot hope to cope with it.'[47] He included a comment, 'It is the same old story of the cavalry all over again!', the meaning of which is not entirely clear but perhaps refers to 'empire building' by that arm. He believed that a Major General overseeing Royal Armoured Corps activities would encourage the primacy of armour instead of all arms co-operation. Rather than a RAC Commander he advocated the appointment of a Director of Military Training to train all three arms in closest possible association, to tie the infantry & gunners to the armour, and not the converse, and teach the RAC how to get the best from their tanks when thus supported. A RAC Brigadier under the DMT would advise and supervise training of tank regiments. But in the end Auchinleck acceded to Brooke's suggestion and McCreery arrived in Cairo on 27th March as Major General RAC, a month after Harding, also in the rank of major general, had been appointed Director of Military Training.

Like Lumsden, Dick McCreery was a former CO of the 12th Lancers. Earlier in the war he had been Alexander's chief staff officer at 1st Infantry Division, then commanded 2nd Armoured Brigade in France in 1940 during the expedition to northern France in an ill fated final effort to bolster the French army after Dunkirk. On return to England he was promoted to command the newly raised 8th Armoured Division. He was relatively advanced in his thinking on armoured warfare, for his experience in France had convinced him of the need for all arms cooperation. He continued to emphasise in August 1941 the importance of sufficient infantry and artillery in armoured formations, citing German experience in Russia where panzer divisions were finding their advance slowed by diversions to mop up the encircled Russians, a task best suited to infantry.[48] This was an impressive insight, since at that stage little information was emerging from the Soviets. Nor was he parochial or careerist in his views on the primacy of armour: he opposed forming RAC Group HQs since RAC officers would inevitably be chosen to run them while infantry and gunner officers were likely to be sidelined and deprived of experience, so that the army as a whole would suffer and the introduction of a tactical doctrine for handling armoured divisions would be delayed. In the autumn of 1941 his division's performance in Exercise 'Bumper', the biggest land forces exercise held to date in Great Britain, impressed not just his immediate superior, Lieutenant General Harold Alexander, and the Commandant of the RAC, Martel, but also Brooke, then C-in-C Land Forces. When Brooke was disturbed by the failures in North Africa in the winter of 1941, he insisted that McCreery be appointed major general overseeing the RAC in the Middle East. Auchinleck was reluctant to accept him in the role, at least in part because Auchinleck had his own ideas as to how armoured forces in the desert

47   JRL GB133 AUC629 to Brooke 12/1/42 and AUC640 to Brooke 15 January 1942.
48   Richard Mead, *The Last Great Cavalryman: The Life of General Sir Richard McCreery* (Barnsley: Pen and Sword, 2012), p. 31.

should be organised and managed but also perhaps because his own rather austere, obstinate character and provincial Ulster and Indian Army roots did not sit well with McCreery's Etonian and cavalry background. Theirs was not a happy relationship. It did not help that both were capable of suddenly losing their temper and neither were willing to compromise on matters of principle. Brooke wrote after the war, 'I had not expected that he [McCreery] would be practically ignored and never referred to by the Auk on the employment and use of armoured forces.'[49] On arrival, McCreery met with Auchinleck on 3 April 1942, then spent his first month familiarising himself with the units, commanders and organisation with which he would be dealing in a theatre that extended from the Western Desert to Iraq. It was not until the beginning of May that he was back in Cairo in a position to influence policy on training and tactics. By 8 May Dorman Smith was also back in Cairo taking over from Galloway as a Deputy Chief of the General Staff, and it is quite possible that at that stage McCreery was, as his biographer says, invited to the C-in-C's major conferences but that 'he was not a member of the inner circle, which was dominated not by Corbett but by an increasingly influential Dorman-Smith.'[50] His presence would not have been welcomed by either, for Corbett saw himself as having responsibility for doctrine, while Dorman-Smith had never cared for McCreery since Staff College days, christening him 'Dreary McCreery'. And with Eighth Army committed to the Box system and brigade groups, McCreery's doubts on the viability of both would have made him awkward company in tactical conferences, especially after he and de Guingand war gamed Operation Buckshot, the plan for advancing from Gazala, and demonstrated the vulnerability of the 'cowpats' to armoured attack. Once the Gazala battle had started on 27 May McCreery's concern was the replacement of armoured vehicles for the fighting units and reforming battered regiments, a task carried out with great efficiency by his command. But on 20 July he was confronted with a reorganisation proposed by Dorman-Smith that the armoured divisions should be broken up and each armoured brigade should be combined with two infantry brigades to form mobile divisions. According to Dorman-Smith 'the RTC generals (Gatehouse) agreed but the project was violently resisted by the Cavalry generals (McCreery)'.[51] The row festered: on 23 or 24 July the proposals for mixed divisions were again rejected by McCreery who 'refused point blank to end the traditional separation of armour and infantry into their own divisions.' Auchinleck threatened to sack McCreery 'in blazing fury and sent him away.'[52] McCreery's biographer mentions another meeting on 26 July, when he is said to have met the Auk and Harding to discuss proposals for reorganisation, the Auk becoming very angry but agreeing to consult all armoured

49   Danchev & Tolman, *Brooke Diaries*, p. 235, Note for 3 March.
50   Mead, *McCreery*, E-book Chapter 13, loc2084.
51   Liddell Hart Centre for Military Archives, DS letter to R.W. Thompson, 17 June 1964.
52   Graecen, *Chink*, p.224

commanders.[53] McCreery was not removed at this stage, for on 28 July he wrote home 'I had a real set to with my boss 2 days ago and I hope I have cleared the air a bit. I cannot be just a yes man and did not come out here just to sit in our office whilst others give most unsound advice on matters they know nothing about!' But on 29 July, in the presence of Harding and Dorman-Smith, McCreery reacted violently against a further proposal to add a fourth squadron to armoured regiments in order to maintain regimental effectiveness after initial casualties. This could only be done by breaking up and amalgamating existing cavalry regiments, seriously upsetting the traditional cavalry regimental system. This, and the re-grouping of infantry and armour into mobile divisions, appeared to McCreery 'to strike at the heart of the sacrosanct cavalry idea. Auchinleck, generally so tolerant, suddenly became angry' and declared that if McCreery would not obey orders he would have him removed. He sent him off and wrote to Brooke accordingly.[54] In a letter to Corelli Barnet after the war, Dorman-Smith says of the proposals that McCreery 'resented them totally and was damn rude to Auk who fired him on the spot, reporting the matter to the CIGS.' [55] A related argument and row continued between Auchinleck and Messervy (now at Eighth Army HQ as a Deputy Chief of Staff), who submitted to Auchinleck a 'paper advocating return to traditional "Divisional" basis, in place of the tendency towards battle groups of tanks, artillery and infantry on which the "Auk" had always been keen.' He took the paper himself to Auchinleck. 'I could see the "Auk" getting more and more furious as he read it, and he kept jabbing his pencil into it. Then he tore it to pieces.'[56]

Brooke had been anxious to visit Egypt since the beginning of July to see for himself where the problems might lie. He finally arrived in Cairo on 3 August together with, to his dismay when it was proposed, Churchill, who always relished an opportunity to get closer to the action. It is possible that Churchill was influenced into travelling to Egypt by receiving Auchinleck's Appreciation of the military situation in Egypt, which was despatched to Whitehall on the 27 July.[57] The Appreciation was in fact written by Dorman-Smith and bears witness to the lucidity with which he could identify the salient factors in a given situation and persuasively suggest a course of action. Unfortunately, the course of action was not to Churchill's liking. It involved remaining on the defensive throughout August, preparing to receive an attack by the reinforced Afrika Korps, and not launching Eighth Army's own offensive until the latter half of September when the new formations arriving in Egypt would be fully trained. But the loss of Tobruk had put enormous pressure on Churchill, weakening his position at home, severely damaging Britain's international standing and raising

53 Danchev & Tolman, *Brooke Diaries*, p. 235, Note for 3 March.
54 Mead, *McCreery*, p .63.
55 CCC, BRNT2 letter 3 July 1958.
56 Maule, *Spearhead General*, p. 204.
57 Greacen, *Chink*, p. 228.

questions among allies about Britain's commitment to winning the war. He was also about to break the news to Stalin that there would be no Second Front in Europe in 1942, just as the Red Army was reeling from the German summer offensive. The planned Allied attack on Vichy French Morocco and Algeria in the autumn would not be an adequate substitute in Soviet eyes and would be likely to meet much more determined resistance from French Vichy forces if Rommel remained undefeated in Egypt. Churchill therefore thought it vital that he should assess the situation in North Africa for himself so that he could press for action in the only theatre where Britain was challenging German ground forces.

Churchill and Brooke both agreed that Auchinleck should continue in command of the Middle East and that a commander for Eighth Army should be found to serve under him, but it was not at all clear who that should be. They flew out from London to Egypt on the evening of 31 July in separate aircraft, touching down at Cornwall, Gibraltar and Malta and landing within half an hour of each other at Cairo at 6.30am on 3 August, commencing a series of meetings immediately after arrival. Brooke met and was very unimpressed by Corbett, then met with Messervy and Auchinleck. Churchill favoured Gott as the new Eighth Army commander on the basis of his reputation, then suggested that Brooke himself should take command. Brooke believed as did many others that Gott was overtired, and though sorely tempted to accept the position, he recognised that he was a novice to the desert and was better employed as an influence on Churchill in his war management. The logical candidate, if not Gott, was Bernard Montgomery, the rising star in British Home Forces, already lined up to command British troops in the planned Allied invasion of Morocco and Algeria but with a history of being a difficult subordinate to Auchinleck.

At meetings on 4 August Auchinleck made clear that despite his previous experience of Montgomery, he was prepared to work with him, but Brooke knew both of them and was concerned that in practice this might not turn out well. He suspected that Auchinleck might interfere too much with Montgomery, 'ride him on too tight a rein and consequently be liable to put him out of his stride.'[58] Churchill still preferred Gott for Eighth Army but developed doubts about retaining Auchinleck as commander in chief after a visit with Auchinleck to Eighth Army headquarters at El Imayid, an isolated spot a dozen miles from the front between the Ruweisat Ridge and the sea, infested by flies and exposed to the summer sun. In this spartan, and to Churchill disagreeable, atmosphere, he heard from Auchinleck of his intention not to launch an offensive until the second half of September and became more short tempered as the exposition continued. Dorman-Smith described briefing Churchill in the Operations room as 'a little like being caged with a gorilla.'[59] Uninspired by what he heard, Churchill declined the opportunity to go through the army's plans with Auchinleck's commanders and left Eighth Army HQ prematurely to visit RAF headquarters, where

58   Danchev & Tolman, *Brooke Diaries*, p. 291.
59   Graecen, *Chink*, p. 236.

his spirits were revived by a more congenial and positive atmosphere, and where he would certainly have had his negative view of Auchinleck reinforced by Air Marshal Tedder, who had been disappointed by Eighth Army's leadership during the summer.

On the following day McCreery's dispute with Auchinleck entered the picture when Auchinleck told Brooke that he found McCreery 'inadequate and disloyal' and wanted him removed.[60] Brooke agreed, but then met Dorman-Smith to whom Auchinleck had left the task of explaining his proposed reorganisation of the armoured divisions.[61] Brooke was not impressed, finding that McCreery's proposal for the organisation of armoured divisions 'conforms to home except for some minor differences and is much sounder than the Auk's wild schemes.'[62]

27. Dorman-Smith and Brooke, 7th August 1942. (Imperial War Museum E015298)

60   Liddell Hart Centre for Military Archives, Liddell Hart papers, LH11/1941/92 Talk with D-S 2/11/42.
61   Liddell Hart Centre for Military Archives Thompson Papers, D-S Correspondence with R W Thompson, 17 June 1964.
62   Danchev & Tolman, *Brooke Diaries*, p. 312.

On 6 August McCreery met the Auk, 'was subjected another long bully' and was threatened with dismissal if he continued to resist the reorganisations.[63] That evening Brooke spoke with Churchill, who had now made up his mind about Auchinleck and suggested moving him to a lesser command covering Palestine, Iraq and Persia, while Lieutenant General Alexander was brought in from England to take command of the Middle East and Gott took over the Eighth Army. This was agreed but on the next day Gott's aircraft was shot down as he flew back to Cairo for three days leave prior to taking up command. He was killed, and, after Brooke had successfully resisted Churchill's preference for 'Jumbo' Wilson to command Eighth Army, Montgomery was summoned.

How far McCreery's conflict with Auchinleck had influenced Brooke's decision to accept a clean sweep at both Eighth Army and Middle East HQ is impossible to say, though while inspecting armoured units with the CIGS after the decision had been made, McCreery found Brooke 'v. helpful and encouraging!'[64] Auchinleck was told that Alexander would be the new C-in-C Middle East and that Montgomery would take over Eighth Army. Auchinleck was offered and refused the position of C-in-C of a new command covering Palestine, Iraq and Persia. On 9 August, in one of his last decisions as C-in-C Middle East Auchinleck informed McCreery that he was to go back to Great Britain and be replaced in Cairo by a brigadier, downgrading McCreery's post. An hour later, Alexander called on McCreery to tell him that he was to remain in the Middle East as Alexander's own Chief of Staff. Montgomery arrived in Cairo on 12 August and, with Rommel's attack expected before the end of the month, took over actual command the following afternoon. This angered Auchinleck who had expected a more dignified and less hasty exit and found his plans and conferences cancelled without notice.[65]

The clashes of personalities at senior levels of Eighth Army may seem trivial and even absurd given the issues at stake, but what a New Zealand observer called the 'crosscurrents and personality conflicts that bedevilled the Eighth Army' were clearly detrimental to its efficiency and therefore need to be considered.[66] At their heart was the uncertainty caused by the lack of a workable doctrine for armoured warfare. Given this absence of a common philosophy on which tactics could be based, it was almost inevitable that the default position for commanders became what suited their own particular arm or unit. In the British army at the time this sentiment was reinforced by the identification most felt for their own regiment or arm.

Social and class issues accentuated legitimate differences of opinion. Dorman-Smith was highly critical of what he saw as the Guards and cavalry clique, even including Brooke amongst them courtesy of Brooke's service in the Royal Horse

63   Mead, *The Last Cavalryman*, Ebook Chapter 14, loc2200.
64   Mead, *The Last Cavalryman*, E-book Chapter 14, loc2200.
65   Hamilton, *Monty*, p. 604.
66   Bates, *Dance of War*, p. 102.

Artillery. Dorman-Smith was acknowledged as a maverick but more sober individuals had similar views. Freddie de Guingand, intelligent, urbane and not in the least self-serving, saw Auchinleck's dismissal in class terms, writing to him on 8 August that it was 'a decision obviously arrived at so as to turn aside criticism from its rightful target. I'm afraid it is a victory for the old and privileged school.'[67] Horrocks, summoned to North Africa by Montgomery to command the armoured corps, asked to be assigned a less prominent role because, given his origin in the humble Middlesex Regiment, he knew from his experience of an armoured division in England that it would be impossible in the desert to command established cavalry generals with more exalted backgrounds.[68] Horrocks and Dorman-Smith had been contemporaries though not friends at both school and Sandhurst, and this was one of the few subjects on which the two might have agreed. Dorman-Smith's belief that the priorities of McCreery as Commander RAC were too often personal and regimental was justified. When a senior officer from a tank regiment was needed for a brigadiers' battle course, the Military Secretary, in charge of appointments, sent an officer from an armoured car regiment, the 12th Lancers, instead of an officer from a tank regiment. The commandant of the training establishment in question, 'naturally protested thinking the MS didn't know the difference between a tank and an armoured car. However was told to shut up as the man had been personally selected by Dick McCreery for this very important job.'

The Military Secretary later informed him that the appointment was forced through because

> Lumsden and McCreery wanted to prevent this chap commanding the 12th Lancers [but] they didn't want to hurt his feelings – by code of the old school tie – so sent him to the METC to make it appear he was being promoted!....And then they wonder why the British Army loses so many battles![69]

Lumsden and McCreery were not only friends but both were also former COs of the 12th Lancers, and it was no doubt this shared background that also allowed McCreery to ignore the intemperance under stress that Lumsden displayed throughout his time as a divisional commander, describing him as 'magnificent ... always calm, encouraging and thinking ahead'.[70] As has been noted, this was not a view shared by others, then or later. During Alamein Montgomery found him 'excitable, highly strung and easily depressed.'[71] And Gatehouse who commanded 8th Armoured Division under Lumsden during Alamein told Liddell Hart that 'on the advice of many senior officers in the Cavalry, I made it a point to get any orders he gave me in writing' because 'very

67   JRL GB133AUC991, Letter from de Guingand, 8 August 1942.
68   Hamilton, *Monty*, p. 717.
69   IWM, , Tuker Papers, Letter from 'Donald', 19 August 1959.
70   Meade, *McCreery*, p. 35.
71   Hamilton, *Monty*, p. 836.

early I discovered that if such [verbal] orders "came off" he was very quick to take the praise, but that if they did not he would flatly deny having given them.'[72]

Dorman-Smith had quixotically advised Auchinleck against acceptance of the offer of the new command in the Middle East even though it would have included a job for him. He was summoned to meet Alexander on the 15th and did so, expecting to be told that he was to succeed Corbett as Chief of Staff Middle East,[73] but was instead fired in favour of McCreery.   He returned to England, aggrieved and resentful, particularly when his rank of temporary major general was not confirmed and he reverted to brigadier. Back in London he met Liddell Hart who kept a record of their conversation in which Dorman-Smith described the 'modern defensive battle' plan which Eighth Army would have adopted had he and Auchinleck not been superseded. It was to consist of a chequer board of defensive localities 10,000 yards square each with two infantry battalions and eight 25-pdrs, surrounded by a minefield. The bulk of artillery was to be kept mobile and to be concentrated where threats appeared:

> Everything inside the chequer was fluid, except for the pivots and they were mutually supporting – at artillery range, not infantry ranges … On the rear flank of this disposition were placed the heavy armoured divisions ready to meet an attempt by the enemy to by-pass the defensive chequer, or to strike the flank of the enemy if he tried to attack the flank of the defensive disposition. The light armoured division was posted further south-west to intercept the enemy's probable flanking movement.[74]

The operational orders actually issued in July 1942 on the basis of Dorman-Smith's plan differed from Liddell Hart's account. They began with instructions for the four British infantry divisions in the Alamein line to withdraw on news of Rommel's attack to ten 'Observation Posts' on prominent features where they would split into battlegroups, up to nine for each division, so not more than battalion strength each. Some would man strongpoints – boxes by another name – spaced 10,000 yards apart to provide mutual support, others containing the bulk of the artillery were to manoeuvre between them. But in reality the crucial 'heavy armoured divisions' did not exist. The only formation then capable of facing the Afrika Korps was 22nd Armoured Brigade under 'Pip' Roberts, who in Dorman-Smith's plan found he spent his time reconnoitring different positions that he should occupy in different tactical circumstances:

---

72   Gatehouse to Liddell Hart quoted in Neil Barr, *Pendulum of War*, p. 132.
73   Information from Christopher Dorman-O'Gowan.
74   Liddell Hart Centre for Military Archives, Liddell Hart Papers, LH11/1941/92 Talk with D-S 2/11/42.

It was all rather reminiscent of the situation in the Gazala line some three months earlier in May. Then we had reconnoitred and planned our defensive positions in many areas which we might be required to occupy in a variety of circumstances. In any event, we had not been given sufficient time to occupy the one selected to deal with the German advance round Bir Hacheim and so were defeated in detail. Certainly on that occasion we recovered our balance and had the remainder of the battle been handled differently, might well have wrested the initiative from Rommel. However, at Alam Halfa at the end of July 1942, the multiplicity of plans as far as 22nd Armoured Brigade was concerned did not inspire the greatest confidence.[75]

Lieutenant General Brian Horrocks, arriving on 15 August to take over XIII Corps and prepare for Rommel's imminent attack, was equally dubious. The plan positioned 22nd Armoured Brigade three or four miles south of Alam Halfa, with four different counterattack plans. It ignored the prominent feature at Pt 102, which could be seized by the Germans and from which they could dominate the Alam Halfa Ridge. 'With this point in their hands they would then be able to advance north and attack the Miteirya Ridge [sic] from the south and thus cut Eighth Army in two.'[76] Horrocks took 22nd Armoured Brigade under his control and stationed it at Pt 102 where Roberts 'was ordered to hold this position at all costs but not to launch his Grant tanks in any attack without reference to Corps.'

Dorman-Smith's previous opposition to 'box strategy' seems to have been based on his perception of boxes as being static and defensive but it is difficult to see how his 'modern defensive battle', reliant on a network of defended areas, would have been any improvement. Given the Afrika Korps' tactical abilities and the numbers and quality of its tanks at this time, such a dispersion of units could only have been to Rommel's advantage, for by the end of August his troops were numerically at their peak relative to the Eighth Army, and the 'Observation Post' tactic would have had the effect of dispersing what by then was Eighth Army's greatest strength, its artillery.

Dorman-Smith's career did not long survive his return to England. After much lobbying he did succeed in getting command of a brigade in Great Britain, which later came under the command of a Corps led by Ritchie, also by now back in England. This awkward situation was resolved by giving Dorman-Smith another brigade in Italy, in a division led by a man he had treated with considerable lack of respect many years earlier. After commanding it competently for a few months, he was sacked in circumstances which were arguably unjust. Doubly aggrieved over his dismissal in North Africa and then in Italy, he waged a long campaign to have his rank as major-general restored, took legal action after the war against both Montgomery and

---

75   Roberts, *Desert to Baltic*, p. 93.
76   TNA CAB 106.654: Battle of Alam Halfa – Lt-Gen Sir Brian Horrocks. Horrocks clearly meant the Ruweisat Ridge.

Churchill over comments in their memoirs, and became a ready source for historians who were willing to be critical of either of them. He contributed his insider's view for John Connell's *Auchinleck,* Correlli Barnett's hugely influential *The Desert Generals* and R W Thompson's *Churchill and the Montgomery Myth.* His only published comments on the North African campaign were in three articles he wrote for Purnell's *History of the Second World War,* a part-work edited by Barrie Pitt under the auspices of Liddell Hart that appeared in the late 1960s.[77] Auchinleck met Dorman-Smith again ten years after the war, staying with him in Ireland and having his son to stay in Suffolk. Dorman-Smith felt on meeting again that they were not the same men, 'for each of us had been destroyed.'[78] He left his voluminous papers and correspondence to the John Rylands Library in Manchester, at that time independent of any government or educational institution, and of whose current strap line, 'a glorious, unrepentant celebration of imagination and learning', one feels he would have approved. It is the measure of Dorman-Smith's relationship with Auchinleck that following his lead Auchinleck also bequeathed his papers to the John Rylands Library. A sympathetic and balanced biography, *Chink* by Lavinia Graecen, was published in 1989 and, at the time of writing, an edition of his letters is planned.

Corbett's career did not last long either. There was a moment of farce when Churchill on arrival in Egypt was told by Corbett that Auchinleck had appointed him 'in command of the Army. In fact I have been living with my kit packed for the last week.' This was certainly the worst decision Auchinleck ever made, for 'poor Tom', as he is often referred to, for all his hard work and loyalty was 'uniquely stupid' according to Montgomery's Intelligence chief Bill Williams, and 'a complete fathead' in the words of de Guingand.[79] It is not known whether he had time to unpack his kit before he was definitively dismissed. After arousing Brooke's contempt by telling him that he wanted to leave the army because he was tired, he was returned to India, kit and all, and given command of 7th Indian Division only to be supplanted by Messervy for the campaign in Burma. After the war he retired to Kenya, where, decent enough man that he was, he fell out with his fellow British settlers over their racism. Hamilton suggests that by appointing Corbett to lead Eighth Army Auchinleck may have intended to exert control through Corbett as he had done through Ritchie.[80]

Auchinleck's reputation was soured by his rather graceless rejection of the role of C-in-C of the new, minor, command in Persia and Iraq – it was not considered good form to refuse a senior job in the middle of a war – but he was redeemed through his achievements when appointed C-in-C in India for the second time. He directed the huge logistical operation behind Slim's formations in Burma, and the recruiting and training of the Indian troops that formed the backbone of 14th Army's military effort,

---

77   *Purnell's History of the Second World War,* No. 34 p. 950 and No. 36 pp. 983, 992.
78   JRL GB133GOW1/2/15, p. 5.
79   Hamilton, *Monty,* p. 571.
80   Hamilton, *Monty,* p. 573.

with great efficiency. His career ended with the independence of India in 1947. His marriage was under strain through his time in North Africa and broke up in 1945, and after some years in London and then in Suffolk he retired to Morocco in 1967, rarely visiting Great Britain and avoiding direct involvement in post war arguments over North African generalship. His qualities as a man and a soldier inspired great admiration and a number of biographies, all of them laudatory.

6

Montgomery

Montgomery was already well-known in the army as a trainer of troops, a stickler for physical fitness for all ranks and intolerant of sloppiness. He had earned a reputation as a battlefield commander in France in 1940 when his 3rd Division retained its cohesion in the retreat from Belgium, making a critical night march across British lines of communication to plug the gap created by the surrender of the Belgian Army. In a campaign in which at least one British Corps commander and a divisional commander suffered a nervous collapse, he set a standard that was rewarded by rapid promotion to Corps and then Army command. As an unusually dedicated professional, he had long kept a notebook with names of colleagues and juniors whom he respected and who might be of use later. De Guingand, who was made chief of staff of Eighth Army less than a month before Montgomery's arrival, had known known him for years. He was the polar opposite of Montgomery in character, amusing, sociable, fond of female company, drink and gambling. He was also highly intelligent, hard-working and able and therefore featured in Montgomery's black notebook of likely officers. Before the war he twice failed the Staff College entrance examination, presumably through not preparing adequately for it, but Montgomery had secured him a place through a 'nomination'. This was a legitimate though exceptional process and saved de Guingand's career. Even so, in August 1942 he fully expected to be removed from his post by Montgomery, but after sharing a car with the new army commander on the journey to the front and being quizzed on the army's situation, he found that he was to remain as chief of staff in a role close to the German conception of the job, empowered to take decisions in the name of the commander as well as being intimately involved with planning operations and managing the staff.

The speed of Montgomery's assumption of command, barely twenty four hours after his arrival, was due not just to his ego but to the critical situation in which the army lay, with an attack expected at any time and no adequate plan, as he saw it, in place. His first act was to emphasise that by virtue of his arrival, all had changed. Introducing himself to the staff he announced that the bad times were over, that there would be no further withdrawal and that 'we are going to finish with this chap

Rommel once and for all.'[1] He moved army headquarters from its fly-infested site at El Imayid to Burg el Arab on the coast where communications with the RAF were infinitely easier, cancelled all orders for retreat or withdrawal, and restored relations with the Dominion divisions by his promise to fight divisions as divisions, not as battlegroups or brigade groups. As Freyberg wrote later,

> 'after the abolition of the Brigade Group battle there was no disagreement between the NZEF and the C-in-C on questions of battle policy, and harmonious relations were maintained up to the finish of the war.'[2]

The authority that Montgomery stamped on his new command was welcomed by many, but his forthright style was not to the taste of some of the 'old desert hands'. McCreery had experienced Monty's caustic manner in England in December 1940: 'What an unpleasant man Montgomery is!', he commented after an exercise in which two of his regiments were criticised.[3] On encountering Monty for the first time, Carver was among those who found Monty's manners and attitude, to the older officers at 7th Armoured Division HQ for example, offensive.[4] But it is clear that in North Africa by August 1942 the existing style of leadership in Eighth Army, as well as its doctrine and its tactical choices, had failed. Montgomery made much needed changes in all three of these areas. And to those already on his wavelength, he was capable of charm as well: 'Pip' Roberts, wounded in June but now out of hospital and commanding 22nd Armoured Brigade, wrote home that Montgomery 'has the reputation of being a bit of a "tiger", but today meeting him for the first time I only had the impression of quickness & efficiency & considerable interest in officers & men, all with a very pleasant manner'.[5]

There were two chief objections to his new style of leadership. The first amounted to not much more than distaste for the perceived vulgarity of his showmanship and thirst for publicity, placing him at the level of a vote-seeking politician, not a group admired by the officer class of the day. It demonstrated that, by the criteria of some, Montgomery was not a gentleman and, even worse, didn't care. Anthony Eden's private secretary recorded in his diary Montgomery's 'reputation of being an able and ruthless soldier and an unspeakable cad.'[6] But Montgomery's experience over the previous two years had been not with the largely pre-war volunteer or regular troops of

1   Hamilton, *Monty*, p. 625.
2   National Archives of New Zealand, WA/11/6, Freyberg to Kippenberger, 5/11/1947, quoted in Professor Neil Barr, *Pendulum of War: Three Battles at Alamein* (London: Jonathan Cape, 2004), p. 210.
3   Mead, *McCreery*, E-book, Chapter 12, loc.1776.
4   Carver, *Out of Step*, p. 134.
5   Liddell Hart Centre for Military Archives, Roberts Papers, Letter 17/8/42.
6   John Harvey (ed.), *The War Diaries of Oliver Harvey 1941-1945* (London: Collins, 1978), p. 88.

Eighth Army, but with the newly recruited conscript citizen soldiers of Home Forces, who were less fortified than the desert veterans by the tribal ethos of the regiment. They would have been unlikely to respond positively to the remote paternalism that was Wavell's style of leadership, or to the distant exhortations of Auchinleck. There is no record of Wavell, Auchinleck or Ritchie visiting troops or addressing them other than through somewhat stilted leaflets. Auchinleck seems to have had what can only be described as a tin ear for the sentiment of his men, asking the Army Council in London in the spring of 1942 for a restoration of the death penalty for desertion or cowardice and continuing to press for it throughout the fighting of the summer.[7] Wartime servicemen made up an increasing proportion of Eighth Army and were receptive to a personal approach. They needed to know that the high command appreciated their concerns and were gratified by the presence of a commander who took the trouble to meet them on, almost, a conversational level.

The second aspect of Montgomery's style that was not welcomed by some of his senior subordinates was his determination to end 'bellyaching'. The expression covered a variety of types of complaining, from moans about equipment to disparagement of commanders, but most insidious was the practice of divisional staff officers contacting their opposite numbers at corps level to query orders and get them diluted. This practice was now stamped on. The consensual style of leadership, of which bellyaching was a by-product, was also ended. Councils of war had been workable among the small band that led the Western Desert Force in December 1940, when Wilson and O'Connor could sit down with their principal staff officers and, as they did, recast the planned assault on the Italians. But under Ritchie councils of war became ponderous rounds of discussion and delay, degenerating into a disinclination to obey or to only half-heartedly follow orders. Montgomery made it clear from his arrival that this practice would cease, immediately. An early victim was Major General Renton, who had survived Brooke's initial culling of senior commanders and with two years experience of desert warfare was now commanding 7th Armoured Division. During a planning session on the DAK's expected attack he informed Montgomery that the key tactical decision would be when to 'loose the armour'.[8] Since this was exactly the tactic that had failed in the past and was the reverse of the way in which Montgomery intended to repel Rommel, Renton's card was well and truly marked. 22nd Armoured Brigade, the sole striking force of Eighth Army, was removed from Renton's division and kept under Horrocks' direct control to ensure it was not thrown away in a vain counter attack, to the great relief of the brigade's commander, Roberts.[9] In September Renton was replaced as commander of 7th Armoured Division by another desert veteran but

7   TNA WO163/51: Death Penalty, Army Council paper. Auchinleck's last cable on the subject, on 19 July, 'pressed most strongly' for it, citing the 57,000 missing, the great majority prisoners, among the 65,000 casualties of the summer.
8   Montgomery's *Memoirs*, quoted in Hamilton, *Monty*, p. 647.
9   Hamilton, *Monty*, p. 647.

of a different caste, John Harding. Lumsden and Gatehouse survived Montgomery's axe only until December. Their disagreements with Montgomery during Alamein were put in the 'bellyaching' category, though this was certainly unfair in the case of Gatehouse.

Doctrine is too elevated a term for the policies that Eighth Army had followed in the period up to August 1942. The army's tactics had included seeking a 'clash of armour' with the opposing tank force, attrition through the use of jock columns against enemy supply lines, 'box strategy' in both attack and defence, and then a dalliance with brigade groups and battle groups. A grim joke at that time defined the jock column as a battle group that had been twice overrun by a panzer division. In September, after the battle of Alam Halfa, Montgomery was to write home to his son's guardian that he had fought it 'in accordance with the doctrine that I have been preaching and teaching in England since the Dunkirk days'. By doctrine he meant stage-management of a battle, training for it, and maintenance of his aim, more a question of good practice and professionalism than a philosophy of warfare in the German sense. He substituted the previous regime's plethora of 'boxes', jock columns and battlegroups for his principles of organisation, a clear plan, concentration of force, care in preparation and training, and briefing of troops specifically for the battle in prospect. Peter Roach, a tank wireless operator in 1RTR discovered:

[T]he mood had changed from one of chagrined defeat and humiliation to a hard confidence tinged with wonder. Then – miracle of miracles – we paraded and were told the outlines of the battle to come. This was genius. Has any army before been briefed on how the battle was to be fought? Always it has been do this, do that, and don't think. Now we were considered as of sufficient importance to be briefed. Morale rose another couple of inches.[10]

Harold Pyman, Messervy's chief of staff in June, identified the value of Montgomery's clear thinking:

Throughout his principles held good and brought tired and muddled commanders back to their senses. Here is one of his proved maxims – "Let your soldiers [commanders] know what you mean them to do and give them the means to do it. They will make mistakes, of course, but so will the enemy. It is the side which makes the fewest mistakes which wins in war."[11]

His concentration on the basics and his attention to organisation fitted well with the 'grip' which he exerted over his commanders. No one except perhaps he himself

10   Peter Roach, *The 8.15 to War: The Memoirs of a Desert Rat* (London: Leo Cooper, 1982), p. 59.
11   Pyman, *Call to Arms*, p. 48.

has looked on his plans as demonstrating military genius, but his objectives were expressed with clarity and simplicity, units could be confident that their own and their neighbour's tasks were achievable and that success would follow. In September he wrote in a summary of the lessons to be drawn from his first encounter with Rommel, 'Never react to enemy moves or thrusts... Once you have the initiative it is essential to pursue your own object relentlessly, you must never be drawn away from it by having to react to enemy thrusts.'[12] This contrasts with Ritchie's leadership, which by relying heavily on wireless intercept and other intelligence to counter German plans, had in practice resulted in merely reacting to the enemy.

Criticism of Montgomery has centred on his generalship but has often been driven by distaste for his personality. Other desert generals such as Gott and Auchinleck were more sympathetic characters and their military record is looked on much more charitably. Montgomery valued professional competence before personal relationships and the result was not always attractive. Colleagues such as Horrocks, de Guingand and, later, O'Connor were appreciated and generously treated while they were of service, but Montgomery could be accused of ignoring or discarding them when they were no longer of use. He had some justification for this, for it could turn out that under the pressures of war an individual's competence was short-lived, or surpassed by a newcomer, or that they had been over-promoted. One such, Major General Erskine, had been highly valued as a staff officer by Gott, Horrocks and Montgomery, but in 1944 under his command 7th Armoured Division's performance in Normandy was considered below par and he was soon replaced. He held no grudge: one of 'Monty's pets', as he described himself to his family, his next posting was to head Supreme Headquarters of the Allied Expeditionary Force in Brussels, a gourmet capital even in wartime, which softened the blow. Others who were dismissed were not so forgiving, perhaps not so well compensated, and after the war made their views known. Dispensing with the chummy, collegiate nature of command of the early years of the war, Montgomery lived with colleagues who were to his professional rather than personal taste and he had little social life. A carefully selected band of liaison officers, all young and energetic men who acted as his eyes and ears at any part of the front, seem to have provided him with as much socialising as he needed, and he made little effort to charm his fellows outside their professional relationships. In North Africa he even made it his practice to refuse hospitality from subordinates, eating sandwiches in his car while the staff of the headquarters that he was visiting lunched in their tents.

12   Hamilton, *Monty*, p. 713.

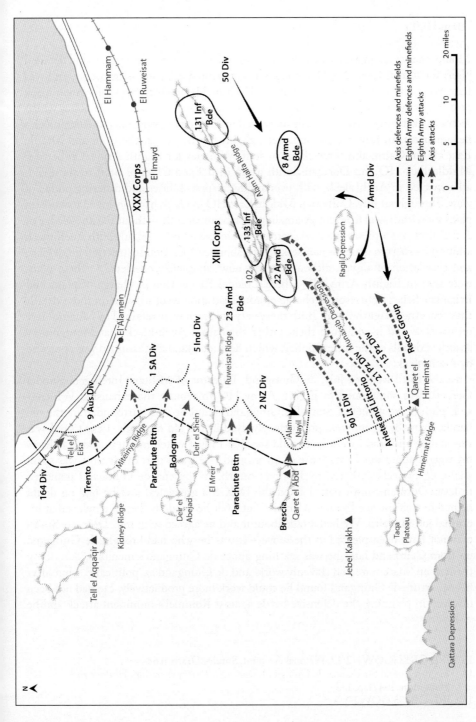

10. Alam Halfa

Alam Halfa

Montgomery's claim in his memoirs, that on arrival at Eighth Army he found detailed plans for retreat from the Alamein position, sparked a lasting controversy, and was fiercely contested by those who felt slighted by him. Having little regard for Auchinleck professionally, Montgomery credited him for a defeatist and unworkable policy which seems to have originated in confusion caused by divided responsibility at Auchinleck's headquarters. In July two headquarters, Eighth Army HQ at the front and Middle East HQ in Cairo, and three chiefs of staff, Whiteley for Eighth Army, Corbett for Middle East HQ and Dorman-Smith as an ill-defined Chief of Staff in the Field, all answered to Auchinleck, with overlapping responsibilities and differing points of view. Throughout July, Corbett at Middle East HQ in Cairo had continued to work on plans for withdrawal from the Alamein position, apparently without the knowledge of Auchinleck or Dorman-Smith. According to Dorman-Smith 'on July 30th Auchinleck allowed Corbett to issue his painstakingly elaborate Operation Instruction for defence and evacuation of Egypt, although it was now completely obsolete.'[13] These plans were sent to Eighth Army HQ where Colonel Richardson in charge of plans and Brigadier Brian Robertson in charge of administration went to work on those details that concerned Eighth Army. Both these very able men were retained by Montgomery on his staff and it was from them rather than from Auchinleck that Montgomery absorbed details of the retreat policy, which he understandably assumed was approved by Auchinleck.

In the third week of July, de Guingand, Director of Military Intelligence under Corbett, was summoned to Eighth Army HQ to replace the exhausted Whiteley as Eighth Army Chief of Staff. De Guingand found he was 'surrounded by the old hands, many of whom were pretty deeply dyed in the old methods. I can't say I was very happy and trod carefully. I could see that I must watch my step, and not throw my weight about until I was sure of my ground.'[14] A great part of his time was spent analysing projects authored by Dorman-Smith. In the end de Guingand managed to lever Dorman-Smith out: 'I liked the DCGS a great deal and he had no doubt helped to stabilise the front at Alamein, but I felt he would be better employed at his normal job in Cairo. We had a talk about it and he agreed with me.' Dorman-Smith may not have been pleased at the move – it was he who had brought de Guingand up from Cairo and later he was scathing about de Guingand's memoirs, describing them as an 'inaccurate and slovenly work' and de Guingand as 'political'[15] – but after his departure de Guingand found he could work more productively. He had not been involved in planning the defensive battle against Rommel's imminent attack and he

---

13   JRL GB133GOW1/2/17, Personal Account, Sundry Drafts p.64
14   Major General Sir Francis de Guingand, *Operation Victory* (London: Hodder and Stoughton, 1947), p. 133.
15   JRL GB133 GOW2/1/3.

was not impressed by the concept left by Dorman-Smith. This involved a network of strongpoints, with concrete, wire and mines, laid out in considerable depth:

> [They] would be occupied in accordance with the situation and from them would be directed powerful artillery fire. I never quite understood how it was to be done, but the artillery was to be concentrated in support of the threatened sector or sectors, and then linked up and controlled from these O.P.'s [Observation Posts]. It was all too uncertain and fluid a plan for a sound defence. There was a great danger of the guns being driven hither and thither, and confusion setting in. Even if they all organised themselves into a fresh command there were many things which could go wrong with these "Master O.P.'s" and so render the plan abortive. Dust, smoke or air attack might well achieve such a result.[16]

Niall Barr's *Pendulum of War* is the most authoritative account of the Alamein and Alam Halfa battles but one might take issue with his verdict on Dorman-Smith's 'modern defensive' system. He states that it was based on 'two defensive zones with a lightly held outpost zone and a web of positions in a main defence zone with mobile battlegroups to counterattack any penetration' and suggests that 'it simply attempted to use German practice and to adapt the tactical method which had worked so effectively for 1st South African Division during the first few days at Alamein.'[17] But all was dependent on the mobile battlegroup being effective in the counterattack which, on recent performance, and outnumbered and outgunned in battleworthy tanks as Eighth Army was in August, was most unlikely. It required the withdrawal of the forward troops to the main defensive zone while under attack, not a manoeuvre in which Eighth Army had a record of success. And it needed the approval of the New Zealand, Australian and South African divisional commanders before the defensive system could even be formally accepted as a plan. The web of positions involved boxes of 'one or two battalions of infantry'. It was by now clear that infantry boxes even of brigade strength had a life measured in hours once the Afrika Korps targeted them, so it is difficult to see Morshead, Freyberg or Pienaar accepting the prospect of a full scale attack by the Panzerarmee on their battalions when their only insurance was the promise of a counterattack by Eighth Army's single and under strength Grant-equipped armoured brigade.

Corelli Barnet in his influential *The Desert Generals* (still worth reading, especially as a window on the ferocity of the Montgomery-Auchinleck dispute) cited the importance that both Dorman-Smith and Montgomery placed on the Alam Halfa Ridge as evidence of Montgomery's adoption of Auchinleck's plan. But given that the Alam Halfa Ridge was twice the height and twice the length of the adjoining Ruweisat

---

16   De Guingand, *Operation Victory*, p. 132.
17   Neill Barr, *Pendulum of War: Three Battles at Alamein* (London: Jonathan Cape, 2004), p. 195.

Ridge over which so much blood had been spilt in July, it is inconceivable that any commander on either side could have regarded it as unimportant. Gott himself was said to have predicted that Rommel's next offensive would come by way of Alam Halfa as it did, 'because that was the only way.'[18] The importance of the ridge was so clear to Montgomery that his very first action after taking over Eighth Army on 13 August was to order the newly arrived 44th Infantry Division up to Alam Halfa. In fact it was the urgent need to do so, with the Axis attack predicted to commence any time after 15 August, that prompted him to take over, as some saw it, prematurely. But rather than emulating Dorman-Smith's plan, which was for a battle based on fluidity and mobility, Montgomery proceeded on the basic principles of organisation and command with which the British army was familiar and made use of the perfectly obvious topographical features of the battlefield.

Brian Horrocks had been summoned from commanding 9th Armoured Division in Britain to take over XIII Corps in Egypt, being in Montgomery's words 'exactly what was wanted for the job ahead.'[19] Horrocks was already attuned to the new, personalised, style of leadership. Having learned in the First World War the importance of a personal contact with the men under his command, he had in the words of Roberts developed the 'wonderful knack of inspiring confidence and enthusiasm wherever he goes and the raised morale he leaves behind quickly spreads to those he has not even seen.'[20] Horrocks described the orders he received as 'to defeat the Germans but not, under any condition, to become mauled in the process' [sic] because Montgomery 'did not want me to suffer severe casualties which would interfere with his subsequent offensive operation.'[21] His defence line from Alamein ran a dozen miles south to the western tip of the Ruweisat Ridge, and from there 15 miles south to the Alam Nayil depression, ending six miles further south at the Qattara depression. The northern half of the line was strongly held by the Australian, South African, Indian and New Zealand infantry divisions while the section south of Alam Nayil was covered by a motor infantry brigade and 4th Light Armoured Brigade of Honey and Crusader tanks under 7th Armoured Division. Horrocks thought that morale was good, but that the troops were 'bewildered, and I think, had lost a little confidence in their leaders.' Training appeared to be 'patchy, still imbued with the "jock col" tactic, unused to concentration and dogfight type of war'. He was impressed by 'a very experienced staff

18   R.H.W.S .Hastings, The *Rifle Brigade in the Second World War, Rifle Brigade 1939–45* (Aldershot: Gale & Polden, 1952), p. 145.
19   Mead, *Churchill's Lions*, p. 211.
20   Captain B H Liddell Hart, Generalleutnant Fritz Bayerlein & Major General GPB Roberts, 'A Battle Report: Alam Halfa (Combat Studies Institute:, Marine Corps Association, 1968) <https://web.archive.org/web/20091228033031/http://www-cgsc. army.mil/carl/resources/csi/hart/hart.asp>
21   TNA CAB106/654: Battle of Alam Halfa – Lt-Gen Sir Brian Horrocks account.

and a particularly good BGS, Brigadier Erskine. They were able to put me wise to the peculiarities of warfare in the desert.'[22]

28. Montgomery, Horrocks (to his right) and Roberts (to his left) planning the Battle of Alam Halfa. (Imperial War Museum E015787)

During the three weeks following Montgomery's appointment, the Afrika Korps' 110 Mk III and IV Special tanks outnumbered and outclassed Eighth Army's 70 Grants. Rommel's remaining armoured vehicles, 90 standard Mk IIIs, the few dozen Marders and standard Mk IVs, and 281 Italian M13s balanced Eighth Army's 400 obsolete Valentines, Crusaders and Honeys. Given Afrika Korps' proven ability in tactics and leadership, any mobile encounter was likely to go heavily in favour of Rommel's men. It was therefore a welcome addition to Horrocks' strength when Eighth Armoured Brigade arrived at the front on 30 August with its 72 Grants and 12 Crusaders, even if as an understrength and largely novice brigade equipped with weary reconditioned tanks it was hardly to be risked in an open battle against the panzer divisions. The brigade was kept under Gatehouse at the eastern end of the

22   TNA CAB106/654: Battle of Alam Halfa – Lt-Gen Sir Brian Horrocks account.

Alam Halfa ridge while 22nd Armoured Brigade held carefully selected positions to the west around Point 102. The 44th Infantry Division held the length of the ridge between them. Horrocks' assessment was that if the Panzerarmee attempted to bypass the ridge either to the east or west, it could be stopped by one armoured brigade and counterattacked by the other. It was known to be short of fuel and so unlikely to attempt any wider manoeuvre. Now that the 44th Infantry Division was present, the ridge itself was unlikely to be attacked. Any portion of the DAK that moved north to directly threaten the rear of the Alamein line would meet 23rd Armoured Brigade's 150 Valentines and be liable to attack by 22nd Armoured Brigade, Eighth Army's heaviest tanks were now all concentrated under a single command within a few miles of each other, supported by the corps artillery and with the RAF on call.

Rommel was expected to move through the southern half of the Alamein line, which Montgomery ordered to be extensively mined, in contrast to the earlier plan of leaving it relatively free from mining to encourage a mobile battle. 7th Armoured Division's cruiser tanks and armoured cars were under instructions to do their best to delay the enemy, while the Panzerarmee's movement would also be harassed by the heaviest possible attacks from the RAF and artillery. Horrocks held two exercises with 7th Armoured Division which turned out to accurately forecast the course of the battle. He also organised a 'telephone battle' on maps with 22nd Armoured Brigade:

> In accordance with the normal custom of those days, the enemy movements and positions were shown in blue and our own movements and positions in red. It may be thought that this telephone battle has not much bearing on a study of the actual battle, but suffice to say that on the day of the battle itself, the blue lines of the enemy's movements – as put on the maps during the exercise – required little alteration to conform to fact.[23]

British intelligence believed, correctly, that Rommel would await a full moon at the end of August before attacking by night and that with 300 Sherman tanks, due at Port Said in early September, he would not delay any further. The critical factor for Rommel was his inadequate reserves of fuel, which threatened to make his operation impractical. Half of the 6000 tons scheduled for delivery in the last week of August was lost when the tankers were sunk by submarine or aircraft. Left with only enough petrol for 150 miles the best he could realistically count on was a tactical victory that wrote down British strength and damaged morale unless he could once again capture British supply dumps. He had restricted ground reconnaissance of the southern sector of the Alamein line in an attempt to achieve surprise, and his troops began their move on the night of 30/31 August unaware of the depth of the triple row of minefields. The Panzerarmee's confidence was dented and their organisation upset by the mines and by heavy bombing from the RAF throughout the night, resulting in delays, confusion

23 Roberts, *A Battle Report.*

and casualties in the move, during which they also faced resistance from the cruiser tanks and armoured cars of 7th Armoured Division. Nehring commanding the Afrika Korps was wounded, von Bismarck of 21st Panzer Division was killed and heavy losses inflicted on the soft skinned vehicles that were essential to exploit a breakthrough. The Panzerarmee's report that day to Berlin gave little grounds for optimism:

> The effects of the attacks was very great, not only in actual fact and from the point of view of morale, but the troops were badly shaken by the fact that our own fighter protection was by no means adequate. The fighting capacity of both officers and other ranks was very considerably reduced by the continuous night attack (lack of sleep, perpetual waiting for the next bomb, dispersal of units etc). Over 400 officers & men were killed or wounded.[24]

Rommel had counted on achieving surprise and on reaching the Alam Halfa area by first light. He expected that British commanders would be as ponderous and as slow to react as ever, would lack the time, as he expressed it, to 'reconnoitre the situation, make their decisions and put them into effect – a period in which there would have been no need to expect serious countermeasures to our moves.'[25] In the event, by dawn on the 31st the advance was seriously behind schedule and the panzer divisions did not come up to the Alam Halfa ridge until mid-afternoon. 15 Panzer began to skirt round it to the east but was halted by darkness and lack of fuel. Meanwhile 21 Panzer wheeled north to engage the tanks of 22nd Armoured Brigade, dug in at the western end of Alam Halfa Ridge with the six pounder anti-tank guns of 1st Rifle Brigade concealed in the folds of the hill. Rather than the British armoured regiments reacting to a flurry of orders and engaging their enemy in succession, the DAK found them concentrated, dug in, supported by their antitank guns and backed by an infantry division and its artillery. Nonetheless the Mark IV Specials took a heavy toll of the Grants immediately facing them, as well as overrunning some of the 6-pdrs. Roberts was forced to order up his reserve regiment, the novice Scots Greys, to fill the gap – they were slow to move and he called out over the wireless, 'Come on the Greys, get out your whips!', shortly after which they appeared and stabilised the situation. By the end of the afternoon he still had some cause for concern, as enemy armour continued to threaten the eastern flank of his position by edging round the defensive line, but the German assault was not pressed quite as fiercely as in the past, and as the light faded the attack died away and was not resumed with any determination the following day, the 1st September. Gatehouse's 8th Armoured Brigade now made its presence felt on the eastern flank of the DAK's advance though it was unable to penetrate the DAK's gun line,[26] the Sherwood Rangers, whose first action this was, losing a number

24   TNA CAB146/15: Part 4, Appendices, p. 199.
25   Liddell Hart (ed.), *The Rommel Papers*, p. 277.
26   Hamilton, *Monty*, p. 682.

of Grants. The static nature of the battle deprived Rommel of his advantage in what he described as 'the greater aptitude of our troops for mobile warfare and the higher tactical skill of our commanders.'[27] Heavily bombed again that night and short of fuel, Rommel went over to the defensive. 8th Armoured Brigade probed at the DAK's lines on 2 September but was held off with some losses.

On 3 September it was clear that the Afrika Korps was beginning to pull out. Montgomery had issued strict instructions that units should not move from the defended areas to pursue or attack retreating Axis forces. His view was that his units, armoured units in particular, were neither sufficiently well trained nor mechanically sound enough to undertake a mobile battle. This was not the line taken by Lumsden, who had no official role in the battle but visited Gatehouse's headquarters 'in a very highly strung state' demanding to know why Gatehouse had not pursued and annihilated the enemy. Gatehouse informed Lumsden that he had, had a long briefing by the Army Cmdr (Monty), and that this had been one of the main points insisted upon – viz, not to be drawn on a wild goose chase on to the muzzles of waiting 88mm guns… H.L. would not believe me and when I repeated I had definite orders on this point, and that I heartily agreed with them, he quivered with rage and left my H.Q. in a hurry.'[28]

Once again the losses of Grants in the firefight between the DAK and 22nd Armoured Brigade had shown how potent the German armour was, for despite remaining on the defensive in carefully selected hull down positions (as far as that was possible for a Grant tank), British tank losses of 67 overall were considerably greater than the German 38. One Grant had been destroyed at 1500 yards before a single British shot was fired from Roberts' brigade, and the inadequate sights of the Grant made it ineffective at ranges over 1200 yards.[29] The value of the RAF and of British artillery fire was shown by the DAK's loss of nearly 300 trucks and the Italians' loss of another 100.[30]

Roberts thought the DAK had lacked offensive spirit and tactical adroitness compared to the past, not using more than 50 of its 200 tanks at any one time:

> The Germans have not been so thrustful as they were earlier in the summer, if they had been they would have taken advantage of that gap in the centre when one squadron of the CLY had been "brewed-up." And then they were slow finding our flanks … Even in a tank it is no fun coming under concentrated artillery fire, but, particularly when that fire is mainly of 25-pdr calibre, that should not halt a

27   Liddell Hart (ed.), *The Rommel Papers*, p. 274.
28   Liddell Hart Centre for Military Archives, Liddell Hart Papers, 9/28/42, Gatehouse to Liddell Hart.
29   TNA WO 169.4251: 22 Armd Bde War Diary 1942, 13 September 1942.
30   Playfair, *Official History*, vol iii, p.391

tank attack. On two occasions it had halted an attack on this day. Obviously, the enemy's morale is not as high as it had been a few months ago.[31]

In a summary to his brigade he emphasised that existing ideas and principles had been strongly confirmed,[32] in particular the importance of keeping the armour concentrated, making the enemy attack on ground of the defenders' choosing and utilising all the firepower from the various weapons of an armoured brigade in co-operation. Defensive fire from the artillery had slowed the German advance, allowing time to bring up reserves to the threatened area. A couple of days later he issued his first Training Instruction to the brigade, very much in the Montgomery style, emphasising fitness, alertness, enthusiasm and keeping troops 'in the picture', but also still feeling it necessary to counter the traditional cavalry mindset: 'In the minds of many, as far as armour is concerned, [the offensive] immediately implies a series of Balaclava charges, albeit supported by artillery. These tactics, although we must be prepared for them as they may be forced on us, will only be resorted to "in extremis".'

The prolonged withdrawal of the Panzerarmee from its salient back through the minefields made a tempting target for Horrocks' XIII Corps, which planned a raid across the Panzerarmee's communications to damage and cut off some elements. By 2 September this was upgraded to a full scale attack using 132nd Brigade of 44th Division supported by the New Zealand Division. The object was to close the gaps in the minefields through which the DAK had advanced and through which it would now have to withdraw. Assembling the attacking force required the redeployment of a South African brigade to cover the positions from which the New Zealanders would attack. The South Africans were slow to comply and delayed the operation by twenty four hours, during which the Panzerarmee continued to withdraw, recovering its balance and becoming better poised to counter attack if necessary. When the British attack was launched, the inexperience of their recently arrived troops showed. 132nd Brigade's night attack failed to achieve surprise, communications within the brigade broke down and heavy casualties were suffered. The New Zealand troops on the other hand had learnt from their experiences during the summer, maintained their organisation and beat off the usual Axis counterattacks with highly effective artillery fire, in a further developement of concentrated divisional artillery. The Australians, supported by Valentines of 40RTR, also attacked along the coast road west of Tel el Eisa. This was the axis most threatening to the Panzerarmee. It met fierce resistance and failed to make any progress. In all, Eighth Army's casualties for the counter attacks amounted to half of the total for Alam Halfa.

31   Roberts, *A Battle Report*.
32   TNA WO 169.4251: 22 Armd Bde War Diary 1942, 13 September 1942.

Alamein

On 2 August Auchinleck had signed off his 'Appreciation of Situation' for the options for an offensive to destroy the Panzerarmee.[33] His conclusions – in fact Dorman-Smith's conclusions, for the paper was authored by Chink in his new role in Cairo as Deputy Chief of the General Staff for Operations, Plans and Intelligence – were that an attack in the northern sector of the front was the only choice. He assessed the Axis southern flank as 'well posted in difficult ground and can be refused [i.e. withdrawn] for considerable distance before his rear areas and communications are endangered.' Concentrating British troops for an offensive in the extreme south would involve depleting the central and northern sectors and thereby inviting a counterstroke, and even if a breakthrough was successful, the distance to the enemy's vulnerable areas meant decisive results would be slow to mature. Breaking through the centre seemed unlikely to succeed without a greater superiority over the enemy than seemed feasible for some time, since the sector opposite the Ruweisat ridge was vital to the enemy's security and correspondingly strongly held, with depressions giving excellent cover to his armoured forces. The northern sector had already been forced back by the Australian capture of tel el Eisa and its security was vital to the enemy since it covered Axis road and rail communications to its supply ports. An assault there was 'certain to meet strong opposition organised in depth and strongly supported by artillery and aircraft. The results, however, of a break through here would have immediate and perhaps decisive effect. Moreover it should be possible to ensure the maximum concentration of artillery on this front without unduly weakening the centre.'[34]

Apart from the local attacks by the Australians, the July fighting had looked for a breakthrough in the centre and a drive to the coast to cut the German communications, forcing a 'clash of armour' in the process. Auchinleck and Dorman-Smith's plan now was to prepare a deliberate attack on the extreme north of the enemy position, disguising this intention by making overt preparations for an attack in the south, and in outline this became the basis of Montgomery's battle.

Other than the attack by 132nd Brigade, Alam Halfa had gone entirely according to plan. It was the first operation to do so since 'Compass' nearly two years previously. The victory produced a surge of confidence among the troops and the staff of Eighth Army. Brooke now had the evidence he needed to control Churchill's impatience at delaying the offensive until October, assuring him that it would succeed when launched as planned, but was at risk of failure if launched prematurely. The additional month of time that Montgomery had secured was put to good use in training specifically for the operation, equipping engineers for mine clearance, practising movement at night and ensuring that troops were fully aware of how the attack was likely to develop and what to expect during the prolonged 'dogfight' that Montgomery was prepared to

33   TNA WO 201/556: Appreciation of Situation, 2 August 1942.
34   TNA WO 201/556: Appreciation of Situation, 2 August 1942.

undertake. Even though the Panzerarmee also used the time to thicken its minefields and increase the depth of its positions, Eighth Army's deception measures left no clue as to the point of attack and thanks to extraordinarily effective concealment of movement there was even less clue as to timing. Shortage of fuel obliged Rommel to station his mobile troops along the forty mile front, since if concentrated at the wrong point he did not have the petrol to move them back. In September Rommel returned to Germany a sick man, replaced by a highly competent armoured warfare specialist, General der Panzertruppe Georg Stumme, who had led armoured forces in Poland, France, Yugoslavia, Greece and Russia. He and his subordinates were confident that they would give a good account of themselves when the inevitable British attack was launched. The British minefields that they had overrun in their attack in September remained in their hands, were used to fortify their own positions and were strengthened. The commanding heights of Himeimat at the southern end of the British line were also firmly in Axis hands. By the time Eighth Army launched its attack, Axis positions were several miles deep, their minefields designed to channel any advance and identify the direction of the main thrust, and their mobile forces ready to counter attack and seal off any penetration.

After Alam Halfa, Montgomery began to reorganise his command. Ramsden had never really been more than a sound divisional commander but promoted beyond his level at XXX Corps, and he was now replaced by Oliver Leese, an old acquaintance from Montgomery's days as a Staff College lecturer. Renton, having been at odds with Montgomery and regarded by others as over promoted in command of 7th Armoured Division, was replaced by Harding, a universally popular choice.

Montgomery had intended Horrocks to take command of X Armoured Corps, the principal strike force of the reconstructed Eighth Army. Horrocks believed from past experience that as a newcomer to the desert and from an unfashionable infantry regiment he would not be accepted by the cavalry generals and brigadiers of the armoured divisions. McCreery, now on Alexander's staff at Middle East Headquarters, made the point that 'it would surely be very difficult for an officer straight out from home, no matter how capable, to command an armoured corps in the desert', and went on to claim that 'Lumsden was the one armoured commander in whom everyone had great confidence.'[35] Lumsden was appointed. Horrocks remained in charge of XIII Corps now on the southern, subsidiary, section of the Alamein line. It included the Free French Brigade, 50th Northumbrian Division and 44th Infantry Division, both somewhat battered after Gazala and Alam Halfa, and Harding's 7th Armoured Division, comprising 22nd Armoured Brigade with its elderly Grants, 4th Light Armoured Brigade with its obsolete cruisers and a newly landed British infantry brigade. New Sherman tanks were arriving but were not allocated to 7th Armoured Division: as Sergeant Wardrop recorded, 'we didn't get them. It was thought that we

---

35   'Recollections of a Chief of Staff' in 12 Royal Lancers *Journal*, April 1959, quoted in
     Hamilton, p. 718.

would be too cunning and not show enough dash.'[36] The Shermans went to the fresher Yeomanry and cavalry regiments of the 1st and 10th Armoured divisions, and to the 9th Armoured Brigade attached to the New Zealanders.

Leese's XXX Corps, consisting of the 9th Australian, 2nd New Zealand, 51st Highland, 1st South African and Tuker's 4th Indian divisions, would provide the infantry assault for Montgomery's offensive. But only the Australian and Highland divisions were up to strength, each with three infantry brigades. The New Zealand and South African divisions each with only two brigades were not capable of sustained operations, and 4th Indian was out of favour with Montgomery. A newly arrived yeomanry formation, the 9th Armoured Brigade, was attached to the New Zealand Division as integral tank support to make up for its missing infantry brigade, and the Australians, the Highlanders and South Africans were also given armour, a battalion of Valentines each. The Australian and New Zealand divisions were by now veterans in every sense, both in the battlewise competence of the rifle companies and in the organisation and staff work of the brigades and divisions. In particular the artillery of both divisions were to prove remarkably adaptable and flexible in producing fire plans at short notice, critical in the battle. The Highland Division, rebuilt from cadres of the original 51st Division that had been forced to surrender in France in 1940, was very much a tribal and family affair. Its commander, Major General Douglas Wimberley, was a former student and admirer of Montgomery from Staff College days and he was relieved to find that under Montgomery divisions would indeed be fought as divisions. In the six weeks between Alam Halfa and the 23 October Wimberley rotated his battalions through the Australians, to give them frontline experience without blunting their élan. The South Africans and Indians played a subsidiary part in the initial assault. Dan Pienaar was as ever difficult to deal with but his South Africans were coaxed into line and fulfilled their part. Francis Tuker, whose 4th Indian Division had more desert experience than any formation other than 7th Armoured, was furious at being given a minor role:

> Monty, having no use for Indian troops, at once put my division on bottom priority for everything. This was the result of Auchinleck's failure as well as of Monty's prejudice. Monty could give good reason for his policy![37]

But he was determined to change Monty's view, and by the end of the campaign his reputation and that of his troops had been fully restored.

Montgomery's initial plan was for XXX Corps to drive two corridors through the German defences in an assault by four infantry divisions supported by nearly 900 guns, taking the Miteirya Ridge which had held out against Australian attacks in July. The corridors would be cleared of mines, and the armour of X Corps would move through

---

36   Forty, *Wardrop*, p. 69.
37   IWM, Tuker papers.

and position itself three miles further on at the Aqqaqir height on the Rahman track, Rommel's supply route to his troops to the south. The Afrika Korps would be obliged to counterattack and should be destroyed on British defences. Meanwhile Horrocks' XIII Corps to the south would draw off as many enemy reserves as possible, and then attack north west to take the supply bases and landing grounds around Fuka 30 miles west of Alamein.

Doubts emerged as the plan was examined. It became clear to Leese, new to the desert and commanding the assault infantry of XXX Corps, that his divisional commanders were not confident that they could break through in a single night's attack, and that they also doubted that the armour would fulfil their role of engaging enemy armour. De Guingand witnessed a briefing given by Lumsden to the commanders of his armoured divisions where it was clear that they also were not convinced that passing through the defended zone in a single night was feasible, given the inevitable confusion with an infantry corps and an armoured corps attempting to move through the same two corridors in the dark and under fire. In the past when commanders or their staff held such doubts, the 'bellyaching' tendency often resulted either in orders being unofficially modified so that the plan lost cohesion, or the subordinate unit accepting its orders with reservations and co-operating less than wholeheartedly.

Montgomery heard the objections and himself modified the plan. He changed the method from a 'breakthrough' to a 'break-in'. Once through the corridors, the armour would form a protective shield behind which the infantry would begin a 'crumbling' process, eating away at the enemy infantry. The German armour could not afford to see their holding troops worn down and would be forced to counterattack before their defence dissolved. With a gift for reducing a complicated problem to its simplest elements, he characterised the forthcoming battle as going through three phases, a 'break-in', a 'dogfight', and 'the final "break" of the enemy'[38]. But he did not pretend it would be easy. The training programme that he had already instituted now included not merely a promise that victory would be achieved but an uncompromising picture of the forthcoming battle for all the troops:

> The infantry must be prepared to fight and kill, and to continue doing so over a prolonged period. It is essential to impress on all officers that determined leadership will be very vital in this battle, as in any battle. There have been far too many unwounded prisoners taken in this war. We must impress on our Officers, NCOs and men that when they are cut off or surrounded, and there appears no hope of survival, they must organize themselves into a defensive locality and hold out where they are.[39]

38 Hamilton, *Monty*, p. 764.
39 Quoted in Hamilton, *Monty*, p. 757.

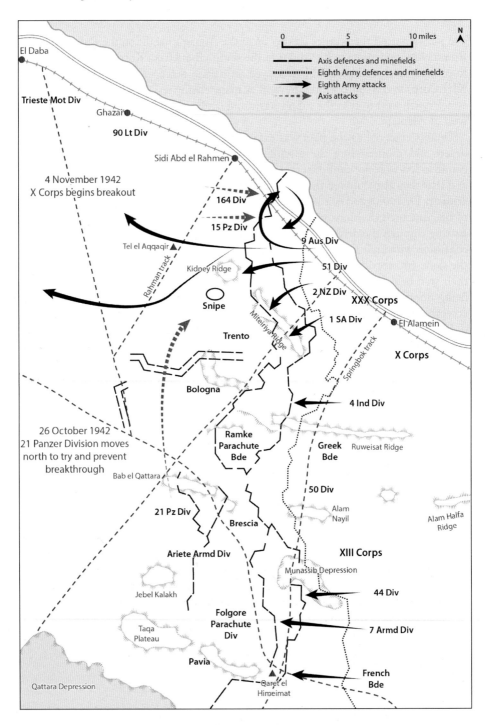

El Daba

Trieste Mot Div

Ghazai

90 Lt Div

Sidi Abd el Rahmen

4 November 1942
X Corps begins breakout

164 Div

15 Pz Div

Tel el Aqqaqir

Kidney Ridge

Rahman track

Snipe

9 Aus Div

51 Div

2 NZ Div   XXX Corps

1 SA Div   El Alamein

Trento

Miteirya Ridge

Springbok track   X Corps

Bologna

26 October 1942
21 Panzer Division moves
north to try and prevent
breakthrough

Bab el Qattara

21 Pz Div

Brescia

Ariete Armd Div

Jebel Kalakh

Taqa
Plateau

Pavia

Qattara Depression

Qaret el
Himeimat

Ramke
Parachute
Bde

Greek
Bde   Ruweisat Ridge

4 Ind Div

50 Div

Alam
Nayil

Alam Halfa
Ridge

XIII Corps

Munassib Depression

44 Div

Folgore
Parachute
Div

7 Armd Div

French
Bde

0   5   10 miles

N

Axis defences and minefields
Eighth Army defences and minefields
Eighth Army attacks
Axis attacks

11. Second Alamein

His realism and grasp on the essentials of the plan was reflected in the most basic practicalities. When asked for an estimate of the duration of the battle, his answer of twelve days was exactly right, and his estimate for Eighth Army casualties – 14,000 – was within a few hundred of the actual figure.[40] Dominick Graham served under him and described him as 'not a clever tactician and he knew that his army was not clever either. Simplicity, direct methods, endurance, obstinacy and emphasizing the positive, if necessary beyond the point of reason, were his hallmarks. They struck a response from soldiers who, like football fans, wanted to win and be on the winning side.'[41] He thought 'Montgomery's enthusiastic references to a "killing ground" or a "killing match" were regarded as rather common by some and "public school" by others', but that most of the army subscribed enthusiastically to that mode of thought.

The opening of the battle on the night of 23 October achieved complete surprise. Rommel was on sick leave in Germany, concerns over ammunition and fuel limited the Axis response, the British artillery barrage stunned the defenders and most of the infantry objectives were achieved at relatively light cost. The 'break in' failed to fully penetrate the depth of German defences on the first night, nor on the second despite a crisis meeting between Montgomery, Lumsden and the commander of 8th Armoured Division, Gatehouse. The armour had great difficulty in reaching the positions intended. Congestion in the corridors, German artillery fire and confusion caused by the dust and dark, slowed progress. It became clear that though it was possible to reach the crest of the Miteirya Ridge British armour could not survive in daylight on the forward slope in view of German anti-tank guns – by midday on the 25th about 250 tanks had been lost, though many were repairable – and therefore could not protect the infantry from counter attack during the infantry's 'crumbling' process. Meanwhile Horrocks' XIII Corps failed to break through in the south, although it exerted enough pressure to distract German and Italian mobile troops from assisting the main defence in the north. On the 28th Montgomery halted offensive operations by Horrocks and withdrew 7th Armoured Division into reserve behind the main battle front.

Stumme had gone forward on the morning of the 24th to see the situation for himself and died from a heart attack while under fire. In his and Rommel's absence, von Thoma of the Afrika Korps took over and followed the practice of immediate local counterattacks against enemy penetrations. By midday on the 24th he was reasonably satisfied. The Panzerarmee reported to Berlin that evening that 'limited counter-attacks appeared to have been successful despite ferocious artillery bombardment which eliminated several battalions… When the German formations were withdrawn to the new front which was to be formed the defence forces would be again in a position to halt the enemy, by exerting all their staying power', and 'reports indicated

40   Hamilton, *Monty*, p. 749.
41   Graham, *Against Odds*, p. 6.

29. Monty 'gripping' subordinates. (Imperial War Museum E015788)

that the enemy attack was halted everywhere and that the main battle line was still in Axis hands.[42]

It had been costly for both sides. The 2nd Armoured Brigade found itself at the extremity of the northernmost corridor through the German lines with their Shermans in hull down positions. It had the advantage over the advancing German armour:

> Our new gunnery methods and our new Sherman tanks showed their worth. For, when the German tanks moved forward, both A and C Squadron began to hit their targets and several of the German tanks went up in flames. This was indeed a morale raising sight, and I felt the Germans were surprised as they turned northwards and moved across the front leaving several wrecks behind.[43]

For the first time in the desert, the German doctrine of immediate counter attack was not paying dividends in destroying the attackers or regaining ground. 15 Panzer

42   TNA CAB 146/17: Panzerarmee daily reports.
43   IWM, Private papers of A.D.R. Wingfield, PP/MR/353 quoted in Hammond, *El Alamein* E-book Chapter 7, loc3696.

lost 75 of its 115 tanks and though many were repairable, further losses on this scale would make a later battle of manoeuvre impossible, though in the south the situation was better: Horrocks' attack had been decisively halted for the loss of only fifteen of 21st Panzer's armour. When Rommel returned to Africa on the evening of the 25th, he changed the policy. Counter attacks would be reserved for decisive blows at key points, otherwise a dogged defence, disputing every yard, aimed at wearing down the attackers, was to be the rule. Properly handled, attrition could work for the defence.

The Australian infantry assault on the 23rd had been the most successful of the divisional attacks and their casualties the lightest. As the most northerly of the attacking infantry divisions, their three mile advance created a salient in the German defences and Morshead now suggested to Montgomery that this penetration be used to continue the crumbling process into the Axis defences but attacking north instead of west. Since July Rommel had reacted strongly to any danger to the northern anchor of his line, and after Alam Halfa he had garrisoned it with the best of the Italian infantry, the Bersaglieri, and with complete German infantry battalions rather than Italian infantry companies interlaced with German companies. Having advanced three miles west since the 23rd, the Australians were ideally positioned to push north, threatening to cut off the German infantry in the coastal sector and to unhinge the entire German defence line. Montgomery's 'crumbling' operation would continue, but northwards rather than westwards, and in a direction that Rommel could not possibly allow to go unchallenged.

While Morshead's men prepared to attack, 1st Armoured Division would maintain pressure on the Miteirya front, in the first instance trying to gain ground by pushing forward two infantry battalions on the night of the 26th, each to form a 'pivot' from which the armour might be able to operate. The southern pivot, codenamed 'Snipe', would be made by the 2nd Rifle Brigade, a battalion sized unit despite its name, reinforced with a total of nineteen six pounder guns. After difficulties finding its objective in the dark, the battalion dug in at dawn on the 27th as best it could, unable to contact the field artillery allocated to its support. Rommel saw the British incursion as having 'the object of extending [a] bridgehead west of the minefields'[44] and he ordered its elimination.[45] Throughout the day the battalion held out against 15 Panzer Division, the Littorio Armoured Division and a Bersaglieri battalion, destroying around forty German and Italian armoured vehicles, before the surviving riflemen were withdrawn in the evening. British armour had been unable to advance to their support due to enemy fire. The other pivot, codenamed 'Woodcock', escaped the notice of the Panzerarmee but pressure had been maintained on the DAK, reducing their tank strength to 77.

The Australian attack was launched on the night of the 28th. The division's two brigades, each supported by a regiment of Valentines, failed to reach its objectives, but

44   Liddell Hart (ed.), *The Rommel Papers*, p. 306.
45   TNA CAB 146/17: Panzerarmee daily reports, 26 October 1942

destroyed a German and an Italian infantry battalion. Rommel was forced to reinforce the coastal sector with the 90th Light Division and brought 21st Panzer Division, with its 60 tanks, to the sector as a mobile reserve. Montgomery ordered the attack to continue northwards on the night of the 30th to pin and absorb the German reserves, while the New Zealand Division, made up to strength with a British infantry brigade, was to attack westwards on the 31st.

The new Australian assault was exceptionally complex. At the opening of the battle on the 23rd, the division had driven west. Then on the 28th it had shifted the axis north. Now on the 30th it was to advance north-east across the road and railway towards the coast, then south-east down the railway to encircle the remaining enemy garrison. A third phase involved a further thrust north-east from its original positions to the sea to cut off any escape along the coast, and another south-west to capture the principal enemy defence post known as Thompson's post. An enormous volume of artillery fire was required to support infantry attacking in so many different directions, and the fire plan involved counter battery programmes, barrages, timed concentrations and three different zero hours, one for each of three stages. At one point the infantry would actually be advancing towards their own guns into their own shellfire, requiring the artillery to shorten rather than increase range as the battle progressed. The fighting reached an unprecedented level of ferocity, some Australian rifle companies being reduced to a handful of men, and the Afrika Korps was repeatedly forced to counter attack to rescue surrounded troops. Rommel was obliged to move his main mobile reserve, 90 Light Division, to the sector.

Eighth Army intelligence noted that all Rommel's troops were committed and the Afrika Korps had no reserves available, giving Montgomery the opportunity to switch from 'crumbling' to 'breakthrough'. He had throughout the battle ensured he had a reserve in hand: 7th Armoured Division had been withdrawn from the fight on the 28th for that purpose, he had been careful not to overextend the New Zealand Division and he had given priority to bringing its 9th Armoured Brigade up to strength after its ordeal on the opening night. To again spare the New Zealand infantry but to make full use of Freyberg's organisation and determination, he placed two English brigades under command of the New Zealand headquarters, each with a battalion of Valentines, while the experienced and reliable New Zealand artillery and engineers provided essential fire support and helped clear minefields. Freyberg had requested and was given a twenty four hour delay to ensure proper planning and organisation, and the operation went ahead soon after 1 a.m. on 2 November. The infantry advanced 4000 yards on a two mile front, lanes free of mines were cleared through the defended area, two armoured car regiments slipped through the final defences, and at 6.15am on the 2nd the 9th Armoured Brigade took up the advance. They were halted after a few hundred yards with very heavy losses but held their ground and enabled tanks of 1st Armoured Division to pass through. They too were brought to a halt opposite the tel el Aqqaqir rise but in the process the DAK lost over 70 tanks.

Rommel and von Thoma now organised a defensive line around Aqqaqir on the Rahman track. This was the supply path to the southernmost Axis positions.

They both knew that the position could only be a temporary shield as they began to withdraw their depleted forces, but they still managed to beat off two further attacks. The first came on the 2 November when Lumsden, 'who had received from General Montgomery a certain latitude in making his plans',[46] ordered a night attack by 7th Motor Brigade on the German line, after which 1st Armoured and 7th Armoured Divisions would pass through and would strike for the Ghazal railway station near the coast fifteen miles behind the original front. 7th Motor Brigade, trained and organised for mobile operations, was perhaps not the best tool for an assault on a defended locality. The attack was hastily mounted, suffered from poor communications and insufficient reconnaissance, and it failed. The official historian remarked that 'information about it is incomplete – in fact, the whole story is very difficult to piece together.'[47] On 3 November Rommel's defence was still holding but the RAF reported columns of troops withdrawing to the west. Montgomery ordered an attack by the 51st Highland Division for that evening, to be exploited northwards by X Corps and westwards towards Fuka and Matruh by the New Zealand division. A map reading failure by 1st Armoured Division, who believed they had already reached the point under attack, led to cancellation of artillery support for one of the Scottish battalions and consequently heavy casualties among the infantry and their supporting Valentines. However attacks by the other two Scottish brigades succeeded and the enemy defence dissolved on the morning of 4 November. The remaining mobile Axis troops were delayed for some hours by Rommel's short-lived compliance with Hitler's 'no retreat' order but in the end made their way to the coastal road, though the Italian infantry were largely abandoned. It now became a question of whether the remnants of Rommel's forces could retreat quickly enough to avoid annihilation from an outflanking move through the desert.

There were three principal bottlenecks where the desert escarpment and coastal road came close enough to the sea for an outflanking force to block the coastal strip and trap the DAK: Fuka (about 40 miles from the last stand of the Afrika Korps at Aqqaqir), Mersa Matruh (90 miles west of Aqqaqir) and Sollum (240 miles west of Aqqaqir). Montgomery intended Freyberg and the New Zealanders to lead the pursuit. He transferred 4th Light Armoured Brigade, composed of Honeys and two pounder-armed Crusaders, from 7th Armoured Division to Freyberg's command, since Freyberg's own 9th Armoured Brigade was too battered for immediate action. But 4th Light Armoured still had to negotiate the mine-free corridors of the battlefield, and congestion there and deterioration of the tracks delayed movement. By the end of the day the New Zealand Division was spread out over twenty miles, its leading elements

---

46 Playfair, *Official History*, vol. iv, p.70
47 Playfair, vol. iv, p.70. These rather elliptical remarks are uncharacteristic of the Official History. The correspondence of the author, Brigadier C.J.C. Molony, does sometimes refer to incidents that he glosses over in the published account. It is not clear what he is hinting at here.

some eight miles south of the DAK's own assembly point. Freyberg was confident of reaching Fuka on the 5th but encountered a minefield at noon after covering thirty miles that day and by dusk only half his force had passed through it. Their presence was noted by the enemy, who withdrew from the Fuka position that night.

Meanwhile the rest of 7th Armoured Division was transferred to Lumsden's X Armoured Corps and moved through the Alamein battlefield to the Rahman track. Its 22nd Armoured Brigade met the Ariete Division south of Aqqaqir and claimed to have destroyed it – 'good battle practice', as Roberts was to describe the encounter, but it took most of the afternoon of the 4th and certainly a significant number of M13s survived to fight again. 7th Armoured Division was eager to lead the pursuit, all the more since it believed it knew the desert better and would move faster than any other formation. But Lumsden gave the division orders to move no further than Daba, 40 miles short of Fuka, while he directed his corps in a short hook, about 10 miles, to el Kharash and Ghazal on the coast, to directly tackle the mass of enemy units that were crowding the roads and tracks leading to Fuka. This was pushing the enemy where he was strongest, and progress was slower than expected due to congestion, darkness, fuel shortage, and delayed and changing orders. Harding of 7th Armoured urged Lumsden 'to release him … to move due west through the desert until he was west of Mersa Matruh; but this did not meet with approval. Had it done so, and Harding been given first priority for petrol supply, he might have have succeeded in cutting off all Rommel's remaining armour and put even more of his forces "into the bag"'.[48]

The 10th Armoured Division under Gatehouse assembled on the evening of the 4th at tel el Aqqaqir, with the intention of reaching el Daba by dawn on the 5th but was halted by pitch darkness after 15 miles. Briggs of 1st Armoured Division had suggested to Lumsden 'towards the end of Alamein' that preparation should be made for pursuit and that fuel sufficient to reach Sollum should be stocked up:

> Herbert [Lumsden] rather laughed at the idea of sending anyone as far as Sollum and said that at this stage Da'aba [20 miles distant] was the objective of his armour... in the event on the 4th November whilst we were moving up to Da'aba Herbert got in touch with me and said "You win. You can go to Matruh." I told Herbert that I doubted if I had the petrol for Matruh, that I thought Matruh was far too near and that I still hankered after Sollum. Well you know the end of that story, how the rain came down and our wheeled vehicles were unable to reach us with the necessary petrol and we were stuck close to Charing Cross [near Matruh] with our petrol tanks empty.[49]

Only at 4.45 a.m. on 5 November did Harding receive orders from Montgomery via Lumsden to strike as far west as Fuka. He pressed to be allowed to make a much

48   Carver, *Harding*, p. 105.
49   IWM, Briggs Papers RB1, letter to Liddell Hart, 3 February 1950.

deeper move to the west of Mersa Matruh but Lumsden refused, and when Roberts' 22nd Armoured Brigade reached the area to which he had been directed, 'it was clear that the birds had flown'. Orders came through for a further advance, but it was Briggs and 1st Armoured Division that were given priority for petrol and movement, although Harding's units were already on the move and better placed to make the interception. Inevitably, 7th Armoured suspected that Lumsden was favouring 1st Armoured Division, his old command, over them. 7th Armoured did catch up with 21 Panzer and Rommel's rearguard near Matruh on 6 November, knocking out 15 tanks and destroying a number of guns, but Harding's tanks were running short of petrol and torrential rain made movement across country impossible for the supply transport. The last chance to intercept the Afrika Korps had gone, for the speed with which Rommel now withdrew – his forces reached the good defensive position at Mersa Brega 500 miles from Alamein by 23 November – gave no opportunities to cut him off once he had cleared the Matruh bottleneck.

The failure to trap the remnants of Rommel's force was unfortunate. The Afrika Korps' rearguard action at Aqqaqir had been highly effective, as fiercely fought by the DAK as any during the main battle and bought time for Rommel to get almost all his German troops on the move. At Aqqaqir British troops did not have the support from massed guns that was so effective in the first week of Alamein. They had only their divisional artillery in support, and not always that in the case of the 51st Division's attacks at Aqqaqir. Lumsden's cavalry spirit seems to have deserted him despite superiority in numbers and quality of armour and there is a hint that he favoured 1st Armoured Division, his old command, over 7th Armoured to spearhead his operations. Montgomery was more impressed by Harding's leadership of 7th Armoured than by Briggs' of 1st Armoured or by Gatehouse's of 10th Armoured Division. He gave Harding the leading role in the pursuit of Rommel from Mersa Matruh to el Agheila, airlifting fuel and replacing some of their decrepit Grant tanks with Shermans taken from the 10th Hussars, much to the irritation of the Hussars. Writing to Harding in December he said that 'the Division has done magnificently. It has shown the whole army how to fight the pursuit battle, how to worry the retreating enemy, and generally how to fight the mobile battle in desert areas and in Jebel country.'[50]

He had not been impressed by Lumsden during Alamein. He thought aspects of his command style unprofessional, in particular his habit of roving around in his command tank out of touch with his Corps headquarters and unaccompanied by his artillery commander.[51] The differences of opinion that had emerged early on 25 October clearly ranked as 'bellyaching' in Montgomery's view, and in December he replaced Lumsden with Horrocks. He removed Gatehouse from Eighth Army at the same time. Oliver Leese, very much one of Monty's men, had proved successful at XXX Corps, and kept his position until he succeeded Montgomery in command of Eighth

50   Carver, *Harding*, p. 107.
51   Hamilton, *Monty*, p. 785.

Army in Italy. Other than Briggs, Montgomery therefore achieved a clean sweep of the summer's senior British commanders in Eighth Army by the end of the year. The men he chose as replacements, and others he was able to introduce or promote over the following twelve months, were much more in his mould. Though Harding left front line command after being seriously wounded in January 1943, he went on to become Alexander's Chief of Staff where he was widely regarded as the driving force behind 15th Army Group's later achievements in Italy. O'Connor escaped from captivity in 1943, and with his reputation and as an old colleague and friend of Montgomery was immediately given command of a corps for the invasion of Normandy. In Tunisia, John Crocker, who had led 3rd Armoured Brigade in France in 1940, commanded a corps in 1st Army in Tunisia with some distinction and Montgomery selected him also for command in the Normandy campaign. All of these men were personable and much liked but were also prepared to drive subordinates in a manner that Creagh, Ritchie, Norrie, Gott, Lumsden and Messervy had found impossible, and that was probably contrary to their natures. Roberts served as a staff officer or commander under all of them and is a witness to this shift in personality type among his superiors. Impressed by Horrocks' charm and humour, he was left in no doubt as to Horrocks' determination to see a job done. When Roberts' attack at the beginning of Alamein failed, Horrocks made it clear to him that he believed Roberts could and should have tried harder.[52] Crocker was universally admired for his integrity and ability but when in Tunisia he saw a chance of cutting off part of the Afrika Korps at Fondouk and Roberts questioned the feasibility of the attack (rightly, as it turned out), it was made very clear that orders were not negotiable.[53] O'Connor reacted equally sharply when Roberts displayed doubts at the opening of the 'Goodwood' offensive in Normandy in July 1944. O'Connor told him that 'the present plans could not be changed and if I felt they were unsound, then he would get one of the other divisions to lead.'[54] Montgomery had introduced a touch of steel to the club ethos of the British Army.

52   Roberts, *Desert to Baltic*, p. 117.
53   Roberts, *Desert to Baltic*, p. 139.
54   Roberts, *Desert to Baltic*, p. 171.

7

The Desert Generals

In May 1942 Brigadier John Harding, newly appointed Director of Military Training of Eighth Army, was concerned about the outlook of the typical British officer. He concluded his first training conference with comments on the army's culture of amateurism:

> Everyone must go all out to win the war. We must overcome the British habit of pretending not to work hard, and must try to increase our output … It is hoped in the near future that a statement on war aims will be produced on a high level. Many officers and men are fighting not only as a duty but through a feeling of patriotism which they do not openly admit.[1]

Harding was looking for a sharper edge to the officer corps. In his final paragraph, he particularly discouraged the notion of being a 'good loser':

> The will to win must be imbued in every man so that it is apparent and not concealed as is natural to the British.

One might think it no coincidence that Harding was educated at a rural grammar rather than an orthodox public school.

In the 18 months following the end of Operation 'Compass', Eighth Army had sorely lacked a commander of the stature of O'Connor, whose leadership up to February 1941 had been outstanding and whose capture that April was a disaster. It would be wrong to discount O'Connor's accomplishments on the grounds that he was opposed only by Italians, for he had a drive and an instinct for command in mobile warfare that was matched by few later British commanders. He empowered Harding as chief of staff to make decisions in line with the ultimate objective, resulting in 7th Armoured Division's change of direction that cut off the retreating Italians. Harding

---

1   TNA WO 201.2591: Notes on Training Conference, 10 May 1942.

later described O'Connor as 'my ideal of a commander in battle, always approachable and ready to listen, yet firm and decisive.'[2] Faced with apparent ineptitude such as the debacle at Mechili in January 1941, O'Connor could be caustic: 'If the Italians were able to move their tanks away at night, I see no reason why we should not have been able to operate ours.'[3] In a note to the divisional commander, Creagh, his tone may not have been hectoring but he clearly was not prepared to accept excuses:

> You say that the Armoured Division will be played out after MECHILI. I'm afraid I can't agree. They will only be played out when there are no more tanks that can move. It is no good failing in the object of our campaign with a reserve of tanks in hand.
>
> No, Dickie, you must do everything possible to get the largest number of tanks on the road by the 10th at latest, no relief of any sort will take place until the next operation is completed and I know I can rely on you to do everything in your power to have the largest possible force ready to move by then.[4]

O'Connor combined drive and aggression with the social conventions of reasonable behaviour. Even while reprimanding Creagh, he was positive in emphasizing his desire to delegate responsibility to the man on the spot:

> I have been considering whether I should have given your division definite localities to occupy rather than general instructions to prevent the enemy escaping. I am inclined to think not, as being on the spot you might have found it better to carry out your task in a different way from any method prescribed by me.[5]

It was not only *Aufragstaktik* he practiced. His 'forward leadership' was exemplified by his presence, without interfering in the battle, at 7th Armoured Division headquarters during the fighting at Beda Fomm, where he was said to have passed the time reading a book, unobtrusive but available in case of need. And Galloway, himself highly rated by Brooke, thought him magnificent, writing

> Never please think that because I emphasize that Dick O'Connor had a completely different problem, his performance was not perfect. You should have seen him. Supreme control coupled with modesty and self-elimination except as

2   Baynes, *O'Connor*, p. 92.
3   Pitt, quoted in Baynes, *O'Connor*, p. 111.
4   Liddell Hart Centre for Military Archives, O'Connor papers, quoted in Baynes, *O'Connor*, p. 112.
5   Liddell Hart Centre for Military Archives, Creagh Papers.

regards his presence always at the place that mattered, made the saga of 1940 in the desert.[6]

No other British commander matched O'Connor's talents, though Eighth Army was unlucky in the toll that accidents took of some who might have rivalled him. Among them was Vyvyan Pope. He was well educated in armoured warfare as any British general of 1940-41, his views on combined arms warfare and brigade groups were validated by events, and he showed clarity in thought and sufficient powers of command to fit him for high rank. He was well regarded by Brooke, whose judgement was generally excellent. His death in an aircrash must be counted as a disaster for Eighth Army. It resulted in the early promotion of Willoughby Norrie to command XXX Corps in the 'Crusader' offensive, before he or most of his troops had time to get to grips with the demands of desert war. Even so, by late 1941 they had fought their way to a victory of sorts. Under Pope's leadership, they would surely have built on that success.

Jock Campbell's death in a car accident in February 1942 was, like Pope's death, also a tragedy, for there is every reason to suppose he would have been a success leading 7th Armoured Division. He had a rare capacity to energize the men and officers under him. Sergeant Jake Wardrop saw him at a firepower demonstration just before he died:

> The man who dominated the whole thing was Jock Campbell. He was big, six feet two, and what a personality … he'd nip up on the back of the tank and watch the target with his glasses. When it was hit he'd be driving up the range in his car while the shooting was still going on. He had a long low-cut Ford and he drove it flat out all the time.[7]

Major Oswald of 7th Armoured Division, a future Director of Military Intelligence, thought Campbell 'thoroughly practical and quick to learn. He was above all things a leader with a magnetic personality, great courage and apparently inexhaustible energy and drive. It is conceivable that with judicious handling by his superiors he might have become the Patton of the British Army.'[8]

It seems he had a greater insight into German technique than any other British leader. He is quoted, unfortunately without the source being given, by a German authority as recognizing the flexibility of the German tank arm's technique:

---

6   CAC, Galloway Papers GLWY 1/6 comments on the Crusader draft chapter in Eric Sixsmith, *Generalship in the 20th Century.*
7   Forty, *Wardrop*, p. 46.
8   IWM, Campbell Papers, 23/1/1963 letter to P B Ellis, Speldhurst, Kent.

It was dominated by a singular characteristic, namely a lack of uniformity. Its methods repeated themselves only very occasionally ... extensive study of armour employment, together with combat experience gave the Panzer arm a proficiency which showed itself in every battle it fought. This guaranteed a combat organization corresponding exactly with the demands of any specific situation and terrain.

Messervy succeeded Campbell at 7th Armoured Division but he was not a success as a commander of armour. Wardrop's view of him, which may or may not have been representative, was 'a silly old man from the Indian Army who had never seen a tank'.[9]

Two Royal Tank Regiment officers who might have been expected to progress further than they did were 'Blood' Caunter and Alec Gatehouse. Brigadier John Caunter, whose nickname was probably a hangover from schooldays where a 'blood' was a hearty solid games playing type, was not a popular man by most accounts. Carver describes him before the war as 'fiery, hot tempered, energetic, enthusiastic',[10] Roberts as 'quick of temper, hasty of decision, generally looked upon by his junior officers as being "difficult" and "prickly"'.[11] His 'caustic tongue and impatience with pretentious fools was apt to upset people', according to Tim Pile, 'but O'Connor thought very highly of him'.[12] He commanded 7th Armoured Division during much of Operation Compass in the absence due to sickness of Creagh. It was he who failed to cut off the Italian armour at Mechili, and afterwards he was sent out to India, writing home to Hobart, 'I think it's a bit steep after being thanked and congratulated by all the high ones! Of course Dickie Creagh does not like me, as I am tanks and not cav., and Wavell takes his views of course.' But he had been an awkward subordinate in the later stages of 'Compass', obstructing the re-allocation of fuel and supplies from his 4th Armoured Brigade during the reorganisation that preceded the drive to Beda Fomm.[13]

He was succeeded at 4th Armoured Brigade by Gatehouse. Gott commended Gatehouse's leadership of 4th Armoured Brigade in the 1941 Winter Battles, describing it as the most successful of the armour during Crusader, 'well trained in a very sound system of support and co-operation between all arms ... especially between the guns of the Bde Grp and the Armd regts. His methods were almost identical with those described in the recent VIII Army directive for AFV training.'[14]

Losses though heavy were reduced by skilful handling and sound administration, but instead of receiving credit Gatehouse was accused of being slow and over-cautious.

9   Forty, *Wardrop*, p. 46.
10   Carver, *Out of Step*, p. 34.
11   Roberts, *Desert to the Baltic*, p.18.
12   Liddell Hart Centre for Military Archives, Liddell Hart Papers, LH11/1942/72 talk with Pile, 24 September 1942.
13   Carver, *Out of Step*, pp. 65-6.
14   JRL GB133AUC659, letter to Auchinleck, 27 January 1942.

He was said to have become tired, losing efficiency and to be 'a difficult subordinate in a long battle'. He was also 'believed to have kept alive the feeling between Cavalry & R Tank Regt ... I do not think it will recur.' Gott recommended him for command of a brigade or a training role, but not for command of a division. Though he did eventually lead 10th Armoured Division at Alam Halfa and Alamein, he was sidelined soon afterwards. He was described during the early stages of Alamein as 'very mulish'.[15]

Comments from Lumsden's contemporaries indicate that he was unlikely to have been a success as Eighth Army Commander, and it is noteworthy that his only advocates were fellow cavalrymen. Michael Carver as a XXX Corps staff officer had enough contact with him to form a clear opinion:

> Lumsden was undoubtedly a soldier and leader of exceptional quality, tough, decisive and clearheaded. He was immensely popular with those under his command, but intense loyalty to his own formation and his full confidence in his own judgement and ability made him a difficult subordinate or equal. He showed little regard for the interests and difficulties of others. Norrie could handle him face to face, but it was not in his nature to force matters to a clash. One of his least attractive traits was to try and browbeat staff officers of other formations, like myself, with lashes from his sharp tongue.[16]

He did not command again during the war but was successful as a high-level liaison officer with the US Pacific fleet, where he was killed in a kamikaze strike on the aircraft carrier on which he was stationed.

'Strafer' Gott's tragic death in August 1942 removed the last desert veteran with sufficient experience to command Eighth Army, and Montgomery, the rising star of Home Forces, was appointed in his place. Whether Gott would have pursued the course outlined in Auchinleck's Appreciation of 27th July is impossible to say. Shortly before Gott took up his last post, Carver discussed with him options for an offensive. Gott's idea at that time was to outflank Rommel's positions either by crossing the Qattara depression or moving round its southern edge. From his pre-war desert journeys Carver knew the difficulties involved, believed that such a plan was unworkable and was convinced there was no alternative to fighting through Rommel's defences. He told Gott that 'we must steel ourselves to find a solution to getting our tanks right through the defences and their minefields by night. There was no way to do it on the cheap. Gott made it clear that he would not be prepared to conduct such a battle.'[17] Admired though he was by his British subordinates, Dominion troops were not impressed by Gott and, other than against the Italians, few of his operations were successful. Gott spent the morning of his death with senior officers of Eighth

---

15   Colonel Richardson, quoted in Hamilton, *Monty*, p. 802.
16   Carver, *Out of Step*, p. 100.
17   Carver, *Out of Step*, p. 132.

Army in what has been variously described as a conference, an exercise and a dress rehearsal for future operations, but it was not an event that made a great impression on the participants. His replacement as Eighth Army commander pending the arrival of Montgomery was Ramsden, once described by Tedder as 'A better specimen of the early Crimean school... I feared that nothing would ever make General Ramsden understand the situation.'[18]. Unsuccessful as a corps commander, Ramsden's appointment to command Eighth Army even temporarily is an indication of how thoroughly the pool of senior officer talent in Eighth Army had been drained.

Having said that there was a depth of ability among the middle ranking leaders, particularly on the staff side. De Guingand remained Montgomery's Chief of Staff to the end of the war, his abilities and charm complementing Montgomery's talents and personality and, arguably, saving Montgomery's career on occasion. Richardson as BGS Plans and Williams as Chief of Intelligence were highly competent, and found their talents were fully used under Monty. Roberts was given command of a brigade at the end of July 1942 and went on to lead 11th Armoured Division in Normandy and was rated − by O'Connor amongst others − as the best British armoured divisional commander of the war. He was also prepared to be as uncompromising with his subordinates as his superiors were with him: after his division's first battle in Normandy he sacked one of his brigadiers, one of his infantry battalion commanders and his motor battalion commander. Harding was outstanding as a staff officer, in administration, developing policy and in handling a crisis, went on to shine under Montgomery as commander of 7th Armoured Division, then after recovering from wounds virtually ran 15th Army Group in Italy as Alexander's Chief of Staff before taking over XIII Corps in March 1945. Carver and Pyman became brigadiers at an early age and reached high rank later. Talent took time to come through in Eighth Army, but when it emerged under Montgomery it was properly employed. And that he could bring Morshead, Freyberg and Pienaar on side so rapidly speaks volumes of the changes he made to the divisive army culture that existed before August 1942.

The club ethos persisted in elements of the British army to the end of the war, despite the dominance of Montgomery and the arrival of the new wave of young commanders, and showed to some extent in the three Eighth Army divisions—50th Northumbrian, 51st Highland and 7th Armoured — that led the assault in Normandy in 1944. Montgomery selected them on the grounds that their experience would be invaluable. All three were certainly battle experienced, but had been overseas for some years, five or more in the case of some members of 7th Armoured. Returning to Great Britain was initially seen as a performance reward and the news that they were to lead the invasion was not entirely welcome. Even before Alamein, 7th Armoured were considered to have lost at least some of their 'dash'. It was recognised that there were fine lines between caution, 'cunning' and cowardice and, respecting what the men had done in the past, their commanders were not always inclined to push their colleagues,

18 Tedder, *With Prejudice*, p.167

subordinates and friends beyond a certain point. 50th Northumbrian Division landed on D-Day and did perform well enough despite some unrest prior to embarkation. But 7th Armoured Division and 51st Highland Division acquired a reputation for being 'extremely "swollen-headed". They were a law unto themselves; they thought they need only obey orders that suited them.'[19] A week after D-Day an opportunity to break through the bocage country and to encircle the key city of Caen was missed by 7th Armoured Division through what their commander, Major General Erskine, a desert veteran along with many of 7th Armoured, acknowledged to be poor tactics.[20] The leading elements of 4th County of London Yeomanry were annihilated at Villers Bocage by a solitary Tiger tank under the command of a famous panzer ace, Leutnant Wittman. The extraordinary drama of the event tends to overshadow the setback to British plans: the division had to be withdrawn from a potentially advantageous position and arguably the campaign was set back by some weeks. Erskine blamed himself for the defeat: 'We had been pushing along at great speed and taking many risks. The damage to 4th CLY was as much my fault as anybody's for urging the speed of advance.'[21] Thereafter, the experience seems to have affected his leadership. After the war he told Robin Dunn's father – they were cousins – that 'he had so many friends in the division that he was not going to ask them to do something today, which he knew they could do tomorrow with far fewer casualties.'[22] This concern was widely shared: there is a touching account of how the officers of 5RTR did their best to keep their long serving Sergeant Wardrop alive to the end of the war, by arranging a training role for him.[23] But Erskine's attitude, a product of the 'club', collegiate and family culture of the British regimental system and army, was far removed from the level of ruthlessness and effectiveness practised by the Wehrmacht or by Patton, or even by Horrocks, O'Connor or Crocker, and there is no reason to suppose that it reduced the total casualty list. 7th Armoured Division's performance in Normandy continued to fall short of what was expected from them, both during the 'Goodwood' offensive in July and in the opening stages of 'Operation Bluecoat', the British army's breakthrough battle in August. At that point Montgomery lost patience, and Erskine, his armoured brigade commander, his artillery commander and the Corps commander were all removed, as were over 100 officers and men of the division.[24] The commander

19   Diary of Major General Verney, GOC 7th Armoured Division quoted in Carlo d'Este, *Decision in Normandy* (London: Collins, 1983), p. 173.

20   Another desert veteran, the New Zealand observer Brigadier Hargest, was also dismayed by 7th Armoured Division's poor tactics, in particular the lack of co-operation between armour and infantry at this time, TNA CAB 106/1060: Hargest Report.

21   Carlo d'Este, *Decision in Normandy* (London: Collins, 1983), p. 193.

22   Dunn, *Sword and Wig,* p. 71.

23   Forty, *Wardrop,* p. 207. Wardrop threatened to volunteer and fight the Japanese should he be removed from the European theatre of operations. He was killed in Germany in the last month of the war.

24   Major General G.L. Verney, DSO, MVO, *The Desert Rats, The 7th Armoured Division in World War II* (London: Greenhill Books, 1954), p.215.

of 51st Highland Division was also sacked. The less tolerant regime that replaced the 'club' mindset significantly improved performance. However, the old clubbability did survive the war. In a telling note to his eventual successor as CIGS, Harding wrote to Gerald Templer in 1948, 'I started my military career as a T.A. officer in May 1914 and I am sure it was mainly the "club" side of the business that attracted the best chaps in all ranks and held them together. It would be foolish now to disregard the British addiction to clubs!!'[25]

And of course club ethos and the new professionalism could on occasion meld effectively. In the final stages of the war, in April 1945, Robin Dunn was given command of the late Jock Campbell's Royal Horse Artillery battery in 4th Armoured Brigade, now commanded by a youthful desert veteran, the 29 year old Michael Carver. Dunn admired Carver:

> He would arrive at my OP driving his own Dingo, hatless and relaxed, and would ask in a friendly way how things are going and whether there was anything he could do to help. He was also a decisive and aggressive commander in action.

He had the reputation for being ruthless in his selection and dismissal of subordinates, and the military establishment on occasion closed ranks against him. Dunn believed that his unpopularity derived from military snobbery resulting from his background in the Tank Corps, 'whose officers were then regarded by some of the cavalrymen and riflemen as their social inferiors, though this was certainly not true of Mike.' Dunn himself was socially very much of the Royal Horse Artillery and cavalry background but was pragmatic in his approach to the military profession. In his view the Royal Tank Regiment on the whole performed rather better in battle than the armoured cavalry regiments. His battery was assigned to support the Royal Scots Greys, one of the 'smartest' and reputedly the wealthiest regiment in the army, that had seen action in the war from Alam Halfa onwards. Dunn arrived at regimental headquarters that April to find that the Greys' colonel had just been sacked by Carver and was hosting a farewell party, drinking champagne with his fellow officers while sheltering from the rain under a tarpaulin. The adjutant suddenly announced he had had a message to say there was a Tiger tank reported at a map reference a few hundred yards away. The colonel

> at once drank down his champagne, stood up and said, "This is a job for me." He called his soldier servant to collect a bazooka and they went off together, Frank [the colonel] wearing a gas cape against the rain, to stalk the Tiger. Soon after they had left, the wireless started crackling again and produced another

25   TNA WO 216/250 Harding to Templer, 8 March 1948.

message which said, "Reference our last message. Map reference in error. Should be 10,000 yards to the east." So poor Frank never bagged his Tiger.[26]

Carver appears to have chosen the colonel's successor well. In his last action of the war, Dunn was greatly impressed by the speed and efficiency that the Greys demonstrated in combined arms mobile warfare against determined German infantry that were supported by significant quantities of artillery. He was delighted to take part in what he described as a 'cavalry action' that lasted three days, the brigade pressed on relentlessly to the point of exhaustion by Carver and Carver's new appointee as CO of the Scots Greys, and taking 'the kind of calculated risk and initiative which had so often been lacking in the past.'[27]

The early war in the desert had been an experience that many of its British participants looked back on with some nostalgia. Casualties then were relatively light, at least compared to the later battles in Tunisia and in Italy, and very much lighter than in Normandy. The Eighth Army was sustained by a universal belief that the war was necessary, was worthwhile and would be won. A German view of the British mindset mentions their 'extensive desert experience, composure and a near fatalism given substance by the optimistic expectation of victory.'[28] Memoirs of the time give a similar picture. Robin Dunn found fighting in the desert 'absolutely exhilarating'.[29] Seton-Watson thought that Operation Compass was 'good fun for almost all concerned'[30] and, like Dunn, unashamedly found the experience of danger in battle exhilarating.[31] Dominick Graham, nineteen years old when war broke out, served in the Norwegian campaign before getting himself transferred to North Africa in 1942 where he found that 'the army was amateur, friendly, and fought as though it were playing a game.'[32] Essentially they belonged to the same club, they soldiered with friends, and if they lost that week's match, there was always next Saturday. They were amateurs at heart. A phrase or sentiment that regularly appears in informal correspondence from the period is 'fair', or 'unfair', in contexts as varied as the granting of leave, the unreasonable dismissal of a respected senior, or the senseless deployment in emergency of small hapless contingents of men. 'Fairness' and 'reasonable behaviour' are not concepts generally linked with a professional outlook, and few would associate them with military life, but they were significant factors in the thinking of the British military hierarchy. They are more to be expected among the members of a club, whose essence is that members should be mutually acceptable to one another, evading disagreements and antagonisms, to be essentially of like mind. Club members join together for

26   Dunn, *Sword and Wig*, p. 82.
27   Dunn, *Sword and Wig*, p. 87.
28   Buschleb, *Operation Crusader*, p. 18.
29   Dunn, *Sword and Wig*, p.46, and in conversation with the writer.
30   Seton-Watson, *Dunkirk – Alamein – Bologna*, p. 59.
31   Seton-Watson, *Dunkirk – Alamein – Bologna*, p. 86
32   Graham, *Against Odds*, p. 7.

reasons quite different to those of a professional trade association or society. They are likely to discourage argument, accept conformity, value tradition and current practices and select new members on the basis of how well they fit with the existing profile. This does not exclude personal differences, but creative and original thought is rarely a priority. Questioning practices requires criticism of the recognised order, so when confronted with a problem, club members may prefer to simply cope as best they can with the immediate difficulty rather than reform their methods, their principle objective being to maintain stability and harmony. Thus after Operation Battleaxe, the British Army displayed its tendency to look for features of the battle that validated existing leadership and tactics. Even after the disasters of the summer of 1942, the suggestion that there might be something amiss with the structure of British regiments caused outrage at the highest levels. In contrast, the Wehrmacht's reporting system, highly critical and honest at both the tactical and operational level, examined their own strengths and weaknesses in a notably professional manner.

It would be unjust not to recognise in the British army, as their opponents often did, the 'hardness and stubbornness which must be admired and which never flagged, even in situations which seemed to be hopeless',[33] This quality underpinned the amateur spirit and club ethos of the British army of the early war years. But Dorman-Smith for one was in no doubt that amateurism was also at the root of Eighth Army's failings. In a letter to John Connell, the biographer of Wavell and Auchinleck, he reflected on his former colleagues:

> There was not the same savage professionalism as existed in the Afrika Korps ... we were an unaggressive, unassertive lot, rather too polite & gentle, perhaps lacking in drive ... But we were extraordinarily unrattleable...we were ultra-detached, recognising nothing as a crisis. Odd to say about a British regular officer, but we were too civilised. Montgomery's vinegar-and-gall was necessary when it came ... Something was wrong with us, not just our tanks.[34]

As an epitaph, it serves well enough.

In tribute to
Major J.B. Colvin, West Yorkshire Regiment
his cousin Captain Robin Dunn, 11 Honourable Artillery Company
and his brother in law Lieutenant General Noel Beresford-Peirse
GOC 4th Indian Division and XIII Corps

***

33   Reidel, Chief of Staff of 15 Pz Div, quoted in Gudmunsson, *Inside the Afrika Korps*, p. 256.
34   JRLGB133GOW, 1/11/2 to John Connell, 2 December 1958.

How can I live among this gentle
obsolescent breed of heroes, and not weep?
Each, fool and hero, will be an immortal

Keith Douglas, 1920-1944

Appendix

Equipment

The perceived inferiority of British tanks affected both the tactics and the confidence of British tank crews. The technical aspects of guns and armour have been in the public domain for many years – what is uncertain is how far and for which periods of time the inferiority complex acquired by British troops was justified. Perceptions and memories do not always reflect the historical reality, and technical inferiority could be blamed when the real problem was inappropriate tactics.

In 1939 British tanks were designed for distinct roles: reconnaissance (light tanks), infantry support (heavy) and exploitation (medium, or 'cruiser' as the British called them in this period). The British light Vickers tank was armed with machine guns only, and like its German opposite number, the Panzerkampfwagen Mark I, was obsolete by the end of 1940. The first British infantry tank, the A11, was a stopgap built to a price and produced in limited numbers but the next version, the A12 also known as the Matilda, was feared by the Germans as 'the heaviest and strongest in the world' in 1940-41,[1] almost invulnerable to all Axis weapons except the 88mm gun until the following year and frequently taken into service by the Afrika Korps when captured. It was popular with its crews for its armour protection but, unreliable if obliged to sustain much more than walking pace, it had difficulty in operating with cruiser tanks that by their nature depended on speed and manoeuvrability. Modifying cruiser tank tactics to suit the Matilda went entirely against the 'cavalry' mindset of many armoured division units, and it was therefore difficult to use it in 'the clash of armour' that British commanders were wont to seek. The Matilda's replacement, the Valentine, remained useful throughout 1942 as an infantry support tank thanks to its fairly good armour protection, reliability and slightly greater speed. Though hampered by its obsolete 2 pounder gun, as late as October 1942 it took a one-for-one toll of

1   Schraepler, p. 117.

German tanks at Alamein when used in conjunction with aggressive Australian anti-tank tactics but it was never a success in mobile warfare since it was outclassed by German tank gunpower soon after it first appeared. Cruiser tanks, whose task was to combat the German medium Mk IIIs and IVs, were the critical issue, and assessing the relative battle-worthiness of these is difficult because of the multitude of types on each side – there were usually three different British models in service at any one time, the mix was constantly changing and the evolution of Axis models complicates the business of assessing their relative effectiveness in action. Looking separately at each period of engagement does at least allow one to try to disentangle the confusion of numbers, technicalities and perceptions.

Operation 'Compass', December 1940 – February 1941

Against the Italians in North Africa in 1940, the Vickers light tanks were useful for little more than rounding up prisoners and were withdrawn from service after 1940. The heavy Matildas were invulnerable to Italian artillery and decisive in assaults on Italian fixed defences but were mechanically not capable of travelling far or fast enough to work with the British A10 and A13 cruisers. The first Italian tanks encountered were hardly more than the equivalent of British Bren gun carriers – their crews not unreasonably tended to abandon them at the sight of British armour. British tank superiority in this period was overwhelming.

The Italian medium tank, the M13/40, did not appear until their 10th Army was clearly in retreat early in 1941 and while its specification was similar to British cruisers, it was inferior in most respects. Though bravely handled it was slow, unreliable, poorly equipped with wireless and suffered accordingly. At Beda Fomm, 112 M13s faced 24 British cruisers,[2] but without wireless could not co-ordinate their attacks, fired on the move and were without significant support from artillery or infantry, while most actions by 2RTR were from stationary hull down positions, supported by 2-pdr anti-tank guns.

'Sonnenblume' and 'Battleaxe', April – June 1941

The Axis response to Italian defeat was to send Rommel and the Afrika Korps to Libya under the operational code name 'Sonnenblume' - Sunflower. The principal German medium tank, the Mk III armed with a 50mm gun, was comparable to the British A10 and A13 cruisers but the German newcomers were in factory condition and greatly superior in numbers. The Matildas of 7RTR, invulnerable to German anti-tank fire but too slow and short ranged – in the desert they needed refuelling

---

2   Liddell Hart Centre for Military Archives, Creagh Papers.

after 20 miles – for manoeuvre warfare,[3] remained in the Tobruk garrison and were critical in holding the town, inflicting heavy losses on attacks by German armour. The first German tank formation to reach North Africa, Panzer Regiment 5, was equipped with the Mark III Model G version and a few Mark IVs, both with 30mm frontal armour though some may have been upgraded with additional plates. Although it is widely claimed that the British 2-pdr gun was ineffective against German armour, 7th Armoured Division's Intelligence summary[4] early in June 1941 relates a different story:

> Results of tests carried out against German Mk IV tanks by 2pdrs in British A13 tanks reveal excellent penetration. Details are given below. These results should be made known to all ranks.
>
> [At] 500 yds: all shots on 20mm side & hull passed completely through and out the other side.
>
> 700 yds   as above, and on 40mm armour penetrated 10-15 mm other side
>
> 1200 yds penetrated 20 & 40mm armour
>
> Against frontal armour, 5 out of 6 shots penetrated thick single and double frontal armour at 500 yds.

For Operation 'Battleaxe' later that month, British armoured brigades with the A10 and A13 cruisers, the A15 Crusader and the Matilda, faced the German MkIII. Their 2-pdr guns were comparable in armour piercing performance to the German 50mm tank gun of that period. The Afrika Korps had now been reinforced with Panzer Regiment 8, largely equipped with the Mk III Model H, which had additional 30mm frontal plates, 'face-hardened', a process that tended to cause solid shot to break up. On 15 June, Pz Regt 8 had 82 operational tanks, while Pz Regt 5 had 96, most of which lacked the additional plates.[5] Total British numerical strength in cruisers and infantry tanks was similar to the German total. If a tactical plan had been found to enable the Matildas to work with the cruisers, their invulnerability should have been decisive. Even so, despite heavy losses of equipment and eventual defeat, all British reports on the offensive were determinedly positive: their analysis was that their tank units had outfought German units and only minor changes to tactics and procedures were needed. 7th Armoured Division reported:

> In every case when met with determined and resolute opposition, and in spite of their superior numbers, the enemy have given ground before our tks and guns.

3   Liddell Hart Centre for Military Archives, Creagh Papers, letter to Beresford-Peirse, 29 May 1941.

4   TNA WO 169/1147: Intelligence summary, No. 44, 5 June 1941.

5   T L. Jentz (ed.), *Panzertruppen*, (Atglen, Pennsylvania: Schiffer Military History, 1996), p. 166.

It is so far apparent that the Germans display a lack of manoeuvrability in their actions, and for this reason the enemy does not have the same effect with his large masses as we should, had we similar numbers.[6]

British armour had been outnumbered in the tank versus tank encounter as the result of the Matildas being deployed separately from the cruisers in an infantry support role, where they came to grief on German 88mm guns. As far as the cruiser regiments were concerned, their feeling was that their tanks and guns were fine, more of the same was all that was required.

A serious deficiency in the cruisers at this time was the inadequacy and limited number of wireless sets, making for difficulties in command and control. At one point, half a dozen tanks without wireless disappeared in the direction of the enemy, never to be seen again. British tanks were unreliable as well. Not only did this mean losses through breakdown, but the hours of extra maintenance that crews were forced to devote to their machines each night added to the strain they were under and may have encouraged their practice of withdrawal from the battlefield each evening, a routine that allowed the DAK to recover their own damaged vehicles. Early cruisers and Crusaders began to show signs of wear after 500 miles and needed complete overhauls after 1000 miles. German Mk IIIs and IVs initially suffered badly in the extreme conditions of the desert, but remedies were quickly found and some are recorded as being in good condition with 4000 kilometers on their odometers. American tanks were more durable than the British and needed less maintenance: Honeys were renowned for reliability and the Grants seem to have achieved 1500 miles between overhauls.

Not appreciated at this stage was the advantage German tank crews had in ammunition and in tank 'survivability'. German armour piercing shells contained a small explosive charge that detonated after penetration with often devastating results, while the British solid shot relied on kinetic energy and fragmentation of the shot and debris from the target's armour plate for destructive effect. And British tanks lacked the German ammunition stowage compartments that gave significant protection to the highly flammable propellant. British Crusaders in particular were notorious for catching fire after being hit. Even General Ravenstein of 21st Panzer Division commented to his captors in December 1941 on the Crusaders' propensity to burn.

Winter Battles, November 1941 – January 1942

In November 1941, A13 cruisers and A15 Crusaders made up 7th Armoured Brigade. 22nd Armoured Brigade had arrived in the Middle East equipped with Crusaders, and 4th Armoured Brigade had been re-equipped with American M3 light tanks, known as Stuarts or Honeys to the British. Deployed as cruisers, these had the virtues

6   TNA WO 169/1173: 7th Armoured Division War Diary.

of speed and reliability but their armour was weaker, the gun was not significantly better than the Crusader's, and their fighting compartment was awkward for a battle tank. German medium tanks had now mostly been up-armoured with 'face-hardened' 30 or 40mm plates attached to the front of the superstructure and turret so that their frontal armour was better protected against 2-pdr fire.

30. The factory fitted, 'face-hardened', spaced armour that gave the Panzer Mk III and IV frontal protection proof against British 2-pdr anti-tank fire. (The Tank Museum Bovington 4868-A3)

Factory fitted spaced armour made the Panzer Mk III and IV frontal armour proof against British 2-pdr anti-tank fire. British wireless sets were now better and more numerous though by no means universally provided. British optimism survived the opening stages of the winter battles and crews initially overestimated the numbers of enemy tanks they had destroyed, to the extent that their reports seriously misled their high command – given the effectiveness of the additional 'face hardened' plates on German tanks' frontal armour, it is possible that when British crews saw the tracer of their shells strike an opposing tank they wrongly reported its destruction. And the reluctance of German tanks to catch fire may have resulted in the same vehicle being repeatedly targeted and hit, and repeatedly reported destroyed. Though the significantly inferior Italian machines had not improved during the year, Italian armoured units surprised British commanders by their performance. They combined effectively with their anti-tank guns and infantry, and fought with so much resolution that a myth spread that some Italian tanks were manned by German crews.[7] It was clear after the winter battles that the Stuart/Honey was not really much of a battle tank, and that the Crusader needed significant numerical advantage to compete against the Mk IIIs, and was difficult to maintain in the field as well as much more prone than German tanks to bursting into flames. At the close of December 1941, just when it appeared that British armoured forces finally had the measure of their enemy and confidence was high that Rommel was on the run, the single British armoured brigade following up the German retreat was badly mauled by a numerically smaller force from the Afrika Korps, losing 70 from 108 tanks.[8] A majority of the losses were mechanical – the Crusaders in particular were worn out and failing fast while the German tanks were newly arrived and therefore mechanically sound as well as being the latest models. Then in the last ten days of January 1942 the fresh and inexperienced 2nd Armoured Brigade and its accompanying Support Group were both trounced by the Afrika Korps in an opportunistic attack. 2nd Armoured Brigade was left with only 18 tanks having lost 41 in battle, and another 53 that could not be recovered after running out of petrol or breaking down. The Support Group had been operating in columns unsupported by and too distant to support the armoured brigade and duly lost most of its guns.[9]

British conclusions from the winter fighting were that their equipment was at a disadvantage against the German, and that their approach to war in the desert needed a change of method or personnel. Auchinleck wrote in December,[10] 'We have, as you say, a hell of a lot to learn about handling armour on the battlefield' and in a letter to Churchill he gave a re-assessment of the Italians:

> Before the fighting started, judging by last year's experiences we were inclined to dismiss the Italian M13 tank as valueless and, indeed, to leave the whole of the Italian armoured Ariete division out of our calculations. We were wrong in this. The Italian tanks and the Italian armoured division have fought well and had an appreciable effect on the battle.[11]

It was of course not the Italian tanks that were so potent, but their deployment with anti-tank guns and infantry that made them effective. And it was the failure to deploy

---

7   TNA WO 201.364: Crusader operational reports.
8   TNA WO 169/1294: 22nd Armd Bde War Diary.
9   TNA CAB 106.662: Messervy's Report, February 1942.
10   JRL GB/133/AUC524, 6/12 to Arthur Smith.
11   JRL GB/133/AUC/628, to PM 12/1.

armour and artillery together that sealed the fate of 2nd Armoured Brigade and its Support Group, as much as the weakness of its Crusaders.

Gazala Battles, May-June 1942

In April and May one or two squadrons in each British cruiser regiment were re-equipped with the American M3 Grant, which had the advantages of an adequate gun, fair reliability and excellent armour. Its ability to fire a reasonably sized high explosive shell against anti-tank guns was a major advance and should have made a difference on the battlefield. Its disadvantage was the positioning of its 75mm main gun in the hull, allowing only limited traverse and making fully hull down positions impossible, and the gun's medium velocity made accurately judging the range, difficult in desert haze, dust and smoke, more than usually important. Its poor sight was also a handicap. Some regiments were short of training on their new vehicle, receiving their Grants only days before the German attack. Its armour was largely proof against the most numerous German tank, the Mk III, and frequently withstood a dozen or more hits from enemy fire. As far as Crusaders and Honeys were concerned, Eighth Army's assessment of 1 May 1942 reckoned Crusaders and Honeys needed odds of 3:2 against German Mk IIIs. Confidence was low enough to believe that odds of 1:1 against the German Mk II and the Italian M13 were also required, despite the fact that the British 2-pdr far outranged the Mk II's 20mm gun[12] and the M13 was inferior in every respect except its capacity for HE fire. Auchinleck's comment on his copy of this letter, in red crayon, that 'leadership and tactics must be our real standby' was true enough but offered no actual remedy.[13]

In May 1942, the Germans began to receive improved Mk III and IV tanks, known as 'Specials' to the British, and mounting much superior guns, though quantities of these were initially very limited. More importantly, they fielded a few 88mm guns mounted on halftracks and a good number of captured Russian 76.2mm guns,[14] highly effective anti-tank weapons more mobile, more numerous and less conspicuous than the 88mm. A number were mounted on redundant tank chassis and christened Marders, only lightly armoured but efficient tank destroyers.[15] British analysts during the summer noted that most Grant losses were to shells greater than 50mm calibre and given the limited quantity of 88mms and even fewer Mk IVs with the new 75mm gun, a significant number must have been to Marders and to the towed 76.2mm gun. The speed with which Grants were identified and knocked out during the initial stages

---

12 Jentz, *Tank Combat in North Africa*, p. 53.
13 JRL GB/133/AUC 832, letter from Auchinleck, 1 May 1942.
14 The 76.2mm gun was in fact derived from the obsolete British 3" AA gun, surplus stocks of which were sold to the Soviet Union and converted to field artillery. Quantities were captured by the Wehrmacht and were adapted to fire German anti-tank ammunition.
15 It appears that not more than one *Abteilung* (battalion sized unit) was equipped with Marders, to a maximum of 27, at any one time.

of the summer battles confirms this improved German capability. The standard Mk IV tank was now also provided with hollow charge ammunition which made it more effective against all British tanks.

By the summer 1942 the Italians had marginally updated their M13, giving it an improved engine, and renamed it the M14, but they also fielded the Semovente, a turretless version of the M13 with a 75mm gun mounted in the hull which with a hollow charge shell was effective against British armour. Production was limited (250 over an 18 month period) and it is unlikely that more than two dozen were deployed at any one time. Italian armoured formations were now supported by 88mm guns or by their own 90mm equivalent, which gave them improved defensive capability against British armour. There are few references in British accounts to Italian armour confronting British tanks other than defensively. Mechanical frailty and the inadequate wireless of Italian tanks continued to hinder the Ariete and Littorio divisions ability to keep pace with the Afrika Korps. Italian tank strength fluctuated wildly, from 240 on 26 May to 16 by 1 June, to 54 on 8 July, and 40 on the 31st[16]

It is difficult to argue that Eighth Army was inferior to the Axis in armour at the beginning of the decisive Gazala battle on 27 May. Their 167 Grants outmatched all German AFVs except the Mk IV Specials, which only became operative after the start of the battle and might have numbered half a dozen by mid-June, the Marders, of which a couple of dozen may have been shipped during the summer, and the limited number of older Mk IVs with hollow charge ammunition. The Grants would have completely outclassed the bulk of the German armour, the 223 standard Mk IIIs. German Mk IIIs and IVs, now all up-armoured, certainly had an advantage over the 257 Crusaders and 149 Honeys, which before the end of the summer were withdrawn from the main battle and grouped into a Light Armoured Division. The 166 Valentines were by now outclassed in their cruiser role, and like the 110 Matildas suffered against anti-tank guns in their infantry support role. With support from heavy anti-tank guns, the Italian M13s and Semoventes proved influential though not decisive in action. In the end, it was German and Italian combined arms tactics rather than their equipment or numbers that gave them an advantage, and the German victory came despite numerical and qualitative British superiority, and to judge by Dunn's comments after looking over some knocked out German tanks in June, it was also aided by a certain German moral ascendancy:

[I] decided that everything German was unattractive, their food, their clothes and above all the smell and the hard, ruthless lines of their tanks [but] was fascinated by the tanks. Everything was so neat and well thought out: the ration boxes, the compartments for blankets, the escape hatch for the driver in the floor; the commander's seat in the turret with the thick bullet proof glass all the

16   Walker, *Iron Hulls, Iron Hearts,* p. 149.

way round, giving him a great field of view. The log books in every case were kept right up to date. It was all so simple and efficient.'[17]

Mersa Matruh, June 1942

British tank recovery systems were well organised by the spring of 1942 and provided damaged vehicles got to workshops they could often be returned to the front quite quickly. But when from mid-June defeated British units were forced off the battlefield, recovery of their damaged or broken down tanks was impossible, so front line tank strength by late June fell to about 60 Grants and as many assorted cruisers. This was nonetheless by then about double the total tank strength of the Afrika Korps and it is a measure of Auchinleck's lack of confidence in his army that despite initially ordering a stand at Mersa Matruh after the fall of Tobruk, in the event he felt unable to challenge Rommel. Mersa Matruh was again a German victory despite British numerical and qualitative superiority.

First Alamein, July 1942

Throughout the subsequent retreat to Alamein and the July battles, British armour was numerically superior to German and the preponderance of Grants meant it was not outgunned tank for tank. Rommel recognised this reality when he called off his last attack on 8 July, thereafter remaining on the defensive until late August. Throughout, Eighth Army was numerically and qualitatively superior. This time, they managed a draw.

Alma Halfa, September 1942

After British losses in the summer, it took time to reinforce the Eighth Army thanks to its immensely long supply chain, whether materiel came from Britain or the US. The Panzerarmee was able to rebuild its forces more rapidly and by the end of August 1942 it enjoyed over Eighth Army its greatest numerical and qualitative advantage in armour of the campaign. In particular, the Mark IV Specials, described by their users as 'outstandingly good',[18] decimated the Grants of 22nd Armoured Brigade. But German numerical and qualitative advantage were foiled by appropriate British tactics, resulting in a British defensive success.

---

17 Dunn, p. 278.
18 TNA CAB 146/15: DAK tactical report, p. 210.

Alamein, October 1942

By October, the Eighth Army had a very distinct advantage in armour over the Panzer Armee. If one compares the numbers of roughly equivalent models, the figures are:

British		German/Italian
Sherman	252	40 Mark IV, including 30 Specials
Grant	170	89 Mark III Specials, plus
		50 Marders/Semoventes
Crusader 6-pdr*	78	102 Mark III
Honey	119	278 M13 and M14
Valentine	194	

* Armed with a 6-pdr gun, the Crusader was quite an effective tank, and crews liked its low profile – it was two feet lower than the Sherman.

At Alamein, the chief killer of tanks was the anti-tank gun. German anti-tank guns at the start of the battle numbered 290 50mm, 68 76.2mm, and 86 88mm. Though some German reports claim the 50mm anti-tank gun was not effective against British Shermans,[19] and the same would apply to the gun of the Mark III Special, German test data show they and the 6-pdr were almost identical in effectiveness. But at Alamein the high explosive capacity of the Shermans and Grants, now with improved sights, began to counter the threat from anti-tank guns, and where field artillery could be brought into play, combined arms tactics, widely adopted at last, were used to good effect. Roberts' 22nd Armoured Brigade had three regiments of artillery available and he used them: he reported to Major General Richardson towards the end of November 1942 that 'once out of the minefields we had practically no casualties in this Bde. We have got the 88mm guns fairly well taped now & knocked out a good many of them'.[20] Similarly, in the final stages, the Sherwood Rangers' Crusaders, the updated version with a 6-pdr gun, came across the German rearguard. The Sherwood Rangers had first seen action as a tank regiment at Alam Halfa, where they charged forward into a screen of anti-tank guns, losing a number of tanks. 'We made every mistake in the book, but fortunately the battle only lasted a few days and then we had six weeks in which to sort ourselves out, reorganise and train, and learn from our mistakes'.[21] Keith Douglas rejoined the regiment towards the end of Alamein and witnessed their newly acquired technique:

19   TNA CAB 146/17: Panzerarmee daily reports – ineffectiveness of 50mm gun at Alamein.
20   Liddell Hart Centre for Military Archives, Roberts Papers , Letter to Richardson, MG AFV, 14 November 1942.
21   Holland (ed.), *An Englishman at War*, p. 263.

The 88s were waiting for us as we came abreast of the crashed Stuka, and their grey bursts and ricochets came bouncing round us and the armoured cars, who scuttled back to our line. Between the armoured cars, the Crusaders, and the O.P. we brought the twenty-five pounders down on them and destroyed one. The others limbered up and pelted away behind their tractors, across the plain, pursued by our shells.[22]

British anti-tank guns took a heavy toll on the German armour before Rommel halted the immediate counter-attack policy. The motor brigades of the armoured divisions held sixteen six pounder anti-tank guns in each infantry battalion, and a similar number of two pounders were integrated into the line infantry battalions. Additional 6-pdrs were held within divisional anti-tank regiments to be deployed where necessary. The famous episode at 'Snipe' is the prime example of their effectiveness, but it was not unique: on the 25 October, Corporal Main's battalion was attacked by approximately 40 Mk IIIs and M13s.

A heavy barrage was brought down on our positions, also machine-gun and mortar fire. Since we were in the front with our machine-guns, as the tanks drew closer we had to stop firing and take cover in our slit trenches. Our sixteen six-pounders engaged the tanks, several firing at one particular tank, so that the closest was knocked out fifty yards in front. The Battalion was credited with fourteen tanks ... From the right came cries of 'You rotten Pommie bastards!' The Australians strongly objected to us knocking out the tanks with six-pounders before they came within range of their two-pounders.[23]

It was later that evening that Rommel halted the policy of local counter-attacks.

22   Douglas, *Alamein to Zem Zem*, p. 53.
23   IWM, Private papers of D.A. Main, 87/35/1 quoted in Hammond, Chapter 7, loc 3831.

Bibliography

Primary Sources

National Archives (Kew)

CAB 44/97	Operation 'Aberdeen'.
CAB 106/654	Battle of Alam Halfa – Lt. Gen. Sir Brian Horrocks' Report
CAB 106/662	Maj. Gen. Messervy's Report, February 1942
CAB 146/15	Part IV, appendices
HW 1/676	Report on German tactics, 26 June 1942
WO 32/9581	Bartholomew Report on campaign in France 1940.
WO 106/2235	Operations 26.5-2.7.42 Report of Court of Enquiry
WO 163/51	Army Council Paper on Death Penalty.
WO 169/401	9th Lancers War Diary, letter 22 April 1942 from Lt Col E.O.Burne
WO 169/1174	Eighth Army Int. Review No.4, 'German Tank Tactics in Libya'.
WO 169/1185	7 Support Group War Diary Jan 1940 – Dec 1941
WO 169/1294	22 Armd Bde War Diary
WO 169/4006	1 Armd Div, Op Order 15
WO 169/4210	2 Armd Bde War Diary
WO 169/4216	4 Armd Bde War Diary
WO 169/4251	22 Armd Bde War Diary ,1942
WO 169/5077	2 West Yorks War Diary
WO 190/283	Military Attaché Berlin reporting views of German General Staff, 1934
WO 201/357	Operation 'Battleaxe': Lessons of the campaign.
WO 201/358	Eighth Army Operations, September 10th to November 17th 1941
WO 201/364	'Crusader' Operational reports
WO 201/379	Lt. Gen. Ritchie's Report on Ops May/June 1942
WO 201/452	Notes on main lessons of recent operations Sept/Nov 1941

WO 201/527	Brigadiers Harding & Watkins' discussion 27.12.41 & Notes on Employment of Armour, 4 January 1942
WO 201/2586	Middle East Training pamphlet No. 10, Lessons of Cyrenaica Campaign, December 1940 – February 1941
WO 201/2644	Report on Indian troops 1943
WO 201/2695	Maj. Gen. Messervy personal correspondence, letter to Lt. Gen. Godwin-Austen , 27 January 1942
WO 201/2696	Report on withdrawal El Agheila – Gazala, Jan-Feb 1942
WO 201/2769	Intelligence report Enemy Ops, April – June 1941
WO 201/2870	Lt. Gen. Martel's Report on Operation 'Crusader'
WO 201/2871	Lt. Gen. Norrie's Report on Operations, May 26 – July 8 1942
WO 231/93	Command Study in North Africa
WO 231/260	Army Training Manual No 43, May 1942, Demands of Modern War
WO 231/281	Army Training Instruction No 2 1941, Army Tank/Infantry Co-operation
WO 232/7	Interrogation of senior German officers, 1945
WO2 36/1	Mersa Matruh & Tobruk, Semi-Official Correspondence: letters from Lt. Gen Erskine
WO 259/73	Auchinleck to Brooke, 20 February 1942
WO 279/57	Staff Conference at Camberley, 17-20 January 1927

John Rylands Library (Manchester)

GB133AUC, Papers of Field Marshal Sir Claude Auchinleck, KGCB, GCIE, CSI, DSO, OBE
GB133GOW, Papers of Major General Eric Dorman-O'Gowan, MC

Churchill Archive Centre (Cambridge)

Papers of Lieutenant General Thomas Corbett, CB, MC
Papers of Correlli Barnett
Papers of Lieutenant General Sir Alexander Galloway, KBE, CB, DSO, MC

Liddell Hart Centre for Military Archives, King's College (London)

Papers of Brigadier John Alan Lyde Caunter.
Papers of Major General Sir Michael O'Moore Creagh
R.W.Thompson's correspondence with Maj. Gen. Eric Edward Dorman-O'Gowan (formerly Eric Edward Dorman-Smith) (1960-1974)
Papers of General Sir Richard O'Connor
Papers of Brigadier George Davy, GB0099 Davy Manuscript memoirs & notes

Papers of Major General Percy Hobart, 15/11/11 Account by Major General Gott of
    actions of 7th Armd Div, 18 Nov – 27 Dec 1941
Papers of Lieutenant Colonel Liardet

Imperial War Museum (London)

Papers of Major General R. Briggs
Private Papers of Sir Robin Dunn – 94/41/1
Papers of Lieutenant General Sir Francis Tuker
Major General Strawson, *General Sir Richard McCreery,* privately published memoir,
    7533

Bovington Tank Museum Archives

3rd Royal Tank Regt War Diaries
5th Royal Tank Regt War Diaries
3rd County of London Yeomanry War Diaries
4th County of London Yeomanry War Diaries
8th Hussars War Diaries
10th Hussars War Diaries

Documents Possessed by Author

Lieutenant General Richard O'Connor's 'Order of the Day', February 1941
Transcript of Conference on 'Armoured Warfare in World War II' held at Battelle
    Memorial, Institute, Columbus, Ohio, May 10 1979, Guest speaker General
    Major Friedrich von Mellenthin

Published Sources

Allport, Alan, *Browned Off and Bloody-Minded: The British Soldier Goes to War 1939-
    1945* (Newhaven & London: Yale University Press, 2015)
Barr, Neil, *Pendulum of War: Three Battles at Alamein* (London: Jonathan Cape, 2004)
Bates, Peter, *The Dance of War: The Story of the Battle for Egypt* (London: Leo Cooper,
    1992)
Baynes, John, *The Forgotten Victor: General Sir Richard O'Connor* (London: Brassey's,
    1989)
Beevor, Sir Antony, *Inside the British Army* (London: Corgi Books, 1994)
Behrendt, Hans Otto, *Rommel's Intelligence in the Desert Campaign* (London: William
    Kimber, 1980)
Bennett, Ralph, *Ultra and Mediterranean Strategy* (London: Hamish Hamilton, 1989)
Bidwell, Shelford & Graham, Dominick, *Fire-Power: British Army Weapons and
    Theories of War 1904-1945* (Boston: Allen & Unwin, 1985)

Boyd, David, *Elites and their Education* (Windsor: NFER Publishing Co., 1973)

Buschleb, Herman, *Operation Crusader: Tank Warfare in the Desert, Tobruk 1941* (Philadelphia & Oxford: Casemate Publishers, 2019)

Carver, Field Marshal Lord Michael, *Dilemmas of the Desert War* (London: Batsford, 1986)

Carver, Field Marshal Lord Michael, *Harding of Petherton* (London: Weidenfeld & Nicholson, 1978)

Carver, Field Marshal Lord Michael, *Out of Step* (London: Hutchinson, 1989)

Carver, Field Marshal Lord Michael, *The Apostles of Mobility: The Lees-Knowles Lectures of 1979* (London: Weidenfeld and Nicholson, 1979)

Carver, Field Marshal Lord Michael, *The Seven Ages of the British Army* (London: Weidenfeld and Nicholson, 1984)

Carver, Field Marshal Lord Michael, *Tobruk* (London: Pan Books, 1972)

Clayton, Anthony, *The British Officer* (London: Routledge, 2007)

Cloake, John, *Templer. Tiger of Malaya: The Life of Field Marshal Sir Gerald Templer* (London: Harrap, 1985).

Condell, Bruce & Zabecki, David (eds.), *On the German Art of War: Truppenführung* (London: Lynne Reiner Publishers, 2001)

Citino, Robert M., *The Path to Blitzkrieg* (Mechanicsburg, Pennsylvania: Stackpole Books, 2008)

Connell, John, *Wavell: Scholar and Soldier* (London: Collins, 1964).

Clayton, Anthony, *The British Officer* (London: Routledge, 2007)

Danchev, Alex, *Alchemist of War: The Life of Basil Liddell Hart* (London: Orion Books Ltd, 1999)

Danchev, Alex & Todman, Daniel (eds.), *War Diaries 1939-1945: Field Marshal Lord Alanbrooke* (London: Weidenfeld and Nicholson, 2001)

Demeter, Karl, *The German Officer Corps in State and Society 1650-1945* (New York: Frederick A. Praeger, 1965)

d'Este, Carlo, *Decision in Normandy* (London: Collins, 1981)

Dinardo, R.L., *Germany's Panzer Arm in WWII* (Mechanicsburg, Pennsylvania: Stackpole Books, 2006)

Doherty, Richard, *British Armoured Divisions and their Commanders 1939-1945* (Barnsley: Pen & Sword, 2013)

Donovan, John, (ed.), *A Very Fine Commander: The Memoirs of General Horatius Murray* (Barnsley: Pen and Sword, 2010)

Douglas, Keith, *From Alamein to Zem Zem* (London: Faber & Faber, 2009)

Dunn, Sir Robin, *Sword & Wig* (London: Quiller Press, 1993)

Fennell, Jonathan, *Combat and Morale in the North African Campaign* (Cambridge: Cambridge University Press, 2011)

Forty, George, (ed.), *Jake Wardrop's Diary* (Stroud: Amberley Publishing plc, 2009)

French, David, *Military Identities: The Regimental System, The British Army & the British People c.1870-2000* (Oxford: Oxford University Press, 2005)

Godwin-Austen, Major A.R., *The Staff and the Staff College* (London: Constable, 1927)

Graecen, Lavinia, *Chink: A Biography* (London: Macmillan, 1989)

Gross, Gerhardt, *The Myth and Reality of German Warfare: Operational Thinking from Moltke* (Kentucky: Kentucky University Press, 2016)

Graham, Dominick, *Against Odds* (Basingstoke: MacMillan Press, 1999)

Griffiths, Paddy, *WWII Desert Tactics* (Oxford: Osprey, 2008)

Gudmunsson, Bruce I., (ed.), *Inside the Afrika Korps, The Crusader Battles 1941-42* (London: Greenhill Books 1999)

Guingand, Major General Sir Francis de, *Operation Victory* (London: Hodder and Stoughton, 1947)

Haig, Major the Earl, *My Father's Son* (London: Leo Cooper, 1999)

Hamilton, Nigel, *Monty: The Making of a General, 1887-1942* (London: Hamlyn Paperbacks, 1992)

Hamilton, Stuart, *Armoured Odyssey* (London: Tom Donovan, 1995)

Harris, J P & Toase, F.N., *Armoured Warfare* (London: Batsford, 1990)

Hartshorn, E.P., *Avenge Tobruk* (Cape Town: Purnell and Sons, 1960)

Harvey, John (ed.), *The War Diaries of Oliver Harvey* (London: Collins, 1978)

Hastings, R.H.W.S., *The Rifle Brigade in the Second World War, 1939-45* (Aldershot: Gale & Polden, 1952).

Hislop, John Archibald, *A Soldier's Story, Memoir of a British Officer in the Indian Army, 1935-1947* (Newhaven: Newhaven Publishing, 2007)

Holland, James, (ed.), *An Englishman at War: The Diaries of Stanley Christopherson* (London: Bantam Press, 2014)

Howard, Sir Michael, *Captain Professor* (London: Continuum, 2006)

Howard, Michael, *Otherwise Ocuppied* (London: Old Street Publishing, 2010)

Jackson, General Sir William, *The North African Campaign 1940-43* (London: Batsford, 1975)

Jentz, Thomas L., (ed.), *Panzertruppen* (Arglen, Pennsylvania: Schiffer Military History, 1996)

Jentz, Thomas L., *Tank Combat in North Africa* (Arglen, Pennsylvania: Schiffer Military History, 1998)

Katz, David Brock, *South Africans Versus Rommel* (Guilford, Connecticut: Stackpole Books, 2018)

Kennedy, Capt. J.R., *This Our Army* (London: Hutchinson, 1935)

Knox, Macgregor, *Common Destiny* (Cambridge: Cambridge University Press, 2000)

Latimer, Jon, *Alamein* (London: John Murray, 2002)

Lee, Christopher, *Carrington: An Honourable Man* (London: Penguin-Viking, 2017)

Lewin, Ronald, *Man of Armour: A Study of Lt. General Vyvyan Pope* (London: Leo Cooper, 1976)

Liddell Hart, Captain B.H. (ed.), *The Rommel Papers* (London: Collins, 1953)

Liddell Hart, Captain B.H., *The Tanks: The History of the Royal Tank Regiment, Vol.II* (London: Cassell, 1959)

Liddell Hart, Captain B.H., *The Strategy of Indirect Approach* (London: Faber & Faber, 1941)

Luck, Hans von, *Panzer Commander* (New York: Dell Books, 1989)

Macksey, Kenneth, *The Tank Pioneers* (London: Jane's, 1981)

Macleod, Col. Roderick & Kelly, Denis (eds.), *The Ironside Diaries, 1937–40* (London: Constable, 1962)

Martel, Lieutenant-General le Quesne, A*n Outspoken Soldier,* (London: Sifton Praed, 1949)

Martel, Lieutenant-General le Quesne, *Our Armoured Forces* (London: Faber & Faber, 1945)

Mason, Philip, *A Matter of Honour: An Account of the Indian Army, its Officers and Men* (London: Jonathan Cape, 1974)

Maule, Henry, *Spearhead General: General Sir Frank Messervy* (London: Odhams Press, 1961)

Mead, Richard, *The Last Great Cavalryman: The Life of General Sir Richard McCreery* (Barnsley: Pen and Sword, 2012)

Mead, Richard, *Churchill's Lions* (Stroud: Spellmont 2007)

Mellenthin, Major General F.W. von, *Panzer Battles* (London: Futura Publications, 1979)

Ogorkiewicz, Richard, *Tanks: 100 Years of Evolution* (Oxford: Osprey Publishing 2008)

Pile, General Sir Frederick, *Ack Ack* (London: Harrap & Co., 1949)

Pitman, Major Stuart, *2nd Royal Gloucestershire Hussars* (Uckfield: Naval & Military Press Ltd, undated but originally published 1948)

Pitt, Barrie, *The Crucible of War: The Western Desert 1941* (London: Jonathan Cape, 1980)

Playfair, I.S.O., *The History of the Second World War: The Mediterranean and the Middle East, vol. iii* (London: HSMO, 1966)

Playfair, I.S.O., *The History of the Second World War: The Mediterranean and the Middle East, vol, iv* (London: HSMO, 1966)

Pyman, General Sir Harold, *Call to Arms* (London: Leo Cooper, 1971)

Roach, Peter, *The 8.15 to War: The Memoirs of a Desert Rat* (London: Leo Cooper, 1982)

Roberts, Major General G.B.P., *From the Desert to the Baltic* (London: Kimber & Co., 1987)

Ross, Gordon, '*Breathless Hush in the Close': The World of the Public School* (London: Weidenfeld and Nicholson, 1977)

Schofield, Victoria, *Wavell: Soldier and Statesman* (London: John Murray, 2006)

Schraepler, Hans-Albrecht (ed), *At Rommel's Side (*Barnsley: Frontline Books, 2009)

Seton-Watson, Christopher, *Dunkirk – Alamein – Bologna, Diaries and Letters of an Artilleryman 1939–1945* (London: Buckland Publications Ltd, 1993)

Stewart, Adrian, *Six of Monty's Men* (Barnsley: Pen & Sword, 2011)

Strang, Jeremy, *The British Army and the People's War* (Manchester: Manchester University Press, 2000)

Strohn, Matthias, *The German Army and the Defence of the Reich* (Cambridge: Cambridge University Press, 2011)

Tedder, Air Marshal Lord, *With Prejudice* (Boston, Massachusetts: Little, Brown & Co., 1966)

Trevelyan, Raleigh, *The Fortress: Anzio 1944* (London: Leo Cooper 1956)

Trythall, Antony John, *'Boney' Fuller: The Intellectual General* (London: Cassell, 1977)

Tuker, Lieutenant General Sir Francis, *The Pattern of War* (London: Cassell, 1948)

Tuker, Lieutenant General Sir Francis, *Approach to Battle* (London: Cassell, 1963)

Turner, David, *The Old Boys* (New Haven & London: Yale University Press, 2015)

Verney, Major General G.L., *The Desert Rats: The 7th Armoured Division in World War II* (London: Greenhill Books, 1954)

Vernon, Brigadier H.R.W. (ed.), *"Strafer" Gott* (Winchester: Culverlands Press, 1983)

Walker, Ian W., *Iron Hulls, Iron Hearts* (Marlborough: The Crowood Press, 2006)

War Office, *Field Service Regulations, Vol. III: Operations: Higher Formations 1935* (HMSO: London, 1936)

Wavell, General Sir Archibald, *Generals and Generalship, The Lees-Knowles Lectures 1939* (London: The Times Publishing Company, 1941)

Journals

Colvin, James, 'Eighth Army Operations May-July 1942', *Journal of the Society for Army Historical Research,* Summer 2019, Vol. 97, No. 389.

Dinardo, R.L, 'German Armour Doctrine: Correcting the Myths', *War in History,* 1996, (3) 4.

Dorman-O'Gowan, Maj Gen Eric, 'Rommel Drives East', *Purnell's History of the Second World War,* No. 34.

Dorman-O'Gowan, Maj Gen Eric, '1st Alamein: The Battle that Saved Cairo' and 'Alamein: The Aftermath', *Purnell's History of the Second World War,* No. 36.

French, David, 'The Mechanisation of the British Cavalry', *War in History,* 2003 (10) 3.

Gudmundsson, Bruce I., 'The Seventy-two Gun Battery', *Military History Quarterly,* 1991 Spring, Vol. 3, No. 3.

Electronic Sources

Liddell Hart, Captain, Generalleutnant Fritz Bayerlein and Major General G P B Roberts, *A Battle Report: Alam Halfa,* (Combat Studies Institute: Marine Corps Association, 1968)<https://web.archive.org/web/20091228033031/http://www-cgsc.army.mil/carl/resources/csi/hart/hart.asp>

Anthony Brett-James, *Ball of Fire: The Fifth Indian Division in the Second World War* <http://www.ourstory.info/library/4-ww2/Ball/fire07.html#ch14>

Broadcast Media

The Desert Generals Pt 1, BBC Northern Ireland 2006

Index